P9-CCJ-029

O C E A N

GREENLAND

CANADA

Vancouver
Island

Vancouver
Victoria

U. S. A.

P A C I F I C

O C E A N

MEXICO

A T L A N T I C

O C E A N

SOUTH

AMERICA

FIJI
Savusavu

anga
arbour
Auckland

NEW ZEALAND
Wellington
Christchurch
Queenstown

Midlife
Runaway

A Grown Ups' Guide to
Taking a Year Off

Lynda Cronin

First published in Canada in 2000 by
Macmillan Canada, an imprint of CDG Books Canada

Canadian Cataloguing in Publication Data

Cronin, Lynda, 1948-
  Midlife runaway : a grown ups' guide to taking a year off

Includes index.
ISBN 0-7715-7685-4

1. Travel. I. Title.

G151.C75 2000   910'.2'02   C00-931274-9

This book is available at special discounts for bulk purchases by your group or organization for sales promotions, premiums, fundraising and seminars. For details, contact: CDG Books Canada Inc., 99 Yorkville Avenue, Suite 400, Toronto, ON, M5R 3K5.

1 2 3 4 5 FP 04 03 02 01 00

Cover and text design by Gillian Tsintziras, The Brookview Group Inc.
Cover photo: Yukimasa Hirota, Photonica
Author photo: Destrubé Photography

The five stages of travel referred to on p. 12 are from *Economics of Outdoor Recreation*, by Marian Clawson and Jack L. Knetsch (The Johns Hopkins University Press, 1966).

Macmillan Canada
An imprint of CDG Books Canada Inc.
Toronto

Printed in Canada

To Peter,
who makes all my dreams come true

ACKNOWLEDGEMENTS

A lot of people have helped to make this book a reality.

My sincere thanks to those free-spirited runaways who generously shared their experiences: Jamie Alley, Chris Beauchemin, Sheila Beauchemin, Judy Birch, Derek Denny, Jan Denny, Dana Hayden, Bryan Kingsfield, Bev McLean-Alley, Carla Matheson, Gabrielle Matheson, Neil Matheson, Catherine Panter, Diane Perry, Mary Lou Wakefield. I have been able to use only a small portion of their reminiscences, but I hope they feel some of the essence of their trips in this book.

Thank you to the family and friends, old and new, too numerous to mention individually, who eased our way, welcomed us into their homes, fed us, housed us, soothed us, and introduced us to the wonders of their parts of the world.

A huge thank you to my faithful friends and informal editorial committee, Barbara Coyne and Linda Graham. Barbara held things together for us at home while we were on the road, and she and Linda devoted weeks of their time to reviewing the first draft and subsequent revisions. They provided constructive criticism with honesty and gentleness, and their unflagging enthusiasm kept me going through the occasional tough times.

Thank you as well to my agent, Robert Mackwood, an "all-round swell guy," for his confidence and professionalism and to my editor, Jennifer Lambert, whose careful eye and sensitive suggestions greatly improved my initial effort.

I also want to thank the Royal Bank Financial Group for generously sharing with me their research and information on extended leave possibilities in the private sector.

Finally, but foremost in this as in all things, thank you to my husband, Peter Heap, whose love, support, and encouragement made the trip and the book possible.

CONTENTS

INTRODUCTION

Have you ever wanted to run away from home? I don't mean at 5, or 8, or 14, but as an adult? To forget your responsibilities: children, aging parents, sisters, brothers, friends, bosses, staff, the demands of a job gone stale? To run away from the reality of impending middle and, worse, old age? To be free, afloat in a world of endless possibilities. Not for always. But for a while.

I have. And I did. And you can too.

For as long as I can remember, I have wanted to see the world. As a child, I soaked up stories of unknown and exotic places. I'd hear "Once upon a time, in a far-off land…" and I was hooked.

I've fed my addiction pretty well over the years. At 18, I boarded the train from Montreal to Vancouver to start an independent life in a new city. At 21, I joined the annual migration of Canadian university graduates to Europe (conveniently ignoring the fact that I hadn't yet been to university), hitchhiking, hostelling, and generally hanging out. The idea, supposedly, was to enlarge our experience and enrich our lives. In my case, it was more a matter of having a good time until the money ran out.

That was probably the last truly free period of my life—the last occasion my time was entirely my own. I could wile it away however I liked, worthily or unworthily, with no one, particularly myself, making any explicit or implicit demands. I loved that feeling! I have hugged the memory over the years, distorting it in the process, undoubtedly, but taking continuing comfort from its essence.

Don't get me wrong, the subsequent years have been good ones. I've been more fortunate than anyone has a right to expect. I discovered the joys of night school and proudly obtained the university degree I had no use for in my teens. After revelling in the single life of the 1970s, I married unexpectedly and happily in my mid-thirties. Peter and I have a strong, loving relationship, a comfortable home in Victoria, and a network of good friends—all of which support, stimulate, and encourage me. I've had interesting, challenging, and well-paid jobs that have subsidized almost annual trips to wonderful places around the globe, and in one instance allowed me to live in Mexico for two years. I love my life and I know how fortunate I've been.

So, what's the issue here? Well, real life has a way of getting under your skin. After thirty years of working, even the most fascinating job contains an element of "been there, done that." After fifteen years of marriage, even the best relationship can sometimes seem a little ho-hum. I was getting stale and bored and boring.

Then came a year when, true or not, the world seemed to be closing in. My best friend, Barbara, relocated to Victoria from Toronto, but an unexpected death in her family and difficulties finding work didn't make things easy. My sister and niece arrived from Italy, where my sister had lived for most of her adult life. Much as I love them, it was a bit like adopting a family of refugees. Their knowledge of Canadian life, and the English language, in my niece's case, was either non-existent or locked in the 1960s. Helping them get settled was a labour of love, but it was a labour, particularly after my sister's leg was demolished in a run-in with a truck. (Thirty-five years in the hot spots of Europe and she's fine; eight months in quiet little Victoria and she's hit by a truck while crossing the street!) Peter's mother moved to Victoria the same year. And my mum, in her eighties, was having health problems.

All of these people are loved and welcomed parts of our lives, and each is individually undemanding. Cumulatively, however, there is no denying they made an impact—particularly on a couple with no children and, therefore, fairly minimal responsibilities previously.

Health problems of my own and an unexpected hysterectomy made it impossible to continue to pretend, even to myself, that I was still young. As I approached 50, I could hear Peggy Lee crooning in my ear, "Is that all there is?" My soul was shrieking, "Get me out of here!" This was my midlife crisis and, puny as it might be by other people's standards, it was real and painful to me.

The travel bug hit with renewed force. I felt time running out and the need to see and do everything. I needed to prove to myself that there was life, creativity, and excitement in the old girl yet. I wanted to travel the world, with no itinerary and no deadlines, going where I wanted when I wanted.

At one level, I thought and talked about it as a journey of discovery. A chance to rediscover who I was and determine what I wanted to do with the next phase of my life. An opportunity to see different places, meet new people, and find out if fresh experiences could help me understand and appreciate what I had. In truth, all I really wanted to do was run away.

Some people are born to travel, others have travel thrust upon them. Peter is among the latter. Prior to our meeting, his independent travel experience consisted of a solitary and somewhat manic driving trip through the Maritimes. Since we've been together, he has allowed himself to be enticed to beaches in Mexico, Hawaii, and the South Pacific, to the cities of Europe, trekking in Nepal, camping with Ahka villagers in northern Thailand, sailing through the Tahitian islands, and kayaking in British Columbia. His occasional mild protests have gradually given way to enthusiasm, but I doubt if he would ever have originated the idea of wandering around the world for a year.

Fortunately for me, he's an easygoing guy and he spoils me wonderfully. It also helped that he was getting more than a little bored with his job and ready for a change of his own.

Peter and I were privileged to be able even to consider the possibility of running away. I was self-employed. My consulting practice would be relatively easy to wind down. Peter worked for the British Columbia government, which offered the possibility of taking leave without pay. We were far from rich, but neither did we have any debts. We owned our own home. And we didn't have any children to hold us back. We would have to deal with the repercussions of leaving our two cats (those of you who live with cats will understand how terrifying a prospect that was). Generally, though, with a little bit of saving, our escape could be relatively straightforward.

We decided to take a year off and go wandering.

I know there are others with similar dreams. This book is for you. Your situation will undoubtedly be different from ours. It may well be more complex. If you really want to do it, however, you probably can. This book is to help you start thinking about how to transform your midlife dreams into reality.

When we started planning, I looked for resources, ideas, answers to what I thought were simple questions. There wasn't a lot of help to be found, at least not easily, and certainly not in one place. Peter and I learned by trial and error what worked for us and what didn't, what we needed to do and what we could have done. Since then, I've spoken with other people who have done their own runaways and who have been kind enough to share their stories with me—and with you. I've changed their names to give them some privacy, but every word of the inserts throughout the book comes from them and every feeling is real.

Marie was 50 years old when she took an unpaid leave of absence from her job in the provincial government. Her husband and her best friend had both recently died, and she was seriously burnt out. During her fifteen months off, she drove across Canada, built a retirement cottage in Ontario, did volunteer work at a Tai Chi centre, and travelled to Europe.

Margaret and her husband, **Bill**, were 46 and 48, respectively, when they took leave from the provincial government—a year in Bill's case; ten months in Margaret's. Their children are grown and living on their own. Margaret and Bill's first two months were spent exploring North America in an old camper van. Then they flew to Costa Rica for three months of volunteer work and studying Spanish. From there it was on to Ecuador for a month and a final three months travelling in Central America and Mexico.

Patrick and **Helen** took 1-year-old Sophie to Europe for ten months—two months travelling and the rest of the time in the south of France. For Helen, then 35, it was a reward to herself after completing her master's degree; for Patrick, at 43, it was a break from twenty-five years of uninterrupted work.

Suzanne, at 44, and **Trevor**, at 47, fulfilled a lifelong dream when they took their 12- and 10-year-old daughters to sail the South Pacific for ten months. Suzanne left her job as a writer and public relations consultant; self-employed Trevor put his business on hold for a year.

John and **Ruth** were 43 and 45, respectively, with adult children, when they took leave from their jobs—John's as a civil servant and Ruth's as a nursing teacher—to travel and do volunteer work in South America. This was their second runaway, having spent a year in Mexico twelve years earlier. It changed their lives.

Janet was 38 when she took a one-year leave of absence from her job with a Crown corporation and headed to the south of France with her husband and two children, 6 and 3 years old. She hoped the experience would bring the family closer together. Instead, it drove them apart.

Jocelyn and **Ian** were 39 and 42, respectively, when she handed temporary custody of her store to a colleague and he took a leave of absence from his government job. They packed up 13-year-old Donny and 10-year-old **June** and headed off to camp their way around Australia, New Zealand, Vanuatu, and Fiji for nine months. They just wanted to have fun. And they did.

At 33 and 31, **Mike** and **Heather** were not exactly in midlife when they left jobs and home to spend six months riding their motorcycles through South America. But their trip was a conscious departure from the planned and, in Heather's words, "milquetoast" life they had lived to date and, as such, it has lessons to offer the older escapee.

At the other end of the age and experience spectrum are **Rita** and **Larry**. They had done a runaway ten years earlier. When they set out this time in their early fifties to circumnavigate the globe on their 47-foot sailboat, they thought they were retiring from nursing and the family business. Unexpected business and financial problems brought them back after two-and-a-half years of freedom. They are still working to recover lost ground.

Peter's and my experiences and those of these travellers will not be yours. Every person's runaway is unique. But there are some commonalities, and other people's experiences may provide you with a better sense of what to expect on your own voyage of discovery.

A good friend and occasional travel companion, Bob, once explained very seriously to Peter and me that there are five stages to every travel experience: anticipation; travelling to your destination; the on-site experience; returning home; and remembering. In homage to Bob and the many laughs we've had analyzing our trips this way, the book is organized around these stages. Main chapters offer practical advice, based on Peter's and my experiences and that of the other runaways. Excerpts from my travel journal will give you a feel for what one person's runaway was like.

So, if you're ready, let's hit the road together.

September: On the Way

We're off! After three years of wishing and hoping and thinking and praying and planning, we have finally set out on our great adventure. But who would ever have guessed how wrenching the starting, the parting, would be? All these months I've been dying to get away from everybody and everything. I've been gone five hours and I miss them dreadfully. Isn't it classic? Now that we're leaving, I realize how much I love our life.

Stage I

Wishing and Hoping and Dreaming and Planning

ONE
ARE YOU SURE YOU WANT TO DO THIS?

Running away for awhile sounds like a great idea. But it's not for everyone. Some people's lives are too complicated; there's just too much to leave. A lot of people can't afford it; it is very much a middle-class privilege. Other people have different dreams.

For many of us, however, particularly in midlife, running away makes perfect sense.

WHY?

The reasons frequently come down to basic issues around the fragility of life and the sense of passing time. Some people know this from direct experience. Others have seen friends and family members die before they could realize their dreams. Margaret told me about Bill's father who worked hard all his life so he could retire early. He retired at 55 and died at 56 after being ill for a year with cancer.

In the two years prior to making our decision, Peter and I lost three good friends. For others, the connection was even closer. Patrick had cancer in his twenties and is very conscious that life has no guarantees. Marie's decision was prompted by a barrage of personal tragedies.

> My husband died, my best friend died, other people I knew died. And my mother got Alzheimer's when she was 55 years old. I suddenly thought—I want to do some things that I really want to do for me before I either get sick or die—and while I still have the enthusiasm and strength to do them.
>
> Marie

Reasons change over time. People who have run away more than once may do so for very different reasons.

> The first time, my job disappeared. I got a crummy one I

didn't like and Ruth didn't like her job, so we quit. We thought—things aren't going well, let's bugger off. The second time, we both had good jobs and took leaves of absence. This time, we thought—we've got a great life and we can arrange to take the time off, so we'll do it. It was just taking a break. And we like each other, so the thought of spending a year together without so many distractions was quite appealing.

John

Turning 50 was a watershed for Peter and for me, as it is for many people. It may be the first time that some of us start to acknowledge seriously that our years on the planet may be limited. We remember the dreams of our youth, review what we've accomplished to date, and realize that time may be running out. If we're going to do it—whatever *it* is—it may be now or never.

For some the issue is one of personal challenge—defining, or redefining, their self-image. Heather liked the idea of stepping outside what was easy and comfortable for her, of doing something different, something unexpected: "I've always sort of followed a pattern, done what was expected of me. I wanted to step outside my normal, milquetoast routine and do something not everybody else does."

For others, it's the culmination of a dream. Larry had always dreamed of sailing around the world. His library is full of books on sailing and round-the-world trips: "My father sailed before me, so it was just a natural progression."

Sometimes it's simply a matter of shaking off the dust of routine and having fun.

It was great just to get away and forget everything. Just break the habits...getting up in the morning, getting the kids to school, going to work...just the same predictable old routine.... Get away from watches. Get away from telephones. Get away from bills...hockey and ballet and volunteer work at the school. All that stuff.

Jocelyn

Whatever your reason, it helps to understand why you want to make a break from your norm. The clearer your reasons, the better chance you have of designing a runaway that works for you. But, if you're not clear about why, don't worry. Runaways have a way of adapting themselves to your needs.

WHAT ABOUT THE KIDS?

Peter and I are classic middle-class, double-income, no-kids professionals. Our decision to take off was relatively simple. If you have children, things will be more difficult.

Older children, going to university or independent, obviously present less of a challenge. Similarly, at the other end of the age spectrum, you can carry healthy babies just about anywhere. Toddlers, however, are already individuals with distinct personalities. You need to assess how well your little one is likely to respond to change.

Things become even more complicated if your children are still in school. Teenagers, in particular, are not notoriously open to changes in routine. How enthusiastic are your kids about the idea? How will they react to leaving their friends, school, sports, familiar places for a while? Are they mature enough to handle the lack of stability?

> At first I was sort of freaked out because I thought I'd forget about all my friends and stuff. But then I got used to it and thought it would be cool.
>
> June, 13 years old

School becomes an issue. You can arrange for the kids to continue their studies on the road, staying in touch with teachers by correspondence or over the Internet. How successful this is likely to be is another matter. Are your children good students? Will they suffer from a lack of routine or do they have the discipline to study away from home? Do you have what it takes to help them focus in a shifting environment? How supportive are their teachers?

> I had a curriculum outline and I had some textbooks. But what gave me a great deal of confidence was the support of

their teachers. I couldn't have done it otherwise. They really endorsed and supported our belief that learning should focus on the people and the experiences we were going to have along the way. They gave us the curriculum outline, but told us to feel free to deviate whenever and however we wanted. And we did.

Suzanne

Not everyone is a fan of trying to bring school with you on the road. When you think about it, the adults are trying to get away from their jobs while telling the children to bring theirs with them.

The people we ran into who did home schooling said it was a real chore. You don't have the time. You cart all this extra luggage around, all these books, and everybody we talked to said it's not worth it. It's just not worth it. You're trying to get away from things and here you are taking that one thing that's already difficult. If your children are fully self-motivated, go do it. But if they need to be reminded to do stuff, forget it. That is one aggravation you don't need. If there was any aggravation at all, that was it—trying to get them to do their homework.

Jocelyn

The more of you there are travelling, the more issues there are to be considered.

PARENTS ARE ANOTHER MATTER
The folks left back home present other complications. Many midlifers are responsible for the care and support—financial, physical, or emotional—of aging parents. How are they going to get along without you for a while?

Peter and I were fortunate. Peter's mother is the youngest, healthiest senior citizen imaginable. His sister lives here in Victoria and has always played the major support role in her mother's life. While we had to cope with the usual guilt feelings about leaving anyone, we had no worries about Yvonne's health or well-being while we were away.

My mother presented a different set of issues. Mum's in her eighties, and her health isn't always great. We had to consider long and hard whether there was a risk that something serious might happen while we were unreachable. Fortunately, while Mum's heart may be medically suspect, emotionally it has no problems at all. My mother has retained her sense of adventure along with her independent spirit. She made it quite clear that she would be outraged and offended if we didn't follow our dream because of her: "Don't you dare use me as an excuse not to go. I'll get along just fine. Besides, I've always dreamed of seeing the Taj Mahal and I don't think I'm going to do it for myself now, so you'll just have to do it for me."

Despite some concerns, we decided to go. My mother could die in a minute or live for another fifteen years. We each had a sister in town to provide support, so we weren't leaving our mothers alone. Our mothers supported what we wanted to do, if somewhat bemusedly in the case of Peter's. Most critical, it was really important to us to do it. We simply had to go. It had become crucial to our sense of what we wanted to do with our lives. Not going was too high a price to pay.

A certain psychological preparedness is essential if you're going to make the trip work. I don't mean that you should become cold-hearted and stop caring about the folks at home. You couldn't if you tried. You do, however, have to accept that something may happen while you're gone. Someone you love might die or be hurt and you won't be able to be there. Until you're comfortable with that possibility, you are probably not ready to go.

Suzanne's father-in-law died while they were in South Africa. Suzanne and Trevor had known his health wasn't good when they left, but they were at a point of no return. They would cross that bridge when they came to it.

You can't know in advance what might happen. You can only prepare yourself to accept that there are consequences of your actions and be willing to live with them.

You can't live your life worrying about people dying. They could die while you're at the grocery store. When Trevor said goodbye to his dad that day down at the wharf, in his head he was thinking this might be the last time. When he hugged him, he gave him a damn good hug because you don't ever know. But you've got to do what you've got to do.

Suzanne

Peter and I were lucky. Our mothers made it through the year with no problems. Our friends were not so fortunate. Each of our closest friends lost a parent while we were away. Barbara's mother died while we were in Australia, and Jack's father, Ken, who was also a dear friend of ours, died when we were in Israel. In both cases, we were fortunate that we were at least reachable. We could talk to Barbara and Jack on the telephone and grieve together at a distance. But it was a horrible experience to be so removed from a friend's pain. We each in our turn felt selfish and guilty. We wanted to be with them. We knew we should have been there to help.

The days following news of the deaths were among our lowest of the trip. We each considered the possibility of returning home for at least a while, but it just seemed too complex. We tried to relieve our consciences with frequent telephone calls and letters but, in our hearts, we knew that we had failed people who mean the world to us. I still don't feel good about it. I wish it had been different. But I do not regret going on the trip.

Consider your own situation very carefully. Is there a real danger that someone will fall ill while you're gone? What kind of contingency plan can you put in place? Can you deal with the guilt should the worst happen? How important is it for you to go? Only you know how much you can handle.

PETS ARE PART OF THE FAMILY

Those of you without pets will think the rest of us are crazy. But those of us who share our lives with cats, dogs, rabbits, budgies, gerbils, and other furred, scaled, and feathered beasts know that their comfort and happiness is critical to our own. Leaving them behind requires thought and planning. Taking them with you requires even more.

Some runaways can be done with some pets. Bringing your dog

along on a driving trip in North America is a great idea. It can make your trip more enjoyable and, if it's a big dog, can increase your security. Bringing your cats along can be done—our friends, Bob and Mary, did it—but do you really want to? Taking animals to Europe, Southeast Asia, or other parts of the world is probably more trouble than it's worth. If the companionship of your pets is critical to your happiness, plan your runaway around various countries' quarantine requirements and the animals' comfort. Otherwise, it's probably wise to make arrangements for them to await your return at home.

Our solution to the pet dilemma was to offer a reduced rent to a tenant who would take our house complete with two cats. We have always assumed that a familiar physical environment is at least as important to Jerome and Georgia's sense of security as we are. Humbling as this notion is, we were proven correct.

If the house-sitting alternative isn't available to you, start asking around early in your planning whether friends, colleagues, or family members would be willing to take care of your pets while you're gone. You might be pleasantly surprised how many people are happy to have a foster pet.

WORKING IS AN UNFORTUNATE NECESSITY FOR MOST OF US

Then, of course, there's your job. Will you have one to come back to? Not all employers are as progressive as Peter's. Your firm may not look too kindly on your desire to leave them for an extended period of time. You will need to speak with your boss about the possibilities for a leave of absence, preferably with a plan in place for how they can handle things while you're gone. You'll want to have some frank discussions about how secure your job is. Will the same job be waiting for you on your return or will you have to accept what's available at the time? Realistically, you have to consider how likely your employer is to deliver on any promises. A lot can change in a year. With the best intentions in the world, promises made now may not be able to be kept a year later.

If you are self-employed, you have to consider the impact of being out of the loop for a while. If clients have to turn to someone else in your absence, they may not be interested in changing back when you return.

Handing your business over to a colleague temporarily may ease the break, but it doesn't always work out the way you planned. People have their own ways of doing things and you can't control matters while you're gone. You could find yourself having to rebuild on your return.

> I would encourage people to take a look at their career plans and take a long hard look at what they'll need to do when they come back. Maybe talk about it with somebody objective, because I don't think you can see your own situation clearly. You sort of assume that you'll take a little break and resume where you were. And you can't just do that.
>
> Janet

It's important to be realistic about how employable you are. In midlife, we're perhaps not quite as attractive to potential employers as we think we should be.

Be honest with yourself about how comfortable you are leaving your job, especially in mid-career. There's not much point in taking a year of your life to get away from it all if you're going to spend large parts of your time worrying about what you'll do when the experience is over.

HOW ABOUT YOU?

More important than any of these external factors, however, is an honest assessment of who you are and how much change you can tolerate. Don't kid yourself. There is enormous stress associated with any change. No matter how much you want to do this, how well organized you are, how much money you have, how secure your job prospects are, shaking up your established patterns will have a tremendous impact. Your self-image and your assumptions about the world will be under constant challenge.

Before we left, I mentioned to a friend the idea of writing this book. "I've got the title for you," he said helpfully. *Risk-Free Runaway.* I was totally insulted. I felt diminished by his assumption that the experience was simply a lark. At one level, I understand what he was saying. We had the money to do what we wanted, and we knew that Peter would have a job of some kind when we returned. Nonetheless, there *is* risk involved, and it is real. We were opening ourselves up to new experiences, testing ourselves, getting to know ourselves and each other better. Self-discovery is an enormous gamble. What if you don't like what you find? How will you deal with the discoveries you make?

Whether you're travelling as part of a couple, as a family, or by yourself, you need to have a good sense of who you are as an individual—although most of your preconceptions will likely be shot down in flames soon into the experience. Just how flexible and adaptable are you? What's your health like? How do you respond to emergencies? How do you deal with boredom? How prepared are you to be miserable occasionally? I can guarantee this is not going to be all sunshine and light.

I don't think anyone can truly appreciate, until they do it, just how much hard work constant travel can be or how much stress is involved in removing yourself from the familiar. If you find yourself stuck in a leaky cabin on a remote Fijian out-island in the middle of an unseasonable gale, or lying cold and sick in an Indian bed far from home, sympathy, and comfort, just how are you likely to react?

COUPLES ARE IN THIS TOGETHER

If you're considering this change as a couple, you'd better be sure you share the same dream. Rita recalls only too well the first time Larry broached the idea of going sailing:

> I was just finishing up my BSN at UVic. I didn't have a job. I didn't have any money. And we were living in my condominium. And he sat down at dinner one night and said, "You know, I've decided I'm going to buy a new boat and go offshore sailing." I hit the roof. I said, "How dare you plan my life for me like this?" And he said to me, "Well, I'm not planning your life—I'm planning my life."
>
> Rita

It also helps to be confident that your relationship is a solid one. When the stresses and strains of being on an unfamiliar road with no one but each other to rely on start building, any cracks in your relationship will start to assume the proportions of the Grand Canyon. It may be a problem if you like to be at the airport three hours ahead of time and he's one of those run-on-at-the-last-minute types. You can deal with this a couple of times a year when you're heading on holidays. But can you handle it on a weekly basis? Or, you know the way he hums unconsciously when he's thinking about something? Cute, isn't it, when you hear it occasionally in the evening or on the weekend? It becomes a whole lot less cute—in fact, it becomes downright irritating—when you're trapped with it twenty-four hours a day, seven days a week.

Heading off with expectations of a change bringing you closer together is probably a sure recipe for disaster.

> There were obvious pressures between my husband and me. I'd been spending so much time at work, I felt that, maybe if I took a break and wasn't working, a lot of the problems between us would have an opportunity to work themselves out.
>
> Janet

It didn't work for them. It probably won't work for you.

PEOPLE CAN BE WEIRD

Some people have an unconscious sense that taking time off work to travel is "wrong." They see it as an abdication of responsibility as an adult member of society.

> Everybody tries to make you feel guilty about leaving.
>
> John

So many times, when we told people what we were planning to do, they'd respond wistfully, "I really wish I could do that." Or, "That's okay for you, but some of us have responsibilities." At first, I felt guilty that we were able to run away. For a while, I was self-conscious about mentioning our plans to anyone. As I examined people's reactions more closely, however, things became clearer.

Those who really were constrained by personal or financial circumstance tended to be supportive and encouraging. They occasionally acknowledged a bit of envy, but they also entered vicariously and enthusiastically into our planning. On the other hand, people who responded with a certain degree of bitterness almost without exception tended to be those who simply had made and were continuing to make other choices in their lives. It wasn't that they couldn't run away; it was simply that they didn't choose to do so. Other things were more important to them. And that's fine. But, they blamed their circumstances—and, at some level, us—instead of accepting their own choices.

> There were people who assumed that it was only possible for us to go because we had money. I don't challenge that, but I know that we made lifestyle choices so that we could afford to do this sort of thing: we drive cars that are ten and fifteen years old, we have old furniture…you make a choice. But the people who choose something else shouldn't think that they should be able to do everything. People shouldn't think that it's just luck. People make choices all the time.
>
> Margaret

When I encounter that attitude now, I remember the British couple we sat next to on the plane from London to Naples. They had been retired for seven or eight years and had never been happier in their lives. Derek told us about the lesson they had learned from their son, Simon.

When he was 17, Simon came to them saying he was fed up, hated school, and couldn't take it anymore. He was going to quit and go travelling. "You can't go travelling," Derek said to him. "You haven't any money." "I do," he replied. "I have one pound." And off he went, with one pound in his pocket. He was gone for seven years. One Christmas Day, he phoned home and reported, "I'm calling from the beach in Thailand. The sun is shining. The weather's perfect. I'm having a great time." Derek looked outside at the rain and cold, and thought of going to work at his "boring" job. He remembers thinking, who's the crazy one here?

Derek retired. Simon eventually came back to England, went to school and is now an investment banker in San Francisco. His parents visit him regularly.

COURAGE, MON AMI

Running away takes more than today's equivalent of one pound and some personal freedom. It requires courage. Peter and I decided to test our courage and try something different. An increasing number of people are doing the same.

> One day, I decided I'm going to do it. I'm going to give up some of the treasures of my life, but I'm going to do it.
>
> Larry

With few exceptions, those of us who have made the temporary break from "real life" have emerged reinvigorated, rejuvenated, more comfortable with ourselves, each other, and our lives.

Only you know if running away is right for you. Take a good look at your personal situation. Be realistic about your circumstances and what level of risk you are able and willing to take. You may need to adjust your timeframe or your expectations of what running away means. Instead of going three years from now, maybe it will be five. Instead of wandering aimlessly around the world, perhaps you'll choose to settle in a house in the south of France to give the kids some stability. Ultimately, though, if an escape from your everyday world is important enough to you, be brave. You can find a way to do it that works for you.

THINGS TO THINK ABOUT

CHILDREN
- Are your children old enough to leave behind or young enough to take along without trouble?
  If school age:
    How enthusiastic are they about the idea?
    Are they good students?
    Can they cope with the loss of routine?
  If you choose to try a home-study program:
    Are they disciplined enough to study on the road?
    Are you capable of supervising their studies?
    How supportive are their teachers?

PARENTS
- How healthy are your parents?
- Is there a support system—siblings, aunts, uncles, grandchildren, friends—you can put in place during your absence?
- Have a contingency plan in case of emergencies.

PETS
- Consider carefully how realistic it is to take your pets with you.
- Start early to find foster parents for your pets.

JOB
- How important is your career to you?
- How comfortable are you with the thought of looking for work on return?
- Be realistic about your job prospects.

YOU AND YOUR PARTNER
- Are you equally enthusiastic about this adventure?
- How strong is your relationship?
- How much do you trust your partner?

YOU:
- How confident are you in your own ability to deal with uncertainty and change?
- How much do you want to go?

September: FIJI
Paradise Postponed

FIJI. Secluded oceanfront home. "Paradise Point." $400 first week, $300 thereafter, $1,100/month.

The ad appeared in a travel magazine. I spoke with the owner, George, a fireman and Harley-Davidson enthusiast from Oregon, and received a letter and pictures portraying a rustic but civilized hideaway near Savusavu on the out-island of Vanua Levu. A perfect, restful way to start our trip. Or so I thought.

SEPTEMBER 3

The first full day has gone about as conceivably well as one could hope. Gopendra, the taxi driver arranged by George, was waiting for us in Savusavu. The house details were a bit overwhelming given our jet-lagged state, but we met our neighbour, Jessie, picked up the keys to the house, did a quick shop so we wouldn't starve to death, and started the process of letting go.

The property is basic, but lovely—on a high point of land in the middle of a coconut plantation, looking south toward a small island and seemingly endless ocean. The house, or houses (the bedroom is a separate building), has its quirks and limitations. It is definitely a do-it-yourselfer's version of paradise. There are solar-powered lights inside, a battery-powered light outside, a propane refrigerator, an oil stove, an electric radio, a battery-powered TV, a generator hookup for the VCR, and God knows what for the water heater, which doesn't appear to work.

It also has peace and tranquility, green grass, red and orange and yellow flowers, coconut palms rustling in the wind, and the sight and sound of the ocean at our doorstep. We've found the mosquito netting to rig up over the bed to add our own touch of romance.

The birds are wonderful. We were greeted by a large blue and grey heron on the coral beneath the cliff; have seen huge, stunning white herons on the small island; have been visited by tiny brown birds with the male displaying a flashy red head; and another starling-like creature who would have walked right in had the screen door not been closed. We have also been visited by hordes of tiny ants—to which I think there is no solution. Fortunately, the house comes equipped with Tupperware of every size.

I'm sure it's a combination of jet lag, fatigue, and culture shock, but I had my first twinges of panic this afternoon. What am I doing here? Why am I forcing myself to wander the globe for the next ten months when I could be comfortable and safe and secure at home? What is it I really want? When I get it, will I be content? Will I die of boredom here? Or exhaustion somewhere else along the road?

It seems to me that we are basically the sum of our contradictions. I want it all—safety, security, adventure, exoticism. I guess part of the reason for this trip is to try to find the balance of these elements that will help me be comfortable with who I am and how I relate to the world around me.

SEPTEMBER 4

The wind died at dawn. For a few hours we thought we were going to have a supposedly typical beautiful Fijian day. But this afternoon, it picked up again and the cloud cover socked in. It may just be my internal workings, but I find a distinctly ominous tone in the weather. It feels as if we're building up to something seriously unpleasant. On the other hand, it may all blow over by tomorrow. What do I know?

The water went off around noon. According to Jessie, it's a common occurrence. The water pipes are laid too close together and too close to the road. The traffic of the old trucks along the road rattles them together and they break. The current record for longest time to fix is two days. Let's hope the workers aren't going for a new one. In the meantime, we have bottled water for cooking and drinking and a huge tank of rainwater for washing and flushing the toilet. The joys of living in the country! I feel like we've rented a cottage in Sooke—a bit like camping with a roof over your head.

One good thing—I've now found out how easy it is to get to

the beach. Answer—dead easy. George may not have been entirely forthcoming about things like water and electricity, but his "ten minutes to the beach" is right on. And it is lovely, particularly the cove just below Jessie's.

Jessie is a figure from a colonial novel. In her seventies I'd guess, possibly her early eighties, with a slight New Zealand accent still. She came to Savusavu as a young bride to live on her in-laws' 300-acre copra plantation. Since her husband's death three years ago, she's been managing the plantation on her own. Her four sons are scattered around the world, and she now lives with Vola—"the daughter I never had"—who moved in at the age of ten to look after Jessie's first son. That was forty-five years ago. Since then, Vola has married, had four children of her own, and been widowed. When Jessie's husband died, Vola's family agreed that Jessie needed her more than they did. Sitting in the living room with the two of them I was transported to a past I had only read about, as Jessie lovingly displayed a grainy black-and-white photo of Vola at 10 with Jessie's son in her arms.

SEPTEMBER 5

Our first truly beautiful Fijian day: wind tamed to gentle breeze, blue sky, golden sunshine. So what do we do? Call Gopendra and go to town.

Savusavu is as stunning as we were led to believe. A calm harbour surrounded by green hills. One main street, meandering alongside the water, lined with small shops. This is the way a South Seas town should look. We did our shopping and had lunch at the café owned and run by Gopendra and his wife, Sharda. Chicken curry, rice, roti, salad, and Cokes for $10—for two of us. They also do take-out and delivery. On the way home, Gopendra talked a bit about the economy and the government. Things are starting to return to normal, he told us, after the coup a few years ago when the Fijian army ousted the democratically elected, Indian-dominated government. But there remains a real sense of grievance. Indians are not benefiting from the new resorts and increased tourist trade, other than indirectly like Gopendra. Hotel jobs go to Fijians and, according to Gopendra, good government jobs are not available to Indians regardless of their education. (This year's coup will undoubtedly make things worse.) On the other hand, Jessie told us about the practice of *kiri kiri*—basically, what's mine is yours. In Fijian culture, you can't refuse a family member, however distant. Apparently that's one reason you don't see many Fijian shopkeepers; they can't sell to a family member—and they have a lot of them. It's hard to make a profit giving everything away.

What a dusk! Stood on the point and watched the herons return to the island and the bats flit from tree to tree. Just came in from gaping at the night sky. The stars are jammed so tightly together you can't tell one constellation from another.

Spotted four kingfishers today in one of our trees. One swooped down in front of me to pick a crab off the lawn and take it back to the tree for dinner.

SEPTEMBER 6

Peter's taking a siesta. I tried, but it wouldn't take. I seem to be suffering from daily siesta-time panic attacks. Today's topic is cabin fever. I'm desperate to be among other people. Before we left, I was feeling peopled out and couldn't wait for quiet time alone. We've only been here four days, and I find myself wishing we were at a resort where we'd have people around. I'm hoping it's just culture shock.

When my anxieties recede (which is most times other than siesta time), I really like it here, and I'm pleased with the way Peter and I are adapting to a totally different environment. Today, we repaired the deck chair, and did a fairly good job for two non-handy types. We took care of the garbage as per George's instructions: organic in the ocean; burn the rest in the pit—after finding the pit, which was no easy feat, and ensuring we didn't set the plantation on fire.

Made it into the ocean for the first time. It's hard to believe it took me four days, but you have to go with the tides here. Morning is swimming time. By noon the tide is so far out you can't swim inside the reef. By the time it rolls back in, it's dark.

We live in a very natural way. With no curtains on the windows, we're up with the sun around 6:00 a.m. By 6:00 p.m., it's dark and we settle in to make dinner, read, write, and play cards by dim solar-powered light. We're usually in bed by 9:00 p.m. and asleep by 10:00.

Saw a mongoose today. Didn't know what he was at first, sort of a large furry squirrel-like creature. Guess we don't have to worry about snakes.

Water's back, but we still haven't figured out how to get the heater to work. Generator's on the fritz as well.

SEPTEMBER 7
Saturday night in Savusavu, Gopendra told us, everyone goes to the dance at the Planters Club. Despite the implications of its name, the PC (Planters Club) turns out to be PC (politically correct). It's an odd mixture of Fijians, Indians, resident ex-pats, and occasional visitors like us. Normally I suspect Saturday night is a hoot. But last night was not a normal night.

The crowd on the dance floor of the veranda-encircled building was sparse—three or four couples moving desultorily to a disco beat. We wandered through to the bar where there were a few more people, but not many. We ordered our beers and strolled out onto the porch, wondering where everyone was. Then we spied some folk going into a backroom. In we followed, to find perhaps fifty people packing the poolroom, eyes riveted on the flickering screen of an old black-and-white television set. It was coverage of Princess Diana's funeral. The sombre tones of the BBC announcer and mournful songs of the cathedral choir filled one end of the room. Disco music intruded at the other. The crowd was transfixed, people hugging each other, tears rolling down cheeks. We stayed only until midnight but heard today from Gopendra that the villagers were quite upset. Many of them stayed up until 4:00 a.m. to follow Diana to the bitter end. They were quite annoyed when the television cameras were stopped at the gates of Althorpe.

SEPTEMBER 8
Fijians are undoubtedly the world's most hospitable people. I telephoned the Cousteau Resort (founded by marine explorer Jacques

Cousteau's son over some serious family objections, according to
local gossip) to make a reservation for dinner:

Hello. Would you have room for two of us for dinner
tonight around 7:30?
(long pause) Two of you?

Yes.

(long pause) Tonight?

Yes.

(long pause) For dinner?

Yes.

(long pause) Does it have to be tonight?

Well, we'd prefer tonight. Do you have room?

Well, (pause) yeeess, I...I guess so...but...

Eventually we realized the phone lines had crossed and I was
speaking to someone in the accounts department of the telephone
company. He didn't seem to mind a total stranger inviting herself to
his home for dinner. He was just a bit concerned that I wanted it to
be "tonight?"
I think we'll eat at home.
No water again today.

SEPTEMBER 10
The rain is bucketing down. Has been since yesterday around noon.
The weather has generally been awful—a couple of nice days, but
overall pretty foul. Yesterday it was very humid and started to rain,
probably because we did our laundry. This morning, the sky was
dark. We did a little shopping in town and had lunch at the yacht
club café before heading home. (Don't let the name fool you. "Yacht
club" is a fancy way of describing a very ordinary café with moor-
age.) Céline Dion was crooning on the sound system, and we could

tell that the man at the table behind us was Canadian when the waitress brought him the wrong order and *he* apologized.

Mum just called. They're enjoying summer again in Victoria, and we're watching the rain in Fiji. I put down the phone and had a little cry. I guess I've got more adjusting to do than I thought.

When the weather is bad, there is pretty close to nothing to do here. I don't know why, all of a sudden, I'm so keen to do things. Probably just because I can't. Peter's reading the *Fiji Times* and chortling. Much to my surprise, he's happy as a clam. I'm the one who's twitchy.

SEPTEMBER 12

Yesterday was the bleakest day imaginable—until today! The sky is an uninterrupted sodden mass of grey from narrow horizon to narrow horizon. Here we are huddled in our somewhat moist cottage, reading, writing and playing gin rummy. This is not precisely the Fiji vacation I had in mind to start our trip.

There is a horrible sense of being totally cut off. We're five kilometres from town, with no car, no functioning radio or television, one dim light bulb in the living area, a sporadic water supply, no weather reports, no people, and rain pouring down. The wind last night almost drove me mad. The bedroom is exposed on a point, with windows on three sides. The rain lashes at us from all sides, and the noise from wind and ocean is deafening. I sat up in bed at 3:00 a.m., terrified, and scribbled the first poem I've written since I was 18:

> wind howl
> ocean growl
>
> tree thump
> heart bump
>
> rain beat
> wet heat
>
> night
> fright

My poetic style hasn't improved in thirty years, but it does capture my mood.

If this trip is about learning about myself, I have learned something about my need to feel connected to other people and other events—particularly when the weather's bad! Jessie calls the weather an inversion and says it can last anywhere from 3–4 days to 3–4 weeks. Arg!

SEPTEMBER 13

It is surprisingly peaceful today. I'd like to say comfortable, but the damp—everything is damp—and the lack of water preclude comfort. Yup, the water's off again! But the wind is calmer and so am I. The ocean's roar has mellowed to a constant growl. The sky and horizon remain socked in, but the grey seems lighter. The rain continues to fall, but it was just dripping this morning, and the wind is damp but soft. At least my headache is gone. We live in hope that the worst is behind us.

It helps to have had a good night's sleep. We've given up on the bedroom. It was impossible to sleep on the point, and running 50 yards in the dark through rain and wind to get to the bathroom in the main building was becoming treacherous. Last night, we tucked up together in one of the single beds that make up the living-room couch and slept the sleep of the dead.

1:30 p.m. We've been reading all morning. When we tell people about our stay in Fiji, they will never understand the range of emotions we've gone through. Last night I was a crazy person. Sitting here now, eating, reading in companionable silence, while the rain falls outside, I am perfectly contented. For the moment.

5:00 p.m. My content is starting to dissolve. In the midst of being walloped at gin rummy, I had a small bout of hysterical laughter as I realized I was sitting here on a tropical island in a house with no running water and no electricity, in the pouring rain. Some kind of cosmic joke.

SEPTEMBER 14

6:00 a.m. Paradise Point, for which I had such high hopes, is quickly becoming an endurance test. I should have listened to Ted the travel agent; he warned me that the place could be rustic. This house is a bit too rustic for my taste. There is still no water or electricity, and the wind is howling again. Everything is damp, smelly, and uncomfortable. Woke up last night around 3:00 a.m., panicky. Shook Peter awake and forced him to sit up and play manic games of gin rummy by the dim light of our battery-operated lantern. If our marriage survives this place, it will be a miracle.

7:30 p.m. Another day of reading and playing cards while the rain falls. There is no sign of a break. Still no water. Electricity returned briefly, and we finally managed to get the radio to work and find the English radio station—had to choose between it and our one dim light bulb, of course. You know we're getting desperate when our idea of amusement is watching a gecko chase a bug along the wall. We're cutting our losses. We've decided to see if we can get a flight out Tuesday morning-basically moving everything up a week.

SEPTEMBER 16—NADI

We made it! I was getting a bit nervous we were never going to get off Vanua Levu. I never thought I'd be so glad to see the back of a South Seas island. But I have learned, among other things, that the South Seas without sun can be difficult to take for any length of time. (Other lessons: Never build a house on a point. Always bring cards.)

Gopendra's father-in-law just died, so Mohammed Hussein (another taxi driver with an extremely confusing family—his brothers are Mohammed Hassine, Mohammed Hassan, and Mohammed Hassain) picked us up. We dropped the keys off with Jessie and were at the airport as requested at 9:30 a.m.—which was a good thing as the 10:10 plane left at 9:45! As entirely appropriate, the water, which had come back on yesterday afternoon, was off again this morning.

I'll miss the flowers, the birds, the butterflies, the bats and, most of all, the wonderful, kind Fijian people, of whatever ethnicity, but goodbye and good riddance to Paradise Point—a misnomer if ever there was one.

TWO
DID YOU EVER HAVE TO MAKE UP YOUR MIND?

Sometimes the seemingly easiest things turn out to be the hardest.

THE WORLD IS A VERY BIG PLACE

We once actually thought it was possible to see the world in a year. Planes can take you anywhere you want to go in about a day. Name a place and you probably know at least one person who has been there. Television makes the exotic familiar. E-mail connects us instantaneously with the other side of the world. The accepted wisdom is that the world is shrinking—until you start putting your trip together.

The most difficult task you face may be deciding where in the world to go, because that means deciding where you will not go. We were loath to give up any dream destination. Back and forth, forth and back we went, debating the merits of one continent over another, one country over a neighbouring one. In the process, we started to define what we wanted from the trip.

First, it was important to both of us to touch base with far-flung friends and family. I hadn't seen my Australian friend, Jennifer, since we had wandered around Europe together in the early 1970s. Peter and I had been telling our friend, Dvora, we'd visit Israel ever since she moved there ten years ago. And we had long ago promised Peter's Auntie Audrey that we would be with her in England to celebrate her ninetieth birthday.

Second, I had always dreamed of visiting India; Peter was keen to see South Africa. We both love the Mediterranean. We could never spend enough time in Greece, Italy, or France. And we'd never been to Turkey or Egypt. Having time to explore that part of the world was high on both our lists.

And finally, sun. I was desperate for sun. There had to be plenty of time for lounging around on beaches.

The trip started to take shape. Shape which would shift and change and transform itself continuously over the next few years of planning.

A YEAR IS NOT AS LONG AS IT SEEMS

Once you narrow down your destinations, you will start to think about how much time you have and how long you want to spend in each place. One of the early and most sensible decisions we made was to set aside time at home at the end of the year off. It didn't make sense to either of us to arrive home from a year of travelling and have to show up for work the next Monday morning. We'd need re-entry time. So we set aside the last two months to get reacquainted with our lives. That left ten months of playtime. But play where? For how long? We began to discover that, if the world is still a big place, so are the individual countries.

We devoured guidebooks on various tentative routes. We read histories of Australia and Israel and novels by authors from India and Italy. The more we read, the more we wanted to see and do. It was clear we could spend the entire ten months in one country and not experience everything.

From previous travels we know that our tolerance for being constantly on the move is limited. Our longest previous trip together was six weeks travelling through Southeast Asia. At about the four-week mark, we got a little ratty—short-tempered, tired, and generally not having as good a time. We discovered that we would rather spend more time in one place and get to know it a bit, than to be always on the go, always seeing something new.

So what was it to be? A month in each of ten countries? Two or three months in three or four places?

TO PLAN OR NOT TO PLAN?

What you think you want to do and what you actually do often bear very little resemblance to each other.

I am a classic Type A personality and a Virgo to boot. Planning is my life. I have lists of everything: to-do lists, people-to-call lists, letters-to-write lists, groceries-to-buy lists. I can't stand disorganization or mismanagement. The point of this is that I'm slightly compulsive by nature. This was my chance to break that mould—if I could.

Part of me just wanted to wander—to have a ticket in my hand to our first destination and then just take it from there. But my essential

organizing character wanted to know what I was going to be doing—
if not all the time, at least in general terms. The battle was on. Plan the
whole trip? Don't plan at all, just go? Plan part of the trip? Maybe plan
the bookends—rent a house in Fiji for the first month and a house in
the south of France for the last. Perhaps we could plan only critical
elements within the trip, such as India, which we both found a bit
intimidating.

Reinforcing my organizational mode was one surprising truth:
planning saves money. And its corollary: flexibility is expensive. It
seems counterintuitive to me, but invariably it proved to be true. I
had assumed that simply wandering would be relatively inexpensive. Not
so. We regularly discovered we could save money by booking ahead,
taking advantage of airline seat sales or package deals. All we had to do
was make up our minds three weeks or a month in advance.

We debated the merits of planning/saving money versus flexi-
bility/spending money. We went around and about and in so many
directions that at various times we totally lost track of what we were
doing. Changing our minds was the only constant.

Ultimately we settled on the great Canadian compromise—what, for
me, was a minimally planned trip:

- We purchased a round-the-world airline ticket (see page 155)—
  it was such a good deal we simply couldn't pass it up—but we
  agreed we wouldn't let it determine where we'd go. If we had
  the chance to try something different—train, boat, car, donkey, whatever—we'd do it. The airline ticket was just to provide
  some structure to the year.

- We rented a house in Fiji for the first three weeks (see page 30)
  to give us time to relax, settle down, and think about what we
  wanted to do next.

- We reserved a bed and breakfast in Auckland, New Zealand,
  for the night of our arrival there.

- We booked a sailing cruise through the Straits of Malacca, simply for personal, romantic reasons. That meant we had to be in

Phuket, Thailand, on December 2 to catch the boat.

• And we had to be in England on March 29 for Auntie Audrey's birthday.

Aside from that, we were on our own.

The planning/flexibility dilemma didn't end with our departure from Victoria. It was a constant of the trip. We'd arrive in Australia and, at some point, have to book a seat on the train from Adelaide to Alice Springs. Or we'd purchase a cheap plane ticket from London to Israel three weeks in advance. Inevitably, every time we made such a commitment, we'd discover some other wonderful place we wanted to stay, or meet someone we wanted to spend more time with. But we'd have to break away to catch our train, plane, or whatever.

CHANGING YOUR MIND IS OKAY

With the exception only of the round-the-world airline ticket and Auntie Audrey's birthday, everything we arranged before leaving Victoria was a disaster. The house in Fiji was "interesting" and the weather so bad we bailed out early. The B&B we booked in Auckland was the only dump encountered in the entire year. The cruise through the Straits of Malacca had to be cancelled because drifting smoke from massive forest fires in Indonesia made breathing difficult and seeing impossible. (Thank goodness we cancelled. The week we were scheduled to be there, two freighters collided due to poor visibility.)

There is no way you can know in advance how you'll like a place, who you'll meet, what the weather will be like, whether you'll be sick or tired. Or any number of other variables that will make you want to stay forever or get on the next freight train out of town.

> Somewhere along the way you switch personas. You become the travelling person as opposed to the home person. And the things that are important to you at home aren't the same things that are important to you when you're on the road. It's very difficult to tell in advance what you're going to need because you're in a different reality.
>
> Margaret

A brief glance at our plans, such as they were when we left Victoria, alongside what we actually did, will give you some idea of how things can change:

ORIGINAL PLANS		ACTUAL TRIP	
Fiji	3 weeks	Fiji	2 weeks
New Zealand	1 week	New Zealand	1 month
Australia	3 weeks	Australia	2 months
Malaysia & Straits	3–4 weeks	Singapore	1 week
India	6 weeks	India	2 weeks
Eastern Mediterranean		England	1 month
(Turkey, Israel,		Ireland	2 weeks
Egypt, Greece)	2–3 months	Israel	3 weeks
England	2–3 weeks	England	1 month
Italy	1 month	Italy	3 weeks
France	1 month	France	3 weeks
Estimated	**10 months**	**Actual**	**9 months**

Our experience was not unusual. Mike and Heather set off for a five-and-a-half-month motorcycle trip through South and Central America and back to Canada. After one week on the road, they realized they could complete their plans, but only by racing around and experiencing nothing. Thus started a constant process of reassessment and changing their minds. Heather now sees it as an important part of their experience: "You don't have an opportunity in normal life to have that kind of freedom very often."

The glory of travelling for an extended period of time is time to fritter away as you like. Sometimes, having no plan is the plan.

> We didn't know where we were going to go when we left. We just knew we were going to go. As a matter of fact, we left thinking we would probably go to the Caribbean. We had no other ideas. Whatever. We just left…. I don't know what finally made us decide to head west into the Pacific again.
>
> Larry

FLEXIBILITY IS ESSENTIAL

Things change. The weather's terrible, so you leave. You find a place you love, so you stay. You get sick. Natural disasters or wars intervene. Margaret and Bill ended up changing their plans to visit Peru because Peru and Ecuador were at war; Mike and Heather were rerouted by terrorism in Colombia and floods in Ecuador.

The best advice is: keep yourself as flexible as your budget and temperament will permit.

This is easier at some times than at others. Your flexibility may be limited by other people's schedules. When friends offer you their house in Yorkshire, you work around their dates. Generally, however, flexibility comes naturally after a while. Travelling in the off-season helps. Contrary to information provided to us along the way, there are almost always two seats left on any train. Sure, at some point, a place you had your heart set on staying is full. But, by that time, you'll be amazed how little you care. This isn't a two-week holiday. If you miss one special thing, you have time to find another.

There has to be a balance, and only you know how much spontaneity you can take. But, if you can, try to stay open to new possibilities. The prized moments will come from doing something you never anticipated, like tracking down the ancestral farm in Ireland, or finding a place, like the Red Centre of Australia, that touches your heart.

PREPARATION IS DIFFERENT FROM PLANNING

For me, preparation (Stage I) is one of the major pleasures of a trip. I read everything I can get my hands on about countries I intend to visit. I plot different routes and dream about specific places. So I wasn't surprised to discover that other people are Stage I fans as well.

> I did tons of advance planning. I did it purely for pleasure. Planning is part of the fun for me. I've researched a hundred trips I've never taken. I like to know what all the options are. But we never book things in advance. We had no plans beyond flying to Costa Rica. We kind of let things happen.

And that was deliberate. For once you have the freedom to do that.

Margaret

Most people who love to travel also love to do advance research. Possibly because it was one of our first stops, we did a lot of reading about Australia. Not just tourism information, but histories of settlement, non-fiction about Australian politics and aboriginal relations, and novels by Australian authors. The reading didn't have a direct impact on where we went in Australia. For the most part, our travel was based on people's recommendations. But the reading gave a richness and a context to our stay that simply arriving and observing couldn't have provided.

In other countries, we tried to make up for lost ground by immersing ourselves on arrival in local histories and authors. This led to some wonderful finds and great moments. People love to help you get to know their country. In Auckland, our B&B hosts, Sally and Gerry, provided us with rival reading lists. We asked the clerk in a second-hand bookstore for help finding their suggestions. Once he understood what we were trying to do, he had his own ideas. Other customers got into the act, and somehow we ended up in the midst of a full-fledged literary debate about the philosophies, styles, and competing merits of previously unknown-to-us New Zealand authors.

> 1st customer: *If you're trying to get a handle on New Zealand, you've got to read Tangi and Tangled Web. They're...*

> 2nd customer: *But they're so depressing. They'll think we're all suicidal.*

> Clerk: *How about One of the Bens by Maurice Shadbolt?*

> 2nd customer: *Well, if you want to bore them to death.*

> 1st customer: *What are you saying? He's terrific. His view of modern society...*

2nd customer:...*is half a century old. Let's get with it. Now, Eldred-Griggs deals with history but he has a modern perspective. And he can write. His Oracle and Miracles...*

Clerk: *Well, I think Paul Thomas's Old School Tie...*

1st customer: *Oh come on. He's deadly. I hated that book. It's so macho. Now, Keith Sinclair's not bad, but if I were you, I'd try these...(thrusting two books into my arms)*

Clerk: *What about Michael King...?*

1st customer: *No. If you want to understand New Zealand, you have to read Rosie Scott's Glory Days (handing a book to Peter).*

The debate lasted about fifteen minutes. The pile of books grew. It cost more than we'd planned, but we didn't want to favour one person's choice over another. We read our way through New Zealand.

Research is not the same as planning. One is broadening, fun, and helpful; the other is limiting and, much of the time, useless. It may save you a bit of money, but it can also get in your way. John and Ruth did a lot of research before they left for their year's travel and volunteer work in South America. They had some ideas about what they wanted to do but, beyond the initial six weeks at Spanish-language school in the Dominican Republic, they made no plans. Using this approach not only shaped their trip, it changed their lives.

> We kept running into people. The kind of people I had never met before. And I guess, had never looked for. We became best friends with a bunch of middle-aged American nuns who lived on pixie dust and spent their whole lives looking after street kids in the middle of Bolivia. It was a trip just to be around them.
>
> John

John and Ruth ended up spending most of their year in Bolivia, working with the nuns and street kids. Since returning, they've restructured their lives to allow them to volunteer around the world for a regular part of every year.

So, prepare yourself and have fun doing it. Read about the places you're thinking of visiting, but take the advice of guidebooks with a grain of salt. Most of them are designed for holiday travel or, in the case of longer trips, for younger people. Talk to people about their travel experiences. Have ideas about what you want to do. But keep your actual plans to the minimum you can tolerate. You'll probably just change them anyway.

A FEW THINGS DO NEED TO BE DONE

Once you've decided what countries you'll be visiting, a few tasks do need to be completed.

First and most important, you need an up-to-date passport that won't expire until at least six months after the conclusion of your trip. Many countries will not issue visas on passports that have less than six months' validity.

The countries that require Canadian citizens to have visas are not always the obvious ones. I was surprised to discover we needed a visa to visit Australia. Obtaining visas is usually a relatively straightforward task. You contact the embassy or consulate of the country, find out their requirements, complete and return their forms along with your passport.

When you're dealing with a longer trip, however, things can sometimes be more complicated. For example, we applied in June for visas to visit India in December, only to discover that the Indian Consulate would not issue a visa more than three months in advance. Three months in advance we would already be on the road. We had to remember to build in time along the way to visit an Indian consulate and be prepared to wait three or four days for the paperwork to be completed. We chose to do it in Sydney, Australia, where we were planning to stay for a few weeks in any event. But you may need to think ahead and perhaps even change your itinerary slightly in order to obtain the visas you need for other places on your route. It's a good idea to bring along some extra passport-size pictures of yourself so you don't have to worry about finding a photo booth or studio wherever you are.

You should also plan in advance to take care of your health, particularly if you'll be visiting developing countries. In some parts of the world, certain inoculations are mandatory; in others, they are advisable. Some of these shots need to be given over a period of time, so it's wise to start inquiring as soon as you decide on your destinations. In Victoria, we are fortunate to have a Travel Immunization Office run by the Capital Health Region. It provides health and immunization information for any country in the world. Other cities may have a similar facility, or your doctor can take care of matters for you.

We were pretty sure we'd want to rent cars in a number of different countries, so we visited the automobile association with extra passport pictures in hand (although we could also have had pictures taken there), paid our $10 each, and received our international driver's licences. We never used them. It may have simply been the countries in which we rented cars, but our Canadian driver's licences were accepted everywhere without question. The international driver's licence may be a useful piece of additional identification, but it doesn't appear to be as essential, at least in the developed world, as it once was.

A number of people put their pre-trip time to good use by studying the languages of countries they will be visiting. Even the slightest familiarity with the language will make your travelling more interesting and enjoyable. I asked my niece to tutor me in Italian before we left. As a result, I was able to manoeuvre ungrammatically through the travel basics—ordering food, finding a place to stay, asking directions. Peter and I both speak French and I speak Spanish, which helped us understand most of what people were saying to us in Italian, even if we couldn't always respond fluently. If you have the time and inclination, I strongly recommend a language course. It's a great way to start your trip early.

VOLUNTEERING

Some of us use our time off simply to have a good time. Others see it as an opportunity to do some good in the world.

> Every summer for the past seventeen years, we've gone to a different country for a month or so. We usually went to poor

countries because that's what we could afford—our dollar went further there. But it was getting to feel a bit voyeuristic. Working with the street kids in Bolivia felt good.

John

Finding the right volunteer work isn't always as easy as you might think. And working in a different cultural environment brings problems of its own.

The volunteer experience was both more rewarding and more frustrating than I expected. It was difficult to find opportunities to volunteer if you weren't prepared to commit at least a year. We wanted to have some of that time for ourselves. Or else you have to pay to be a volunteer and we couldn't afford it.... We finally found something, and I expected that we would arrive and they would put us right to work. In fact, we didn't work nearly that much. We met, we talked, they considered what they'd do with us, we met again. In the meantime, we studied Spanish very intensively. It was great training for the job I am doing now [working on aboriginal treaties], where you have to be patient and allow for the cultural stuff.

Margaret

Nor does volunteer work always turn out the way you expect.

I did volunteer work for eight months, and there was very little about the way I worked as a volunteer that was different from the way I worked for a paycheque. I always had this idea that, if you were doing volunteer work, you wouldn't have the same pressures, but a lot of those pressures you feel from work are internal.... It doesn't matter what you're doing in life, whether you're sitting on a beach or doing what you always wanted to do or volunteering, there is a certain amount of baggage that you carry with you. So the work that really has to be done is in your head.

Marie

For some people, however, the volunteer experience can be life-altering.

> We got deeper into a culture, far deeper into a culture, than we ever had before.... My biggest surprise was how much I enjoyed doing it. Because we were totally useful. Being totally useful for a whole year, after working for the government, was like drugs.
>
> John

You may be as fortunate as John and Ruth and luck into the right contacts and a good volunteer fit when you're on the road. But, if you're serious about wanting to volunteer during your time away, you're probably wise to try to set something up in advance.

RENTING HOUSES AT A DISTANCE

Most travel magazines and newspaper travel sections have lists of houses to rent in various parts of the world. Internet travel sites abound with rental opportunities. Catalogues of stunning-looking houses can arrive on your doorstep in a matter of days. They all sound perfect.

Beware. Renting a house you've never seen, based on the word of a stranger who stands to gain from the transaction, can be perilous. It can also be wonderful. We once rented a house on Santorini, Greece, that was paradise on earth. Then there was Fiji! And it's not only in the developing world that renting a house sight unseen can be hazardous. Janet's experience in Provence is not atypical.

> The septic system failed. Then it started raining and the roof leaked. And the well ran dry two or three times. And then the winds came, and they knocked out the power. And because we're out on this little farm, the power was down for three days and, of course, the pump for the well works on electricity, so we also had no water for three days. And the roof was still leaking....And then it started getting cold in November. There were these radiators around this old stone house, but then we find

out that the lady who owned the house never bought the boil-
er to run the radiators. So she brought out these three little
electric space heaters…. About two weeks before Christmas,
there were five days when we had no heat, no light, no water,
and the roof was leaking. My mother arrived to stay with us. My
husband's family—three brothers and sisters and their families—were coming from the rest of France to spend Christmas
with us. And the kids were sick and we were all freezing and in
the dark with candles. It was just a nightmare.

Janet

Perhaps the trick is not expecting too much. And asking questions.
Middle-class Canadians enjoy one of the highest standards of living
in the world. We have to expect that things will be simpler elsewhere.
But we should be able to expect a certain level of basic amenities. Be
specific about your requirements. Don't be afraid to sound picky. This
is no time to be a "nice" Canadian. Ask:

- Is the house heated? How?
- Is there indoor plumbing? Hot water?
- How far is it to the nearest store/town/beach?
- Do we need to bring our own linens?
- Is there a phone/washer/dryer/dishwasher/television?
- Do they all work?

Request references—previous renters you can contact to inquire
about the place. If you don't feel comfortable with what you hear, look
elsewhere. There are a lot of places to rent out there.

Don't assume anything—other than that things probably won't
work. Have an explicit written agreement with your landlord, including what you can expect if things don't live up to advance billing.
Neither Janet nor we did this, and we ended up throwing money to the
wind as we made alternate arrangements to keep ourselves sane.

If you're thinking of a long-term rental, you might consider renting
initially for a limited period of time with an option to renew.

It was good having the first house rented for the first three months—and only three months. When we found out how cold and dismal and damp it was, well…. It was a good thing.

Helen

SO, WHOSE TRIP IS THIS ANYWAY?

I have a theory that, in every couple, one person is the trip planner and the other is the trip goer. This is probably a survival mechanism. Two planners in one family could result in homicide. In our family, I am the travel person. My places-to-visit list encompasses most of the globe. As one vacation nears its end, I'm already thinking of the next destination. Peter will occasionally object to some particular scheme—"Aren't the Sendero Luminoso killing people in Peru at the moment?"—or have conditions to impose—"I'm only going trekking in Nepal with a company that brings a portable toilet." Generally, though, he is content to leave the organization to me.

This arrangement is fine for a three-week vacation. It doesn't work with a significant chunk of your life.

Everyone involved in this adventure has to buy in—to participate in decision-making and take equal responsibility. There are far too many details for one person to deal with, and the potential for too much to go wrong. If you don't spread the responsibility around, one of you is likely to break under the pressure.

The advance planning is the least of it. On the road, each day is filled with small and large decisions: What do you want to eat? How does this phone work? Where can I buy stamps? What bus do we take to get to the beach? What time does the train leave? From which station? Where are we going to stay tonight? On and on and on.

Unless you're travelling on your own, this is not a solitary endeavour. Part of the reason for breaking away from your own little world is to test yourself on a broader canvas. You can't do that as a passenger.

The issue of shared responsibility may be particularly important for women.

I think what was difficult for Heather was that she's a take-charge kind of person and she found—well, here I am in this country where I don't speak the language, and I need Mike to ask how much this loaf of bread costs. That was very difficult for her—to be dependent on me.

Mike

This may be particularly true if you're involved in a physically challenging form of travel.

Also, physically, on the motorcycle, there were certain things I couldn't do. I couldn't move it in certain circumstances. I couldn't pick it up when it fell over. So, again, I was completely dependent. I felt sometimes I wasn't contributing at all to this trip. That caused a little bit of tension, a little bit of weepiness.

Heather

One solution may be to carve out your own areas of responsibility. Look for tasks that each member of the family can call his or her own. Ian and Jocelyn put the children, June and Donny, in charge of the captain's log—the mileage, the destinations, the expenses. They also rotated some of the regular duties, like cooking. Donny built a camp cooker and cooked on that. It took a little longer—some nights they ate at eight, some nights they ate at nine—but it didn't matter. They ate.

In the planning stage, Peter and I were enthusiastic partners. I took my usual lead in gathering tourism information, while Peter did the historical reading and research he loves. On the road, however, it was a different story. When something went wrong—and a lot went wrong in the first couple of weeks—I felt totally responsible. I was the one who had wanted to run away. I was the one who had felt the need to start by hiding out on a tropical island. I had rented the ruin on Fiji. I even felt responsible for the gale that hit the island. Midway through New Zealand, I was adding exhaustion to guilt. Every day I spent hours poring over tourism information, choosing which bed and breakfast we'd try, suggesting which route we might take, what we might like to see or do. A couple of weeks of this and I'd had it.

In my typical solicitous way, I chose an evening when Peter was flat on his back in bed with the flu to launch my assault. "I can't do this anymore. Why do I have to make all the decisions about this trip? You've got to start taking an interest and taking on some of the responsibility?"

It was painfully clear that our usual vacation patterns didn't work. Peter had to be more assertive. I had to be less directive. If we didn't find some equilibrium, this trip was going to be a disaster. So, together, slowly, we started to develop a different way of travelling together—as partners. Peter started opening up about his needs. We began to take turns making decisions. We discovered that we could pull together comfortably. I felt a weight lift, and Peter made the trip his own. It was then that we really started to travel.

THINGS TO THINK ABOUT

PLANNING
- You can't do everything. The world is bigger than you think.
- More time in fewer places is probably a good idea.
- Keep yourself flexible. There's no way you can know how you'll feel months from now.
- Prepare, but don't overplan.
- Make sure your passport is valid until at least six months after you plan to return.
- Once you know where you're going, check to see if you need visas or inoculations.
- Bring along extra passport photos for visa applications.
- Consider getting an international driver's licence. It's no longer necessary in much of the world, but it may come in handy as additional identification.
- Brush up your foreign-language skills. You'll have a better time if you can speak a bit of the local language.

VOLUNTEERING
- This is one area that does need planning. Try to set up something in advance.

RENTING HOUSES
- Ask questions.
- Be specific about your requirements.
- Ask for the names of previous tenants who can give you an unbiased opinion.
- Get it in writing.
- If you can, rent for a trial period with an option to renew.

RESPONSIBILITIES
- Share responsibilities and decision-making.
- Assign specific tasks.

September/October: NEW ZEALAND
Chain of Friends

I'm going to like New Zealand. The sun was shining when we arrived three days ago and has been more or less faithful since. After one false start—the B&B we had originally booked from home turned out to be a dump—we decided to go with the recommendation of a couple we met in Fiji: The Great Ponsonby B&B. At Cdn$125 a night, it's more than we wanted to spend, but we need pampering.

Ponsonby is a trendy, in-transition neighbourhood about a 20-minute bus ride from downtown. Everything in the B&B works and the water is hot. There's a comfortable lounge to sit and chat with our hosts, Sally and Gerry, and other guests, listen to CDs, and pour ourselves a drink from the honour bar (first drink on the house, thereafter keep a tab). We even have a resident dog and cat. This is more like it!

Sally and Gerry are terrific. Sally teaches school, primarily Maori kids, in a tough South Auckland neighbourhood. Gerry is an old-fashioned left-winger, ex-ship's steward and union worker, reincarnated as a small businessperson. He says he tries to hide his leftist leanings from his primarily business clientele but I doubt he's very successful.

Auckland is an interesting mix of the modern and trendy and the slightly seedy. The physical setting is beautiful—a busy harbour, blue water bounded by softly rising hillsides hugging largely older, nicely lived-in buildings. It's much more multicultural than I expected.

If Fijians win the hospitality award, Kiwis (read, New Zealanders) are definitely in the running for the chattiest people in the world. Throughout the past few days, we've found ourselves in intense con-versations with strangers—in the museum, at the restaurant, at the bus stop. It may be a function of being isolated on a small group of islands at the end of the earth, but these people simply love to chat. You can't do anything according to a schedule because you inevitably end up spending hours just sitting around talking. It's great. You hear about people's personal lives, their views on politics, what shows are hot, whatever.

We've spent our days doing lovely tourist things—visiting museums, taking ferry rides, walking on the beach, exploring shops, etc. Then back to the B&B for a glass of wine, some chat, an occasional trip with Sally to visit local pottery shops. Feels like home.

SEPTEMBER 20—
OMAPERE, HOKIANGA, NORTHLANDS
Leaving The Great Ponsonby this morning turned out to be a major production. We decided to rent a car and wander around New Zealand for awhile, but didn't really have any plans. Gerry decided to make some for us. We had never even heard of Omapere (on the northwest coast of the North Island), but Gerry decided we should see it, stay with their friends, Gay and Allan, and have Allan take us out on his boat. Before we knew it, it was all arranged.

Gerry was, of course, absolutely right. Omapere is rugged and gorgeous, and Allan and Gay are wonderful people. We're actually staying next door with their neighbours, as their house is being repaired, but they are acting as our hosts and treating us as if we were old friends of the family. Gay is half Maori, and it's fascinating to hear her reactions to the political moves by the New Zealand First (Maori-dominated) Party. Signs of integration of Maori culture and language with the mainstream are everywhere, and their legitimate role in the society is a given. Having said that, the Maori still have a long way to go to enjoy the same rights and privileges as the pakeha (non-Maori). The visible poor are overwhelmingly Maori. Gay is clearly torn—proud of Maori accomplishments to date, but concerned about Maori demands rocking the boat. Fundamentally, she accepts that "we're all New Zealanders"—quite a different perspective than you'd hear from many Canadian First Nations.

SEPTEMBER 21—RUSSELL
Today dawned clear and bright, as befits my birthday. We spent the morning on Allan's boat, sailing with dolphins in Hokianga

Harbour. This is an elemental part of New Zealand. It still has a frontier feel to it—although a weekend influx of "lawyers from Auckland" may change that in a few years. For the time being, however, the green-treed hill in the east, sloping to the crescent-shaped bay, is dotted with only a few houses. To the west, a rugged mountain range provides a sharp contrast behind a barren white-sand peninsula. Beyond the narrow opening to the sea, the Pacific Ocean beats against the shore but inside the harbour all is calm.

In the afternoon, we drove for an hour or so across the North Island to the east coast, the Bay of Islands and Russell. Here we are staying with former neighbours of Brian, the manager of the car rental office in Auckland. I feel like we're being handed carefully from friend to friend.

The area is a stunning visual hit of primary blues and greens, and we have another drop-dead gorgeous view of hillside and ocean, small bays and large boats. But things seem strangely plastic after Hokianga. It's much more settled and genteel on this side of the island. Helen and Ray, our hosts, are pleasant but very conservative people, and Ray is an angry man, at least with respect to Maori issues, which are clearly top-of-mind in New Zealand at the moment. He harangued us over tea with quite a different perspective to Gerry and Gay's, and not a particularly pleasant one. It may have been that or the drive, but this afternoon both Peter and I were down—physically, mentally, emotionally.

Fortunately, our mood passed and, by evening, things were looking brighter. We dressed ourselves up (overdressed in Russell terms) and headed off to the Duke of Marlborough Hotel for a birthday celebration of cervina (farm-raised deer) and great New Zealand wine. We have discovered that Kiwis don't dress up, ever, as far as I can tell. They're lovely people but their dress sense is in their mouths. The national uniform for young women seems to be dark brown or black ankle-length hobble skirts with clunky platform shoes.

SEPTEMBER 23—RUSSELL
Russell is a charming little town with an "early settler" feel to it. Old wooden buildings line the waterfront and ramble up the short

downtown streets. New arrivals in soft shades of stucco have taken over the hillsides and hilltops. Russell will always be memorable to me, however, for the most lugubrious tour I've ever encountered. Who would have thought a visit to an historical book bindery could be an emotional experience. The tour guide who showed us around Pompallier House was clearly having major personal problems. He looked as if he were going to burst into tears at any moment.

Kiwis have a strange attitude to service. They are incredibly warm and friendly, but they work at their own pace and think nothing of chatting on the phone about their personal lives while potential customers wait around. They also have an unusual relationship to time and frequently leave five or ten minutes ahead of schedule. (We first experienced this phenomenon with the plane in Fiji. Maybe it's some kind of South Pacific thing.) They must also hate working on weekends, as everything is understaffed on Saturday and Sunday, which is, of course, precisely when you need staff in the tourism industry.

We've been wandering and touristing, exploring the Bay of Islands by boat, catching up on New Zealand history by visiting Waitangi across the bay where the treaty with the Maori was signed, and generally having a relaxed good time.

I spent this afternoon trying to figure out what we should do in the South Island. It seems so big, and I can't get a handle on what the weather is likely to be at this time of year—snow? rain? drizzle? Last night we tucked up in front of the tube with fish and chips. I watched *Hamish MacBeth* and there was a cricket game on for Peter. The simple pleasures.

SEPTEMBER 24—
NGONGOTAHA (OUTSIDE ROTORUA)

So this is travelling. Enormous emotional ups and downs. A long day's drive through alternately beautiful and boring landscapes. Arrival in the rain at another great B&B, the Waiteti Lakeside Lodge, with friendly hosts, Bryan and Val. This is the second recommendation from our Auckland car rental agent. This one, I think, will work.

This evening we headed off to the local therapeutic hot springs, the Polynesian Spa—just us and four busloads of Korean tourists. It was like throwing in a free trip to Seoul.

Over dinner, Peter declared he wasn't feeling well and we left early. I'm feeling sad, mad, and pissed off. Peter and I have been a little edgy with each other today. Part of me wonders if he's as sick as he says or if this is just some way to get back at me because he really didn't want to go to the spa. Another part of me feels guilty because things seem to keep going wrong. First Fiji. Then word that forest fires in Indonesia are spreading thick smoke over all of Southeast Asia, which could threaten our planned time in Malaysia. Now Peter getting sick. I know I'm overreacting, but I don't care. This is not what I had in mind.

SEPTEMBER 25—NGONGOTAHA
Poor Peter—he really is sick—feverish in the extreme. He's been sleeping all day and, hopefully, is feeling a little better. We can stay here one extra day, which is a relief, but the B&B is fully booked on Saturday night. And we have to make a decision tomorrow about ferry reservations to the South Island. Peter and I had an ill-timed argument last night about him taking a more active role in trip planning and not leaving all the responsibility to me. Nothing like hitting him when he's down.

While Peter slept this afternoon, I went for a horseback ride in Whakarewarewa State Forest Park, a bizarre redwood and fern forest—sort of California meets New Guinea—and returned feeling a bit more in control. Tonight, I'll be making chicken soup for Peter and probably ordering in Chinese. Who says we're not living high on the hog?

SEPTEMBER 26—NGONGOTAHA
Forget Chinese. How about fresh-caught marinated smoked trout, homemade pizza and salad and a good New Zealand red? Bryan and Val invited me to join them for dinner last night so, while poor Peter suffered, I was socializing.

Peter's a bit better today—or so he says. And he certainly wasn't

going to miss the performing sheep. One of the yachties trapped in
Savusavu with us had Peter in open-mouthed wonder, and hysterical
laughter, with his tales of the incredible performing sheep of
Rotorua. These sheep became the Holy Grail of Peter's New Zealand
experience, and no mere bout of the flu was about to derail this
quest. The sheep lived up to their advance publicity. One by one,
nineteen separate breed of sheep are introduced. (I had no idea there
were so many different types of sheep. But then, I never knew there
were so many sheep, period. Forty million in New Zealand alone!
That's a lot of sheep.) On call, each comes running up a ramp to
take his (or her?) place on the podium, standing proudly over the
sign bearing the name of that breed. They are aided by mechanical
manoeuvring devices, but it's nonetheless an amazing performance.
Peter loved it, and I have the happy picture of Peter and the head
sheep to prove it.

While Peter rested from the excitement of his morning's success, I
visited the Geyser Park and "Living Village." A volcano erupted
some 250 years ago, covering the "Buried Village." The survivors
moved to the present site, the "Living Village." Approximately sixty-
five Maori live there today—at the end of a tourist route. After
wandering through the geysers, you walk into their village and look
at the people, their houses, their cooking boxes. It's the most intrusive tourism site I've ever visited. These people have been turned into
Disneyland figures or museum exhibits. Buried again.

This evening, Peter lifted himself off his sick bed to go to a *hangi*,
a Maori feast, and cultural performance. The Maori are alternately
forbidding and friendly, separate and New Zealanders. The Maori in
Waitangi refuse to do cultural performances and refer to Rotorua as
Tinseltown. But we enjoyed the evening, thought it was culturally
sensitive, informative, fun, and presented with dignity and pride.

SEPTEMBER 28—WELLINGTON
Yesterday was a travelling day. A long drive to Wellington through
volcanic plateaus and sheep, sheep, and more sheep. Appropriately,
we ate dinner in the Shepherd's Arms.

On Bryan and Val's recommendation, we're staying at yet another great B&B, Holdsworth, two doors away from the prime minister's residence. You can tell this is a government town. Our hostess, Miriam, loves to talk local politics, which are really interesting at the moment as the governing Coalition seems to be falling apart. There appears to be enormous ambivalence among Kiwis about their government and the rigid economic restraint program they've been living with for the past decade. Everyone we speak with is angry about the social and racial problems that government policies are causing. At the same time, they all seem to feel that the economic changes were necessary.

Today started off slowly and got even slower. We rose late and took a tour of the Parliament Buildings with the slowest-speaking tour guide in the world. I thought Peter was going to explode. It took an hour and a half to complete what should have been, at most, a forty-five minute tour. Worse, it delayed Peter's lunch—never a good idea. However, it was one of the few free experiences we've had in New Zealand, so we shouldn't complain.

The Parliament Buildings themselves are a testimony to New Zealand parsimoniousness, peculiarity, or both. The legislative complex consists of three buildings, none of which matches any other. There's a beautiful library, which would have been even nicer if they'd spent the money to put on the planned third floor; an attractive central building, in a totally different architectural style and with only one wing completed; and a hideous modern "beehive" office tower to house MPs. A definite candidate for ugliest legislative buildings in the world.

We're trying hard to keep up with local happenings, but it can be difficult. The biggest news of the day is "the travel rorts scandal." What the hell is a rort? And the "hoons" are acting up. Huh?

SEPTEMBER 30—NELSON, SOUTH ISLAND
An Australian on the ferry informed us that a rort is a deceit, particularly of the system, and can be used either as a noun or a verb. A hoon is a hooligan. I like that word.

The three-hour ferry trip from Wellington, North Island, to Picton, South Island, could have been a BC Ferry ride through

Howe Sound. Even the weather was BC-like—overcast, damp, yet beautiful. We left the rental car in Wellington and picked up a new one on this side—cheaper that way. I love the informality of New Zealand; the car rental "agency" consisted of a woman and her 10-year-old son holding a sign. We then set off on the twistiest road imaginable, through farm valleys and along exquisite coastline. To make us feel totally at home, they threw in some clear-cut! These folk make BC look environmentally responsible; they log right down to the streams.

Arrived in Nelson, the sunniest spot in New Zealand, in—what else?—rain. Once again, the B&B hand-off demonstrates its worth. Walmer House, recommended to us by Miriam in Wellington, is perfect. We are Bob and Janet's only guests and have a private apartment: a small sunroom overlooking the harbour on two sides, a big bedroom also with harbour view, our own kitchen and, best of all, a bathtub! Had my first bath in a month.

Our jinx continues. A half-hour after leaving the Parliament Buildings in Wellington, the building next door caught fire. (In past years, two places, the Lake Okanagan Resort in Kelowna and the Hudson Inn in Quebec, caught fire either while we were there or immediately after we left.) The fire raged for almost forty-eight hours. The building was filled with asbestos and PCBs, so a portion of downtown Wellington was closed off and five government departments locked out for three days. Perhaps we should issue warnings when we're heading somewhere.

I have felt totally giddy all day. The simplest things send me into fits of laughter. I lost it entirely while reading the map and trying to direct Peter. We had to pull over to the side of the road until I could collect myself. When leaving the house today, I said goodbye to Janet and proceeded to walk confidently into the closet. I emerged, however, with pride intact and eventually found the door.

OCTOBER 1—NELSON
One month out. No obvious life-altering revelations as yet. Maybe next month.

OCTOBER 2—NELSON

Yesterday, we fossicked, i.e., we wandered around the countryside looking at arts and crafts. This morning, we hiked. The sun is shining, the ocean is blue and green—a glorious warm sunny day. Lunch on the deck at the Boat Shed sipping Mac's local beer and listening to Céline Dion on the sound system—that woman is everywhere. Then off to Tehananui Beach just down the road to snooze and read and watch kids playing soccer and Frisbee.

Then home to visit with Bob and Janet, and Jim and Penny, the golden Labs. I'm going to hate to leave this place tomorrow. It has been more like staying with friends than paying for accommodation. Last night, Janet and Bob opened a bottle of wine, and we drank and chatted and nibbled on smoked salmon before going out to dinner. The night before, we watched Sir Edmund Hillary's biography on TV together.

Our new friends are an absolute stitch and, in many ways, wonderfully representative of so many New Zealanders we've met. On the surface they appear quite ordinary. Bob is around our age, slightly built, with glasses; Janet is a few years younger, attractive but a very conservative, even prim, dresser. Underneath these unimposing facades, however, beat the hearts of true free spirits. Janet's manic laugh and wild driving are dead giveaways to a raucous and sensual personality. Bob's passion for the environment and the wild country around Nelson shines through his conversation, which is leavened with *Fawlty Towers*–like tales such as mistakenly mentioning to a German tour group that, in the summer, crowded Tehananui Beach is known locally as the Nelson Belsen.

OCTOBER 6—WANAKA

Since leaving Bob and Janet, we've travelled down the west coast, mixing driving with great hikes through primeval forests to beaches with Jurassic Park-like rock formations.

Janet hoped we would meet "some real Kiwi jokers, not just middle-class folk like us," and she got her wish. The west coast of the South Island is renowned for its characters and crazy poets. We stayed one night in Hokitika with Anne and Spencer, a retired fisherman. Breakfast was whitebait patties made with fish caught by Spencer the previous day and a chirpy greeting from Anne: "Looking sparky this morning." Translation: you're looking bright and cheerful. It was such a pleasure spending time with them. If their views are any indication, the Maori are on to a good thing. When I think of some of the extreme reactions I've encountered from fishers in British Columbia regarding aboriginal issues, I am struck by the openness and generosity shown by Anne and Spencer. They voted New Zealand First in the last election and have great confidence in their country's ability to accommodate cultural differences fairly.

Bob and Janet have handed us on to Bindy at The Stone Cottage in Wanaka. Wanaka, we are told, is the Kiwi's Queenstown. By which they mean that, while most tourists go to Queenstown, New Zealanders go to Wanaka. Once again, we have a self-contained apartment, this time right on the lake. The first night, after a long drive to get here, we arranged for Bindy to cook us dinner. Drinks in front of her fireplace, then sitting around the table, eating a home-cooked meal, chatting about life in the country—it feels like having dinner with a friend you haven't seen for a while. And you can't beat the price: NZ$30 each, including drinks and wine. An equivalent meal at a New Zealand restaurant would be at least NZ$100–125. (The comparative Canadian cost would be around $70–80.)

Meal prices in New Zealand are extortionate—and for no good reason that I can figure out. A bowl of soup can be NZ$8; a main course NZ$22 or $23—nothing cheaper. This is for pasta, for God's sake. Restaurants charge for bread! A restaurant lunch will be NZ$30–40; dinner NZ$70–80!

We've been horseback riding and hiking, walking on the beach, watching the sun go down behind the mountains. Yesterday, we drove up the Motakataka Valley into high ranch country—sheep, deer, and cattle everywhere, including on the road. It is a glorious place, but so like British Columbia that it seems a little odd to have come all this way.

OCTOBER 8—QUEENSTOWN

A short drive and Bindy's recommendation led us to the terrace at

Trelawn Place B&B, overlooking snow-capped mountains and the Shotover River. A corgi is resting at my feet while three others race around the yard. The sun is shining, the birds are chirpling, sheep are baaing in the distance.

Kiwis may find Queenstown "too commercial and touristy," but we had to see it for ourselves. Our conclusion: New Zealanders have no idea what "commercial" really looks like. Queenstown is a pleasant small town with a focus on tourism. It's no Coney Island.

Nery and Michael continue the string of B&B hosts who become friends. Like us, they love to travel, and they are filled with good advice about places we want to visit on this trip. Like all Kiwis, they are tiringly active, always hiking, fishing, bicycling, doing something. When you mention you're thinking of spending the afternoon sitting around, reading, writing, enjoying the spectacular scenery, they're always terribly understanding. "Oh yes, of course," they say, providing books and a comfortable place to sit. "But," they go on, "you might also want to…and then there's this fabulous walk to…." The list is endless. They can't seem to abide the idea of doing nothing.

Today, I resisted—at least for the most part. I wrote my mum and did some reading. I did, however, succumb to a solitary walk in the hills, where I found myself doing a Maria von Trapp imitation, singing to the sheep appropriate songs like "I'll think of summer days again and dream of ewe," "Till there was ewe," "Ewe-we-we left me standing all alone-one-one…." You get the idea. New Zealand in spring is a treat—lambs everywhere. So cute. And music lovers to boot.

The country does have its downside, however. The calciovirus has struck with a vengeance, and the roadside is littered with dead bunnies.

10:00 p.m. Just came in from a hot tub under the stars. Saw the Southern Cross for the first time. Sigh.

OCTOBER 9—MILFORD SOUND, ABOARD THE MILFORD WANDERER

People told us about the beauty of Milford Sound, but no one mentioned the tunnel you have to go through to get here. You're driving along a lovely country road in the sunshine when, suddenly, you're confronted with a rough opening in a mountainside. With no warning, it's pitch-black, no lights anywhere. Water drips on the windshield from rocks above. Then it's straight down in the dark, like being hurled into the mouth of hell. You have no idea where you are or what, if anything, is coming. It's terrifying. And New Zealanders just seem to take it for granted. Of course, after one-lane bridges, some shared not only with oncoming vehicles but with trains, not to mention the aggressiveness of Kiwi drivers (for a generally quiet people, they are terrors behind the wheel of a car), I guess nothing fazes them on the road.

After a strong drink, we boarded the *Milford Wanderer*, an old wooden schooner, for an overnight cruise through the sound. We are a motley crew of approximately twenty-nine aboard a vessel that theoretically holds twice that number. There are five shared showers inside, five toilets outside. Our four-bunk "cabin" has walls that don't reach the ceiling and a curtain in place of a door. The weather is iffy—raining at the moment and low cloud—but it's still beautiful. Using the biffy in the middle of the night will be interesting though.

The sound is spectacular—a narrow fjord between steep craggy cliffs with waterfalls rushing to the sea. But, again, it's so like parts of the BC coast as to be weird. In general, New Zealand is much like a miniature British Columbia with warmer water.

OCTOBER 13—CHRISTCHURCH
After another few days with Nery and Michael (how wonderful to be greeted with a big hug and "welcome home"), we drove east across the South Island to Christchurch. We arrived at Hambledon B&B by mid-afternoon, refreshed enough to go to the big rugby match that evening.

My reaction to my first professional rugby game appears to have made me an honorary Christchurchian. At breakfast the following morning, another guest asked about the game. "Who won?" he inquired. "We did," I responded, meaning the local team, Canterbury. Later that morning, our host, Calvin, approached me. "Thank you," he said softly. "We really appreciate your support." I had no idea what he was talking about. That evening, I figured it out when he went on to say, "Even Jo (his wife, who is not a rugby fan) thought it was terrific the way you supported our team." It was the "we" that did it. Calvin is a serious Canterbury fan.

Since arriving in Christchurch, we've been playing tourist—taking the tram tour, visiting the museum, wandering through the botanical gardens, listening to the choir in the cathedral, punting on the Avon. Christchurch appears to be a nice, quiet little place—much like Victoria—but the inhabitants seem to be convinced they are crime-ridden: Jo and Calvin lock the B&B doors during the day and have been the only B&B hosts to ask us for a credit card number up front; Calvin cautioned us not to walk home from the rugby game; the teddy-bear shop downtown has an obvious state-of-the-art security system; the tallest building in town has a large POLICE sign on top, and there's a police kiosk in Cathedral Square; the café where we stopped for coffee asked us to pay in advance. Christchurch either has some strange hidden life or it's a city of paranoids.

OCTOBER 14—CHRISTCHURCH AIRPORT

I have just reread these notes and realized how comparatively little introspection there is in the New Zealand section compared with its Fijian counterpart. The New Zealand experience may not have been as personally revealing, but it has been infinitely more comfortable and enjoyable. Our stay here has given us a chance to find our travelling rhythm. Even better, it has helped me recover my sense of silliness. I once seriously wondered if middle age destroyed your ability to belly-laugh—you know, the deep-from-the-tummy, brings-tears-to-your-eyes, can't-stop kind of laugh. Now I know it has nothing to do with age. Since arriving in New Zealand, I have been having regular fits of laughter for no obvious reason. Anything can trigger one—sheep, half-flush toilets, clothes, expressions, you name it. I just generally feel lighthearted and happy here. I've found myself again.

So, thank you, New Zealand. We've had a great time. And we'll be back. After all, we have friends here now.

THREE
MONEY, MONEY, MONEY, MONEY

So, how much is this going to cost? More than you think.

Peter and I are probably the worst people to talk about cost. We always spend too much on everything. Given a choice between plain and cheap versus charm and comfort at a slightly higher cost, we'll choose the latter every time. Your trip can cost pretty much what you like. It depends on what you're trying to achieve and what you're prepared to put up with. For example:

- Staying in one place costs less than travelling around. Renting an apartment or a house for two or three months will be less expensive than staying in hotels or bed and breakfasts.

- Camping is even less expensive.

Jocelyn, Ian, and the two kids cut their expenses for nine months to approximately $35,000 by camping and using frequent-flier points for their airline tickets.

- Where you go makes a difference. If we had stayed in Fiji, gone to Southeast Asia, or visited parts of South America, things would have been a lot cheaper than spending most of our time in New Zealand, Australia, and Europe.

John and Ruth's year of volunteer work and travel in South America cost them only around $20,000.

- Planning ahead can save you money. If we had tied down our plans in advance, we could have saved on transportation, put together money-saving package deals, and probably found cheaper places to stay.

These choices, however, are as much about the kind of trip you want as they are about finances. Once you decide what type of experience you want and how much money you have, you can make your decisions accordingly.

But be prepared. No matter how much advance research you do, things change. The value of the dollar fluctuates. Local economies go crazy.

Heather and Mike's five-and-a-half-month motorcycle trip through South America cost approximately $40,000.

Even knowing what kind of travellers we are, I was surprised how much we spent. Things are a lot more expensive than they were the last time I took an extended trip in the 1970s. And certain things in certain parts of the world are a shock to a Canadian. Food in New Zealand, for example (see page 65). Will someone please explain to me why restaurant food prices are so exorbitant in New Zealand? We quickly learned to share. Or travel inside Australia. Even for a Canadian, Australia is a big country. It costs a lot to get from place to place, no matter what mode of transport you choose. And, of course, two people cost more than one. A simple truth, but one that only really hits home as you hand over $800 for train fare, not $400.

Rita and Larry estimate they spent approximately $20,000 a year while sailing. That doesn't include expenses back in Canada or the quarter-million-dollar sailboat they called home.

COMFORT IS IMPORTANT
Difficult though it is to accept, travel at 50 is not travel at 20. I'm not as tough as I was. The roughing it I revelled in thirty years ago is simply uncomfortable today. I don't want to stay in a hostel anymore. I want a comfortable bed in a clean room with a private bathroom and, if possible, a degree of charm. I don't want to sit up on a bus or train for four days if there's a stateroom available. I'm willing to be uncomfortable for a limited period of time in exchange for a particular experience. Then I want to be pampered.

Financial decisions can't be separated from your trip goals. Peter has always believed that travel doesn't have to be uncomfortable to be worthwhile. I, for my part, have a high charm standard. Many times we could have opted for a clean, comfortable, perfectly acceptable motel room in the $50–70 range; or stay at a charming bed and breakfast, with friendly and helpful hosts, for $100–125 a night. Invariably we chose the latter. It was the right choice—for us. Some of the B&Bs were even the right financial choice—the breakfasts were big enough to see us through to dinner. Emotionally, there was no question. We felt comfortable and comforted. We made friends we hope to keep for a lifetime. We received more than value for money. The experience was priceless.

Janet's year off, including eight months in France with her husband and two children, cost around $80,000.

OUR COSTS

So, what did it cost us? We budgeted $75,000 for the year. We overspent. We didn't do badly on the actual travel—only 8% over budget.

TRIP EXPENSES BROKE DOWN ROUGHLY AS FOLLOWS

TRANSPORTATION	
airplanes, trains, buses,	
car rentals, gas, etc.	$40,000
ACCOMMODATION	20,000
FOOD	13,000
MISCELLANEOUS	
additional medical insurance,	
shots, guidebooks, photo supplies,	
admission fees to attractions, etc.	3,500
PURCHASES AND GIFTS	4,500
	Total $81,000

The big surprise was not the total but the categories. Transportation, in particular, was a shock. When we bought round-the-world airline tickets (I admit it—we went business class), we assumed we had taken care of the major transportation expenses. We didn't count on how much internal travel would cost in the countries we visited. Over the first three months, we did some serious budget shuffling among categories.

Suzanne figures her family of four spent approximately $50,000 during their ten months away. That doesn't include the approximately $10,000 cost of their 26-foot sailboat.

We had planned to buy a major souvenir in each country we visited— dusters in Australia, carpets in India, etc. That was the first expense to go. A choice between buying things and shortening the trip or staying on the road and accumulating memories was no choice as far as we were concerned.

We tried to budget a hundred bucks a day, for four people, including gas. We didn't quite make it but sometimes we did okay. Sometimes we'd have to do wild camping to catch up.

Ian

We were also able to economize on food, at least once we'd left New Zealand. To our surprise, this didn't turn out to be much of a sacrifice. Originally, we had planned to try great restaurants around the world. After a couple of months on the road, however, any restaurant, no matter how great, loses its appeal. Picnic lunches of bread, cheese, pâté, and fresh fruit were soon preferred to sitting in yet another restaurant, ordering from yet another undistinguished and indistinguishable menu. Dropping into a local pub for snacks and a beer and chatting with the locals was more fun than dressing up for a three-star dinner. Bringing in fish and chips to enjoy in our B&B was a comfort. Cooking, when we had a kitchen at our disposal, was a luxury.

Our real budgeting error had to do with non-trip expenses we hadn't thought enough about. Our focus had been on the trip and what it was going to cost. We had pushed aside all thoughts of some basic expenses that don't go away just because you do: house insurance, life insurance, property taxes. And we were unpleasantly surprised by one large income tax bill. We had neglected to think about the tax implications of cashing in some savings bonds. And the financial wizards in charge of the program that administered Peter's self-funded sabbatical hadn't withheld sufficient tax money at source.

Then there were post-trip expenses. Peter had the option of buying back pension time for the year he had been away from work. This was too valuable in the long run to pass up because of lack of funds at the time. Forty or fifty rolls of film cost a lot to be developed. And living at home, while less expensive than travelling, is not cost-free. Things break down while you're gone and have to be replaced. You still have to eat, pay the telephone, hydro, and other bills.

OUR NON-TRIP EXPENSES LOOKED MORE OR LESS LIKE THIS

SHOULD HAVE BEEN ANTICIPATED:	
residential taxes	$2,000
household insurance	800
life insurance	800
UNEXPECTED:	
income tax	5,000
POST-TRAVEL EXPENSES:	
pension buy-back	6,000
photo developing	500
household repairs	500
living expenses for three months	3,000
Total	$18,600

Our total year costs came in at approximately $100,000—a full 33.3% or $25,000 over our original budget!

Margaret and Bill stayed within their budget of $45–50,000 while travelling for nine months in North, South, and Central America. But they did have to give up their plans to spend a final month in Europe.

When some of the reality of this not-so-slight miscalculation finally broke upon us (I think it was the day in England we received the fax from our accountant about the tax bill), we panicked. Who wouldn't? We thought about cutting our losses and coming home right away. We moped and worried and were generally miserable for a day or so.

Then we started to rationalize. Things really weren't that bad. We had money put aside we could call upon in an emergency. Besides, the trip wasn't responsible—life was. If we had been at home, we would still have paid taxes and insurance, and we would have frittered away most of our income just living. Somehow we managed to convince ourselves things weren't as bad as they seemed.

Patrick and Helen estimate they and Sophie spent approximately $80,000 during their year in Europe.

We continued the trip, albeit taking more care about expenses, and decided to deal with our finances when we got home. Peter is now back at full salary and we're paying off our debt. I don't like owing money. And I wish I had budgeted better. We probably would have made different decisions. But I know we can handle the debt. And we had such a great time, it feels worth every penny.

So don't panic. We were definitely at the high end of the spending scale. Other people seem to have had a better grip on financial reality. (Or there may be an element of selective memory at work.)

Marie's fifteen months off work cost her only about $20,000.

And there are ways of minimizing expenditures on the road. Jocelyn and Ian purchased their airline tickets with frequent-flier points. We were not alone in freeloading off forbearing friends and family wherever we could.

> I was very fortunate. I lived with my sister and her husband for several months and I didn't pay them rent. I did contribute to the groceries and the bills and stuff like that, but they didn't ask for rent. I also lived for several months at the Tai Chi Society. I didn't get an income, but I had free room and board.
>
> Marie

THE OCCASIONAL LUXURY MAY BE A NECESSITY

It's fine to travel on a limited budget, but there are times when a little self-indulgence is absolutely called for. John and Ruth may have won the travel frugality award, but even they advise: "Don't nickle-and-dime yourself to death." Others agree. What's the point of travelling if, when you arrive, you can't afford to do anything.

> While you're travelling on a budget, don't get too fixated on that, because you may have the opportunity to have the experience of a lifetime. We made a mistake in Zermatt. It was going to be the Canadian equivalent of about eighty bucks to get on the aerial tramway to go up and look at the Matterhorn. It's all very dramatic, but we didn't do it because of the cost. Well, you get home now and you think—what a stupid thing. We should have just gone and done it.
>
> Patrick

> So many people are on such a limited budget that they arrive somewhere and they can't afford to go out to eat and try the food, rent a car and drive it inland.... They can't afford to get off the boat. I think it's better to shorten the trip so that you have some money to experience the life of the country. If you're going to a place that has phenomenal waterfalls inland, to go there and not see them seems a shame.
>
> Larry

Some things are worth blowing a little money. I don't regret going first-class on "The Legendary Ghan" from Adelaide to Alice Springs or the Eurostar Chunnel train from Paris to London. They were once-in-a-lifetime experiences. Sometimes luxuries are absolutely essential. One night soaking in a hot tub and sleeping in a clean, comfortable bed in a good hotel may be all it takes to enable you to go on. One three-star dinner may help put a strained relationship back on track.

Be prepared for the last few weeks of your trip to be among the most expensive. As you near the end, holiday patterns start to emerge.

The urge to treat yourself gets stronger. Guilt rears its ugly head. You might feel better greeting the folks back home with something in hand. We take personal credit for the improved fortunes of tablecloth sellers in St. Paul de Vence.

HOW WE SAVED

Saving was easier for us than it may be for many people. We both made good incomes and had no debts. Most importantly, Peter works for the British Columbia government which, blessedly, offers an employee benefit called the Deferred Salary Leave Program. Essentially, this enables employees to fund their own sabbaticals.

DEFERRED SALARY LEAVE PROGRAM

Canada's Income Tax Act was revised in 1988 to allow employees to defer a portion of their salary for what would otherwise be an unpaid leave of absence. With employer and Revenue Canada approval, employees can save up to one-third of their pre-tax salary in an interest-bearing account. Here's how it works:

- The employee banks a proportion of salary for a selected period of time.
- During that time, the banked money accumulates interest.
- The employer provides leave without pay and the guarantee of a job at the same level, although not necessarily the same job, on return.
- While on leave, the employee receives the banked money, either in a lump sum or as regular deposits to a bank account. Taxes are paid only on the money actually received in any given year; banked money remains tax free until withdrawn.
- In some cases, the reduced annual income results in a lower tax rate.

Peter banked one-third of his salary for two years. He then took a year off without pay and received the two-thirds of his salary he had put aside. He could have chosen a longer savings period or shorter time off. The program can be personalized to suit individual finances and wishes.

This program, with the guarantee of a job on return as well as tax benefits, provided the spur we needed. Without it, the idea of taking a year off might have remained a distant dream. But it was just the spur, not the horse. The critical component is wanting to do it badly enough.

Our original plan had been to save one-quarter of Peter's salary for three years. This would have left us more money to live on in the meantime as well as more money to use for our travels. When he applied for Deferred Salary Leave, however, Peter discovered he needed an additional year's employment with the BC government before he would be eligible to enter the program. We were devastated. We'd set our hearts on leaving at a certain time, and we didn't want to delay our departure for a year. But our travel budget called for at least three-quarters of Peter's salary.

In a classic example of the limitations of linear thinking, it took us a week to realize that, just because he couldn't enter the program for another year, there was no reason we couldn't start saving right away. We weren't able to tax shelter that first year's savings, but we were able to save.

For three years, we spent almost nothing on the house or on ourselves. Every time we thought of buying new clothes or renovating the kitchen, we'd ask ourselves which we would prefer, a new suit or travelling around the world for a year. Somehow, the old suit looked better every time. Our intensive savings program was a sign of our desperation to get away. It would probably have been more sensible to have strung it out longer. But our strategy worked for us.

Other people are even more desperate—or more courageous. They sell off all they own to follow their dream. It's an option, but not one I feel comfortable with. Our runaway was intended to be temporary. We always planned to come home. It was important to us that there be something to return to.

> We met a lot of people who had sold everything and put it into the boat. Now, people lose boats. I can't count the number of boats that were lost, sunk, and damaged. And they lost everything.... We didn't sell our house. Even though we didn't know when we'd come back, we had something to come back to.
>
> Larry

Psychologically I think that's really important. There are two sides to it though. Those who just basically sold up had a much more relaxed time of it. They didn't have to worry about leases and tenants. They had their money invested.

Rita

But there was a certain point where they weren't enjoying what they were doing, but they didn't have anything to go back to.

Larry

HOW YOU CAN SAVE

If you really want to run away, you probably can. How you do it and when depends on how much risk you're willing to take. If you're fortunate, your employer may offer some version of the Deferred Salary Leave Program, or possibly even a paid sabbatical program.

The idea of sabbatical leave originated in the academic world. More recently, variations have become common across the public sector. Most teachers and nurses have access to some form of extended leave, as do most federal and provincial civil servants.

The private sector in North America has not been equally whole-hearted in embracing formal extended leave. There are, however, a number of forward-thinking firms that offer some version of sabbatical leave to long-term employees. Royal Trust, for example, has offered a Deferred Salary Leave Program since 1991. More common in the corporate world are various forms of "personal or professional growth" or "social service" leave. A number of corporations, including McDonald's, American Express, and Xerox, support employees who want to return to school or who are interested in volunteering their time in the community.

In general, however, the private sector seems to prefer flexible arrangements. Most firms may not have a formal leave program, but they will try to accommodate the wishes of valued employees with corporate objectives. The competition for talented, highly skilled employees is fierce, and companies are increasingly trying to find creative ways of attracting and maintaining good employees. If you're a valued worker, chances are your employer will be open to at least discussing some form of leave—paid, unpaid, or a Deferred Salary Leave Program—for you. Your company may need some convincing, so go with a plan. Outline the benefits—recharging your batteries, so you return to work a more enthusiastic performer, developmental opportunities for other employees, and so on—and provide your employer with ideas for handling your absence and your return.

What do you have to lose? The worst your employer can do is say no. In this case, you have other decisions to make. You may decide the break is important enough to you to quit your job and take your chances on finding a new one when you get back.

There are other ways of generating some income and minimizing expenses. If you own a house or condo, renting it may provide that added bit of necessary income.

> It was surprisingly easy to find somebody to rent the house. And it was good to have that money coming in to cover continuing costs at home.
>
> Margaret

> I owned a condo, which I rented. I still had to cover the costs associated with the condo, but I didn't have a mortgage. So I was able to use some of the income from renting the condo for my expenses.
>
> Marie

Depending on what you do for a living, it may be possible to find work outside of Canada for a period of time.

You may be able to call on the kindness of family or friends to help you cut back your expenses.

> We lived with a relative from June until December when we left, with no rent or anything, to help us with this trip. That was an incredible boost. Without that, I actually am not sure we could have done it.
>
> Heather

For some people, It may make financial sense to use money from your RRSP during your time away, when your income and consequent tax rate will be lower than usual. But remember, you will be taxed on RRSP withdrawals, so it's wise to get professional advice to make sure this possibility works for you.

Don't give up your dream too easily. Think about your options. Speak with other people—friends, banker, accountant. Be creative and willing to compromise. The ways and means of accumulating the money you need for your runaway will depend on your circumstances. But, once your mind is made up, you can find a way to make it happen.

> Financially we risked a bit. We risked quite a bit. But obviously we felt it was worth it. We're now trying to build up again. We're not exactly depleted, but we need to build up our reserve. If you're going to do it, you have to do it right. That's what the money was being saved for. Something important. And we both very strongly felt that, as much as we believe in saving money for a rainy day, I certainly didn't want to do this trip when I was 70. If we're going to do it, let's do it while we're both healthy and able to do it.
>
> Suzanne

THINGS TO THINK ABOUT

- Everything will cost more than you expect.
- The kind of trip you want will determine how much you spend.
- Conversely, the amount of money you can save will influence the type of runaway you take.
- You're not 20 anymore; midlife travel comforts cost more.
- Speak to your employer about your leave possibilities.
- Put a savings plan in place and start saving now.
- Don't forget to factor in ongoing operating expenses at home.
- You still have to pay taxes.
- Be clear about how much financial risk you're willing to take. Is selling everything you own a realistic option or do you want something to come back to?
- Use your house or condo to generate income.
- Another option might be to use your RRSP, but make sure you get professional advice.

October/November: AUSTRALIA
Complicated Continent

OCTOBER 15—SYDNEY

What a day! Up, down, up, down. The only constant of travelling is that emotions swing like laundry in the wind.

We arrived a couple of days ago and have already given up our brilliant idea of renting an apartment and putting down roots for a month. We've wandered the streets of Sydney looking for an affordable apartment with absolutely no success. This is one expensive city. Anything we can afford, we wouldn't want. Our price range seems to limit us to the King's Cross area which, if not quite the Sodom and Gomorrah Sydneysiders would have you believe, is not my idea of a fun neighbourhood. The porno palaces and drug dealers make me just a little uncomfortable. The axe murderer wandering loose in the area at the moment is an added deterrent.

OCTOBER 21—SYDNEY

We are now comfortably ensconced with Liz Trickett and Bandit the cat at Tricketts Luxury Bed and Breakfast. It isn't what we had in mind, but it's the best of the available options. For awhile it looked as if even finding a B&B was going to be a problem. The B&B network in Australia isn't anywhere near as developed as in New Zealand. There aren't many, and those that exist are booked. None of them could keep us for a month; some could only take us for a few days.

Tricketts is the third place we've stayed since arriving a week ago. For some reason, few Australian B&Bs have ensuite bathrooms. That's okay for a few days but not for a month. So we've made our usual decision—hang the cost and go for the more expensive, comfortable, well-located, atmospheric B&B with private bathroom. We can stay until November 1.

Peter and I had a chat over dinner in the pub about whether our frustration at being constantly on the move and our decision to opt for comfort made us poor travellers. Peter's view is that there is no merit in being uncomfortable. I think we are probably somewhat unadventurous, but I'm coming to a greater acceptance of that being the reality of who I am.

OCTOBER 24—SYDNEY

Sydney lives up to its advance billing. It's a fabulous, fun, lively, beautiful place. We've spent the last week and a half wandering the streets, museums, and art galleries. We've been trying to gain some understanding of Australian aboriginal culture. Thanks to a truly informative exhibit at the Australia Museum, the history is becoming a little more real. And with the help of a gallery owner who sat us down in front of a video about aboriginal art before guiding us through her collection, I'm actually starting to be able to perceive meaning in what were previously just dots and dashes.

Sydney is a much more artistic community than I had expected. Their *Crocodile Dundee* tourism promotion actually does them a disservice. We've taken advantage of it all, from a free street performers' festival in The Rocks, to splurging on tickets to *Eugene Onegin* at the Opera House. And the setting can't be beat. We've cruised the harbour and tanned our still-pale bodies on the beaches at Manley and Bondi.

The city is a wonderful combination of modern metropolis and distinct livable neighbourhoods. Our B&B is in the Glebe area, close to the University of Sydney, filled with bookstores, cafés, and pubs, old-character houses with wrought-iron balconies on leafy, tree-lined streets. We're a 25-minute bus ride from Circular Quay, the central tourist point down on the waterfront, and our Sydney transit pass (one of the world's great bargains—$19 a week for unlimited bus, train, and ferry trips) takes us anywhere we want to go.

Best of all has been seeing Jen again. She is, after all, the reason we're here. It could have been a disaster. It's been twenty-seven years since we met and travelled together through Europe. But I needn't have worried. It was as if we had seen each other yesterday. Jen is absolutely recognizable—funny and direct and open and thoroughly comfortable to be around. While Peter has immersed himself in the local cricket season, Jen and I have had the chance to reconnect and get into some serious girl talk.

Jen's husband, Paul, and their three kids, Nick, Lucy, and Claire, have adopted us and given us the illusion of belonging. Dinner at their place; being filled in on the happenings at school; checking out the latest boyfriend; Peter and the girls exchanging gossip about *Xena, Warrior Princess;* attending the premiere performance of Nick's cello concerto; spending evenings with Jen and Paul in The Nag's Head commiserating over the state of the world. We're feeling very much at home.

The public-policy issues in Australia are even familiar: aboriginal issues; ongoing tension between the forces of conservatism and liberalism; a pedophile-ring scandal; and government downsizing. No wonder we feel at home. Not to mention that Céline Dion is everywhere. You can't sit down in a café without hearing her voice.

OCTOBER 25—SYDNEY
Jen and I took in an extraordinary exhibit at the art gallery—BODY—a representation of different ways of looking at and perceiving the body. A month ago, I had never thought about self-mutilation as art. I'm not sure I knew it existed. Then I heard Sting discussing it in New Zealand and now this exhibit. I thought Australian aboriginal art was tough to understand, but this is another world. Travel is certainly broadening.

OCTOBER 27—SYDNEY
Peter and I, independently, had a spell of *tristesse* today. We were clear before leaving Canada that we couldn't live in each other's pockets for a year, and we acknowledged that we would each need time to ourselves. Little did we imagine that, the first time we tried to go our separate ways for a few days, we'd both be lonely.

It may be that the single biggest revelation of this trip is how much we love our lives. Being in a relatively familiar environment, spending time with Jen and her family, seeing a familiar-looking cat, all remind us of the ordinary pleasures of our normal life.

Yesterday, we had a great time at lunch with Jen and Paul and their friend Penny, laughing, arguing, comparing politics and life in different countries. But returning to Tricketts, I was left with a vague sense of letdown. I think I envied their having real lives to return to. Coming from someone who has never seen herself as work-oriented, it's odd to start thinking that the meaning of life may lie in having meaningful work and the familiarity of friends and family. The journey is inward, not outward and, so far, I'm finding out that, instead of the quiet adventurer I imagined myself to be, I'm actually a gregarious homebody!

OCTOBER 28—SYDNEY

Travel in Australia is expensive—some combination of distance and lack of competition. We've been looking at options for the rest of our time here. Some things are quite reasonable: B&Bs, food, rental cars (at least through the automobile association). Others—trains, planes, and excursions in the interior or on the Great Barrier Reef— are outrageous. The Great Barrier Reef cruise was A$1,400 per person for four nights! Maybe in some other life.

OCTOBER 29—SYDNEY

What a lovely relaxed time we've had these last few days. We're so comfortable in Glebe and seem to be becoming part of the 'hood. People recognize us and we them. We're regulars at the Turkish café and the pub. We've done all the standard tourist stuff and are now just hanging out during the day, getting our hair cut, visiting second-hand bookstores, picnicking in the park. In the evenings, we head to the pub, a movie, or the theatre.

Sydney is a wonderful, fascinating, alive, livable city, but I suspect it's as much like the rest of Australia as Auckland was representative of New Zealand, i.e., not very.

NOVEMBER 7—NOOSA

We're just finishing the first mini-holiday of our trip. We took advantage of a seat sale and purchased an inexpensive one-week get-away to Noosa, a resort town on the west coast in Southern Queensland, just north of Brisbane. It has a mile-long ocean beach with pounding surf and a quiet tidal river. We're staying in a two-bedroom apartment on the river for less than $100 a night, and that includes the airfare from Sydney. In the mornings, we walk fifteen minutes to the main beach and spend hours tanning, reading, and braving the waves. We usually have lunch in town, then walk home for more tanning, reading, a quiet swim in the river, and a nap.

Australians understand the art of the beach. People are so well behaved. There are no boom boxes, no music, just the sounds of the surf and people having a good time.

The birds have been a particular joy. Huge pellies (pelicans) float in stately fashion up and down the river. Red, blue, green, and yellow rosellas (parrots) fly from branch to branch and tree to tree. One afternoon, we took a boat up the river where the everglades are filled with cormorants and darters and golden-brown eagles, and mad kangaroos frolic on the shoreline in mid-afternoon.

From our patio, we wave a daily hello to two dogs who stand proudly at the prows of their respective boats as they cruise up and down the river. One of them can't contain his excitement and barks wildly the whole time; the other, a huge, majestic hound, holds a silent and impressive pose. In the evenings we are visited by Oscar, a showy cream/grey-point Persian cat, who comes to the patio door and yells to be let in. He isn't particularly hungry, although he will take a bit of bacon just to be polite. He lives at the resort around the corner but likes to drop by and be sociable.

We've been drawn into the grand Australian obsession—gambling. Had a successful flutter on the Melbourne Cup horse race, winning A$59.30. We enjoyed being part of the excitement of Melbourne Cup day, when the entire country comes to a halt, but the prevalence of gambling in Australia is quite disturbing. There are ads on TV encouraging people to come to the local pub, drink, and gamble. We originally had trouble finding bank machines in Sydney until we realized you can always find one in a pub, placed there to make it easier for people to get their hands on money to gamble.

The highlight of our stay in Noosa has undoubtedly been our fifteen minutes of fame on Australian television. We were stopped on the ocean boardwalk and interviewed for the program *Front Up*.

In retrospect, we are somewhat embarrassed. The interviewer was really good at his job and had us rambling on about our dreams, life experiences, Peter's once being fired, not having children, even our sex life. With any luck, no one we know will ever see it. There is something absurdly perfect—or perfectly absurd—about setting off for a year to find ourselves and then being interviewed on television about ourselves.

(You can run but you can't hide. So much for no one we know ever seeing the interview. When we returned home in June, our neighbours, Jim and Sue, invited us over for dinner. Jim is from Australia and it was he who originally recommended we visit Noosa, so we were telling them all about our time there. As we regaled Jim and Sue with the story of our interview, strange grins came across their faces. It turns out they had been in Australia in April, visiting family. One evening, as Jim knocked on his sister's door, she flung it open, grabbed his arm, and pulled him into the living room, saying, "Hurry, hurry. Your friends are on the telly." He looked blankly at the screen for a moment and then realized, "My God, that's Lynda." They taped the show and presented us with a souvenir copy.)

I love the Australian way with words. They have this way of making things cute. Bikers are bikies, truckers are truckies, and the five guys who just escaped from prison here in Queensland are *es*capees. Cute but hardly terrifying.

Noosa has been a lovely interlude. The last few days have been a bit rainy and overcast but, overall, it's been a wonderful, necessary break. It's odd to think we should need interludes in what is really a year-long holiday. But we do. We need an occasional break from travelling, from seeing new things, from feeling like we have to do things. Noosa has been perfect. Tomorrow it's off to the Blue Mountains and on to see Australia.

NOVEMBER 8—BLACKHEATH, BLUE MOUNTAINS
Emotional roller coaster again today. Woke up to stunning blue sky and heat at 7:00 a.m. in Noosa and flew to overcast and chilly Sydney. Depression deepened at the Hertz counter where they tried to palm off a dirty, gouged car. I managed to get us an upgrade, but

only after a snit. On the road to the Blue Mountains, the fog and rain set in and so did my mood, culminating in tears of what? frustration? anger? Sometimes it seems as though rain and bad weather are plaguing us on this trip. It isn't true, of course. It just seems that way.

We picked a B&B at random out of a guidebook, based primarily on its reasonable price, and arrived at Montrose House to find the fire lit, fresh scones and tea at the ready. Peter's now playing the piano in the weaving studio while I write this, with Sandy, the Irish setter, at my feet. I'm looking out at a 170-year-old Himalayan pine tree, reputed to have been a gift of Captain (then Governor) Bligh to the French representative to the colony, whose house this was. The house is built on the foundation of the oldest building in the Blue Mountains, originally constructed by convicts to house themselves while working on the railroad. Rosellas are feeding outside the window. Now if only the fog would lift.

NOVEMBER 9—BLACKHEATH

Today I woke up and wanted to commit suicide.

That's Peter's line and not entirely accurate. I didn't actually want to commit suicide until I'd been up for an hour or two.

The fog is still with us. Here we are in an area renowned for its natural beauty, and we can't see across the street. I don't recall weather usually getting to me like this, but today I just went into the trough. Fiji seems to have warped my reaction to the elements.

Our host, Ron, was closer to death than he'll ever know. He insisted on talking about the weather:

I'm so sorry the weather is so dismal...

Last week was so lovely...

It's so disappointing that you can't see how lovely the countryside is around here...

This is so unusual for this time of year...

It's normally lovely in October...

According to the radio, the sun is shining in Sydney today...

Usually, it's the opposite—clouds in Sydney, sun here...

Can someone please explain to me why people think it's going to make you feel better to know that three days ago, when you weren't here, it was gorgeous. And it will undoubtedly be gorgeous again once you leave. Why should you feel better to know that you have been specially selected from the multitudes to be shat upon by fate?

Aside from his fixation with the weather, Ron is a hoot! He's a terrible name dropper and loves the sound of his own voice. In his defence, however, he's actually got interesting things to say. I just don't know how much to believe. According to him, he's an archae-ologist, a specialist in the Zapotecas, has travelled in 40–50 countries, climbed the Matterhorn and in the Himalaya, weaves (the English Queen Mother and the Queen of Sweden have some of his throws), plays piano and harp, carves puzzles, makes jewellery, speaks fluent Scots Gaelic, and has renovated this house and garden. His mother was nominated for the Nobel Prize, the rosella was named after his great (great, great?) grandfather, Sir Hugh Rose, etc., etc. For all I know, it could be true. He does play a mean piano and runs a great B&B.

NOVEMBER 10—BLACKHEATH
Finally sun! We can now see why the Blue Mountains are so popu-lar—and why they were so difficult for the original settlers to traverse. When we were reading about the history of Australia, I could never understand why they had such a hard time making it across the Blue Mountains. Or why the convicts who attempted to escape across them usually came straggling back to captivity. In my hardy Canadian way, I assumed they were simply wimps. I now know better. The Blue Mountains are a sort of Grand Canyon of the Antipodes.

We started with the more touristed areas, the Three Sisters and Echo Point, and were fortunate—there weren't many people around. Then we walked down the approximately 1,000 Furber Stairs, hiked to Katoomba Falls, and on to the base of the Scenic Railway (supposedly the steepest railway in the world) for the uphill journey. It was good to get some exercise again.

Then we visited some of the less touristed hiking areas and scenic lookouts recommended by Ron: Megalong Valley, Shipley Plateau, Hargreaves Lookout, Govett's Leap, Dickens Point, the Wind-Eroded Cave, Perry's Lookdown, and Anvil Rock. The day has been an overwhelming blur of incredible vistas, quiet, bell-like bird calls, wildflowers, scents, the eeriness of blue gum forests, and more incredible views. It's a strange countryside, and it leaves an impression. The tops of the canyons are striated, multicoloured layers of pressed rock, similar to parts of the Rockies and the Grand Canyon. Below, however, is a thick wave of green palms and blue-green eucalyptus sweeping up against the rock. It's possible to imagine a Stone Age tribe still living under that canopy, invisible to the prying eye. These are aboriginal spiritual sites, and they feel like it. You feel in touch with the beginnings here.

NOVEMBER 11—CANBERRA

We're staying in the Australian equivalent of Kanata outside Ottawa—suburbia gone mad. It's reminiscent of the *Star Trek* episode where crew members beam down to a perfect plastic planet. Everything's clean and everyone's smiling and you know something is very wrong.

Getting here was lovely. We drove through rugged and somewhat intimidatingly beautiful farmland north of the Blue Mountains into gentler farm country coming back south toward Canberra. In between, we stopped at the Japanese Gardens in Cowra. There's something weird about the serenity of the Japanese Gardens in a town whose claim to fame is that it was the site of a Japanese POW camp from which a great escape was attempted and some 250 people killed.

Here at the Pines Attic, we're staying with a family for the first time. For some reason, most B&Bs seem to be run by couples or single people. Colleen and Adrian and their two boys, Mathew and Julian, are really nice, but they don't know much about cats. They have just acquired an 8-week-old kitten, Harry, an adorable but basic tabby cat. Colleen told us proudly he was half Persian and half Siamese. And they paid A$122 for him!

NOVEMBER 12—CANBERRA

We've set the cat among the pigeons, so to speak. It may have been Peter's shocked "This is not a $122 cat" or my "I think he has a bit of tabby in him," but Colleen called the woman who sold them Harry. She reported that the mother was Persian/Siamese, the father was Persian/tabby, and Harry was almost "show quality." That woman is wasting her time selling cats. We reassured Colleen that Harry's value surpassed any crass monetary amount.

Canberra is astonishing. A totally artificial, soulless city. A national capital designed by an American on a monumental scale, with a population of only 300,000. You've never seen such huge empty roads in your life. There's a business district, a shopping district, an entertainment district, a government district, a diplomatic district, and God help you if you try to do anything outside the designated district. Canberra makes Ottawa look vibrant and alive. I am mind-boggled by the city and can't begin to analyze what it says about the national psyche. The National Art Gallery is worth visiting and the people are great, but Canberra itself seems totally out of step with what little we've seen of the rest of the country. I couldn't live here on a bet, but I wouldn't have missed it.

New Zealand and Australia seem to be vying for the "world's ugliest parliament" award. The Aussie version is ten years old and, again, designed by an American. Why? The building has a couple of nice touches but generally looks like a bunker topped by a phallic flagpole. The best I can say about it is that its sterility is a perfect mirror for the city.

We returned stunned to the house, craving the normalcy of animals and kids and crested cockatoos in the pine trees. Colleen and I sat in the garden and had a long heart-to-heart. She desperately needed a stranger to talk to. She and Adrian are newlyweds. The boys are hers from a previous marriage. They have been working hard to build a new family together and were all thrilled when she became pregnant. She lost the baby four months ago, just a week after her father died.

There's something about B&Bs. You find yourself becoming a temporary part of different worlds. An almost instant intimacy arises from being a guest in someone's home. And, when it works, you can offer each other some measure of comfort.

We arrived home from dinner tonight and found, waiting for us by the bed, a bottle of port, some Turkish delight, and a bright and beautiful card, hand-drawn by Matthew and signed by all, thanking us for staying at the Pines Attic. I had originally hated the thought of staying in suburbia, but how glad I am we did.

NOVEMBER 13—SNOWY MOUNTAINS
Dead rat, drunks, and Daphne—the three Ds of our Australian ranch experience.

This was to be our horseback expedition into the Snowy Mountains—riding by day, camping under the stars by night, experiencing the Australian Outback in its natural state.

We called from Canberra to confirm our arrival and found out that the others booked on our trip had cancelled. Roz, the owner of the ranch, offered a couple of options. We could link up with a group who had already been out for the better part of a week or we could stay at the ranch house and do day trips into the Snowies. We chose the latter.

We arrived two days ago. We entered the main room and were immediately drawn to the large stone fireplace dividing the sitting area from the dining room. Suddenly, we stopped dead in our tracks, frozen in place by the overwhelming stench of rotting flesh. There's no smell like it. Once you've sniffed it, you never forget it. It seemed to be coming from the fireplace. We backed off quickly, trying to get out of range.

After a few minutes' wait, Roz came hurrying from the backroom. "I'm so sorry I wasn't here to greet you," she said breathily, in a voice uncannily like Sybil Fawlty's. "But there's just so much to do. My husband, John, is at the other property and..." Within the first five minutes, we heard about how hard it was to get good staff, how bad business was this year, and how she and John disagree on just about everything. As she spoke, she neared the fireplace. We waited. She entered the stench zone. "Oh," she cried, giggling shamefacedly. "Isn't it awful (tee-hee)? I think a rat has died under the house (tee-hee). And there's no man around to do anything about it (tee-hee). I just don't know what to do (tee-hee)."

For the next two days, whenever she approached the fireplace, she'd break into embarrassed giggles and go into the "Isn't it awful (tee-hee)?" routine. Roz is a charming woman, a great cook, and must be a competent businesswoman because she's been running this place for more than twenty years. But it never seemed to occur to her to do something about the rat herself.

Yesterday, the weather started off iffy and then got foul. We saddled up the horses and headed up into the mountains with our wrangler, Daphne. Daphne is what I imagined Australian countrywomen to be—tough, good-natured, confident. In her sixties, with hands like leather, she's been on a horse since she was six months old, riding in front of her mother. She knows every inch of these mountains and loves them passionately.

The early sprinkle of rain soon turned heavy. The higher we went, the worse it became. Brief, misleading respites were followed by ever stronger outbursts. The rain slashed at our faces. The wind tore at our clothes. The horses put their heads down and together we slogged on. Water poured from our hats onto our sodden dusters. The temperature dropped. At various times, Peter and I, independently, considered calling it quits, but we had the Canadian reputation as hardy outdoorspeople to protect. If the Australian could do it, so could we.

"Where are we headed?" I yelled to Daphne after about an hour and a half of slow, uphill, treacherous trudging in the mud. "To the lookout," she called back. Peter and I pulled up our horses at the same instant. We stared at each other in horror melting to hysteria. A lookout! One of us started to laugh, then the other, and then we couldn't stop. If we couldn't see Daphne's horse in front of us, what in God's name were we going to see from a lookout? Enough, already. Peter was laughing so hard, he was having trouble staying on his horse. I laughed until I cried and the tears mingled with the rain on my face. And Daphne rode on. As soon as we managed to get ourselves under control, we reined her in. National pride could take a back seat to common sense. We headed down the mountain and home to a hot shower.

Last night we met the "naughty group," as Roz refers to the people she had proposed we join on the trail. Thank heaven we had the good sense not to have anything to do with them. Picture a group of sixteen people—ten men from the Mobil Oil refinery, two couples and a pair of women—on the trail for five days with two female wranglers. According to Roz, the Mobil men arrived drunk and stayed that way for the entire ride.

They returned to the ranch late yesterday afternoon, still drunk. We finished dinner quickly and beat a hasty retreat to our room. I heard them once around four-thirty in the morning, as they did their coyote imitations, howling at the moon and getting the dogs all worked up.

This morning, we headed to the main house to be greeted with the mingled smells of vomit, stale beer, eggs and bacon—and let's not forget the rat. One of the young men had passed out on the couch and was simply left there, wheezing and snoring, while the rest of us had to line up behind him to get our breakfasts!

The Australian attitude toward young men getting drunk and behaving badly is very difficult for a North American to understand or accept. There's a "that's what young men do" kind of philosophy. Over dinner our first night, Roz told us about her eldest son who was drunk one night and tried to leap from balcony to balcony in his university dorm. He fell five storeys and now has a permanently disabled right arm. She told the story with absolutely no trace of anger or disapproval, just a "boys will be boys" placid acceptance. The four women on the "naughty group" ride had a similar attitude—"Terrible isn't it, but that's life."

We're out of here.

NOVEMBER 16—PHILLIP ISLAND
What a great couple of days! Gippsland, along the south coast, has

been a total surprise and revelation. And an enormous relief after the ranch. Rolling green hills—much as I imagine Ireland to look—and 145 kilometres of white sand beach. We've hiked through Wilson's Promontory National Park, enjoyed Saturday night at the Bistro in Foster with half the town's population, and viewed the Penguin Parade.

The Penguin Parade is high on my hit parade. Thousands of tiny Little Penguins surfing in on the tide, struggling across a vast expanse of sand, heading into the grass, calling and chirping for their mates (and vice versa) who are in burrows sitting on eggs. The grasses are filled with the sounds of searching and finding. Every night, these brave little creatures do the same routine, bringing home dinner and then changing places. Some of them are clearly terrified of the open beach, although they don't seem even to notice the people. Others are lame, but they continue on. It was extremely touching. It was also bloody freezing!

NOVEMBER 18—ST. KILDA, MELBOURNE

Some days you feel like you should have just stayed home. I woke up this morning feeling slightly unwell and totally exhausted. All I wanted was to stay in one place for a while and put something back in the tank—read a book, do my journal, whatever. Wouldn't you know this would be the time we can't find a B&B with room to take us for three days.

After a classic few hours of sniping at each other, culminating in a manic circling of a parking garage in downtown Melbourne searching for a non-existent parking space—as close as I've seen Peter come to total meltdown—we finally found at least one night's accommodation at Robinson's by the Sea in St. Kilda, a suburb of Melbourne.

Peter's out getting something to eat. I've now had a short nap and a bath, and things are looking a little brighter. But we didn't get here until 4:00 p.m., and the thought of trying this again tomorrow is almost more than I can bear. I think we need another plan here. Sometimes extended travel seems like one long struggle for survival—something to eat and a warm place to rest your head.

It's so lowering to discover that Peter is the better traveller of the two of us. Another personal myth shot.

NOVEMBER 20—PORT FAIRY

Wendy Robinson is my personal nominee for saint. She clearly recognized the signs of imminent marital failure and took control. On Peter's return, we headed to the lounge to figure out what the hell we were going to do. Wendy provided wine, crackers, salmon spread, a sense of perspective, and advice. We talked about what we were looking for, how much time we had, and made some tentative plans.

At some point, Wendy disappeared. Peter and I relaxed in the company of Periwinkle the cat and Scruffy the dog. Jonathan, Wendy's husband, joined us for awhile and regaled us with the story of his and Wendy's romance. They've been married only three months. They met when he was a guest at the B&B—with a wife and kids in Sydney. As he put it, within three days they "had totally lost the plot."

The wine flowed. We mellowed out.

After an hour or so, Wendy returned, rubbing her hands. "There, that's done," she announced. "You're spending tomorrow night at Caulfields, out by the racetrack. That will give you time to see a little bit of Melbourne. On Monday, you're driving the Great Ocean Road to Port Fairy and staying at Goble's Mill House—you'll love it there—for a few days. Then I've booked you into Victoria Cottage in Robe for a couple of days on the way to Adelaide."

She'd done it all. She'd been on the phone to her B&B colleagues from Melbourne to Adelaide and had laid out the next week for us until we boarded the Ghan, the train from Adelaide to Alice Springs and the centre of Australia, named after the Afghan traders who originally plied this route by camel.

We've been doing as she said, and it's been grand.

NOVEMBER 25—ABOARD "THE LEGENDARY GHAN"

Woke up to a cup of tea and cookies and the beauty of dawn over the Outback. Red earth, saltbushes, eucalyptus trees, soft blue and pink sky, the occasional cattle. I didn't expect it to be so lovely. The

sun is turning the tops of the eucalyptus trees to gold. By noon, I
suspect it will be washed out in the sunlight, but now the landscape
is filled with shades of red, green, and gold.

NOVEMBER 29—ALICE SPRINGS
This time in the "Red Centre" has been fabulous! If I had had any
idea how gorgeous it is and how much there is to see and do, I
would have planned to be here much longer. I can't believe the number of Australians we've met who have never been here and who
discounted the idea with "Why would you want to go all that way to
look at a rock?"

From The Ghan, we checked into the Alice Springs Resort and
had time for a leisurely swim and lunch by the pool before being
picked up for an afternoon tour. Alice Springs is a fascinating peek
into life on the frontier. It isn't quite "A Town Called Alice" anymore—there was even a Burger King until it burned down under
mysterious circumstances last week—but it does retain an edge-of-
the-world feel.

The highlight for me was the Stehlow Research Station, if "highlight" is the right word. The building houses sacred aboriginal
artifacts— so sacred no one can see them. No one, that is, but initi-
ated males of the local tribe. The visitor enters, expecting a museum,
to receive a lecture and slide show. The guide isn't even local—he's
from Western Australia—because there are things certain members
of the local aboriginal group are forbidden to see and they don't
want to take the chance of a mistake.

The peculiarities of the museum are mirrored in the town. The
aboriginal population is almost totally separate from the rest of the
community. The Todd River encircles the town. For most of the
year, it's a wide, dry, sandy riverbed with eucalyptus trees growing in
and beside it. At first glance, the river bed appears empty. As you
watch, however, shadows start to move. Groups of aborigines are
camped under the trees, in a spectral world totally removed from the
town life 100 yards away. They and the white community never
seem to connect. They pass on the street without eye contact. Their
only recognition appears to be as artists or as threats. After dinner

our first night in town, our waitress advised us to take a cab rather than walk the ten minutes to our hotel. "You'd have to cross the Todd, " she warned, in a voice more appropriate to alerting us we were crossing the Styx.

The next day we were up bright and early to be picked up at 7:00 a.m. for a five-hour drive to Ayers Rock. The countryside is simultaneously boring and varied, in a minimalist kind of way. In a terrain so basically similar, small distinctions take on big meanings. After a while, you begin to understand how the aborigines can go from landmark to landmark, as recorded in their paintings. But someone in this country, resident or visitor, is a slob. The road to the Centre is littered with beer cans. My money's on the residents.

Ayers Rock Resort is an interesting example of development in a sensitive environment. One organization operates a campground, apartment hotel, budget/backpacker lodge, medium-priced and five-star accommodation. (Guess which we picked.) There is something for every taste and budget, pulled together by a town square with shops, bakery, deli, supermarket, restaurant, etc. The complex is largely solar-powered, with its own sewage treatment plant. Everything is tucked away in one area behind sand dunes, leaving the rest of the countryside relatively untouched.

We whipped into bathing suits on arrival, hurried down to the pool, ordered lunch, swam, ate, and made the afternoon bus, refreshed and ready to go. Off to the Olgas (Kata-Gahga) and Ayers Rock (Uluru), the only visible formations in a seemingly endless flat desert. Until you've been here, it's impossible to grasp how compelling these piles of rock can be. They are alive. They pulsate with energy, change colour and shape as you move around them. You lay your hand on the stone and expect to feel a pulse beat.

Uluru is particularly impressive, a sleeping giant ready to awaken at any moment. It's easy to understand why aborigines consider it a sacred site. I saw the spikes driven into the rock along the climb line and felt the same discomfort I experience when I see a line of piercings in someone's body.

At sunset, twenty or thirty buses disgorge their passengers. We stand around looking at the rock, wondering what we're waiting for.

We wait and wait and chat and laugh. We've been warned that it—whatever it is—doesn't always happen. Just as we're about to give up, Uluru comes alive. It starts to change colour—brown becomes gold, orange, copper. It glows red against the sky. There are moments in life when you come close to touching God.

We spent our short time in the Centre hiking, viewing cave paintings, visiting water holes, marvelling at the palette of colours in the rocks, visiting the interpretation centre, and generally soaking up the extraordinary feel of a world beyond simple understanding.

One evening, we attended an aboriginal cultural presentation—another strange experience, given that most of the dances and songs are secret. Are we detecting a theme here? Once again, the event was presented by aborigines from another part of Australia, as the local group don't want any of their secrets revealed accidentally.

And we've spent a fair bit of time in the pool. The temperature hasn't gone below 42C since we reached the Centre. Yesterday, it reached 46C. It's like standing in front of an open furnace. I didn't know it could get that hot.

NOVEMBER 30—PALM COVE, QUEENSLAND
From the desert Centre to the sea and the Great Barrier Reef. On the recommendation of friends, we're staying in Palm Cove, a 30-minute drive north of Cairns. Palm Cove is basically one main street wandering its way along the ocean, the beach on one side, low-rise apartments, hotels, and a small shopping plaza on the other. From the pier, you look back to town and all you see are palm and bluegum trees. We're tucked up in a comfortable one-bedroom apartment with a balcony overlooking the ocean.

One of the ironies of Queensland is the presence of all these beaches you can't use. This is stinger season. Stingers are fatally poisonous jellyfish that inhabit the shoreline waters. Here we are with miles of beautiful white sand beach at our doorstep and we have to swim inside a net.

This is another mini-vacation. There's lots to do but we've opted for doing a lot of nothing. Australia is clearly having an impact on us. Last night we ate pizza in front of the TV, along with half the nation, watching the Australians try for a World Cup qualifying spot. We're settling into a lovely, quiet beach routine—me up early for a swim, breakfast on the balcony, off to the beach, lunch on the balcony, Peter watching cricket or golf on TV, me reading on the balcony, nap, shop, back to the beach, shower, stroll, dinner, TV, read, bed.

DECEMBER 2—PALM COVE

The one exception to our "do nothing" routine has been a day trip to the Great Barrier Reef. A huge catamaran picked us up at the pier and, under a perfect blue sky dotted with fluffy white clouds, we cruised for an hour and a half out to the reef. There, in the middle of the ocean, we docked beside a covered platform and a roped-off section of sea about the size of a football field, dotted with floats. Snorkelling equipment was distributed and safety instructions given. We were cautioned to stay inside the ropes and to hang on to the floats if we got tired.

Into the warm water and another world. Deep canyons of pink, purple, and blue coral inhabited by silver eels, fluorescent and iridescent fish of all sizes and shapes. It was glorious. The best snorkelling I've done since a trip to Qamea, Fiji, a few years ago. (The whole trip was terrific—except for the fact that someone may have died! A young Japanese woman was found floating facedown without her snorkel. She was still alive when they airlifted her off the reef, but it didn't look good.)

This week at Palm Cove, coupled with the time in the Centre, has been a godsend before going to India. I'm positively limp with relaxation.

DECEMBER 5—SYDNEY

Back home at Tricketts. Bandit the cat has grown and is even lazier than when we left.

We're heavily into India preparations—laundry, film, shipping stuff home, letters, etc. And what would moving into the next phase be without the obligatory panic attack. We've started reading guidebooks to India, and they make it sound as if we're entering a war zone: don't drink, don't eat, make reservations months in advance. Rationally I know it can't be that impossible to arrange things once we're there. If it is, we'll adapt or leave. Emotionally, however, at least in the middle of last night, I felt like the last thing I wanted to do was leave Australia and go to India.

Australia is a wonderful country. But it's a whole lot more complicated and less straightforward than it likes to pretend. Under its sunny disposition is a dark core. Peter refers to Australia as being in the "sloppy adolescent" stage, not having a clue what it is or what it wants to be when it grows up. Part of Asia? Part of the Commonwealth? Like the Americans? The vehemence of the current debate about whether to abandon the monarchy and become a republic has been a revelation. I had always assumed Australians were far down the republican road. Instead, I find them deeply tied to the monarchy. The media are filled with royal tidbits: Prince Charles's tour of South Africa, his birthday celebration, the Queen and Prince Philip's wedding anniversary. At the same time, American influence is rampant. Perhaps because they're so geographically removed, Australians seem to care less than Canadians about the impact of American culture. At times, Australia seems as much a colony of the United States as it ever was of Britain.

And aboriginal issues are raw and getting rawer. There is still a very deep and ugly racism here, as brutal in its own way as racism anywhere. The growing voices of liberalism and tolerance are fighting hard to be heard.

Australians are truly shaped by their past. I guess we all are, but it seems more than usually evident here. The convict beginnings (except for Adelaide, of course) are reflected in a modern-day distaste for authority and the concept of mate-ism—you and your mates stick together, and there's little tolerance for anyone thinking himself better than anyone else. The shortage of labour in the country's early days has given the labour movement enormous power which continues today. The treatment of aborigines has left a swamp of unresolved problems.

One disappointment has been the animal life. Surprisingly, there hasn't been much. With the exception of a very large lizard at the

Centre, we haven't seen any animals since Phillip Island. The only kangaroos we've spotted since Noosa have been dead ones on the side of the road. Their absence is more than made up for, though, by the birds, which are truly magnificent. There's been an hysterical exchange in the papers about British ex-pats who find the birds too raucous. They're crazy. The birds are just Australian.

This is one big, diverse, tough, beautiful country, and it needs tough people to survive. It is also a much more multicultural country than I had expected. The strong Irish presence everywhere was a real surprise, and Sydney is a veritable United Nations. For some reason, I find people here tend to look more like their ethnic stereotype than they do in Canada. It may be that in Canada I just think of everyone as Canadian.

I didn't expect to like Australia or Australians as much as I do. I came to see Jen and ended up loving the place. But, after two months here, I still don't have a sense that I know or understand the collective Australian psyche much better than I did when I arrived. They are not an easy people to get to know, despite their outward and real friendliness, possibly because I don't think they know themselves very well yet. I can't wait to come back.

DECEMBER 7—SYDNEY

This entry should have been written on board the Singapore Airlines flight to Delhi. I think I may be the only person in the known world to have food poisoning *before* going to India.

We had a wonderful last evening with Jen and Paul. The meal was delicious, conversation animated, and then on to a jazz club for good music and more talk—until 1:30 a.m. when my stomach went wild. After a night spent primarily in the bathroom, absolutely no sleep, and a raging fever, I was in no shape to get on a plane at eight this morning.

What a production for Peter. Was there room at Tricketts? No, but Liz could move her mother in with her and give us her mother's room. Could we change our flight to tomorrow? Only to Singapore, not on to Delhi. Where could we stay in Singapore? No answer at Isabel's; they could be out of town. We have to let Jennifer and Al know of the change so they don't meet us at the airport in Delhi as planned. Thank God Peter's feeling well.

I am now comfortably, if morosely, ensconced in the back bedroom. As always when I don't feel well, it affects me emotionally. My main reaction has been antipathy to the idea of India, once the supposed centrepiece of our trip. Despite my early opposition to the idea of planning, I now long for the surety of an organized plan. I said I wanted to see how I coped with spontaneity. Well, I have my answer—not well! I am what I am—a plan-driven Virgo. By 50, some people may be capable of major structural change, but I don't appear to be.

And, also as always, when things seem worst, something wonderful happens. While Peter was out having dinner and I was feeling wretched and lonely and sorry for myself, Liz and her mother, Elsa, came to visit. They sat on the other bed and we chatted, about life, men, different cultures, whatever. It was so homey and comfortable, like having my mother and sister visit. What a nice note on which to leave.

FOUR
TAKING CARE OF
THE HOME FRONT

From the time you decide to go, your thoughts will be focused on the trip itself. First, however, there are some mundane tasks that need doing at home.

CLEARING OUT THE PAST

Leaving for an extended time gives you not only an incentive but an active desire to clean out your belongings. If you've lived in the same place for a while and you're anything like us, you have a basement, attic, cupboards, and/or drawers filled with stuff—stuff you've been meaning to go through but just never quite got around to. The prospect of having to pack and store everything makes it a whole lot easier to throw things out.

But something more than a simple desire to be tidy kicks in. The whole idea of running away from home implies divesting yourself not only of your everyday life but of stuff. The idea of travelling light takes on a whole new meaning.

Our decision to leave jobs, families, friends, and just go was really a decision to make a major change in the way we lived our lives—to simplify, to clarify, to reach for the essence of who we are. We actively wanted to get rid of things.

Other people had similar reactions. By their second runaway, John and Ruth had, like us, decided to hold on at least to their home base. First time round, however, they cleaned out everything.

> We sold a house, a sailboat, two vehicles, furniture, everything. We had both dragged shitty furniture, relics of different relationships, and memories of past lives to this house, and it was like a purge to get rid of it all. It felt wonderful. We loved it.
>
> Ruth

The lead-in to leaving reinforces this cleansing urge. For the three years prior to leaving, we saved every spare penny for the trip. Our usual buying patterns were totally disrupted. Even if we had wanted to buy something new, we had no money to do so.

The months before leaving were a delighted frenzy of divestiture. Closet by closet, drawer by drawer, we went through the house, dividing belongings into four categories: take on the trip; save for return; put in garage sale; throw out. With every addition to the "garage sale" or "throw out" piles, we felt lighter, freer, younger. The apex of personal liberation was the day I took seven cartons of books to the second-hand bookstore. Even Peter, who has never before been able to part with a single book, managed to contribute a dozen or so to the collection.

The garage sale itself was a celebration. Our enthusiasm was contagious, and a couple of friends joined in with their offerings. The purpose was not to make money but simply to get rid of stuff. Passersby needed only to glance in our direction and we were thrusting things into their hands. Cheers went up as each item left the driveway.

> We were pretty much giving it away at the garage sale. This young couple with a baby came up—I think the price of everything they had came to $70—and they said, "Would you take $60 for these things?" John said, "No. But we'll take $50".... I just loved seeing that stuff go down the driveway.
>
> Ruth

At the end of the morning, everything left unsold was piled into our neighbour's van for delivery to their church thrift shop. The basement was clean. There was space in the closets. We felt lighter than air.

We seldom realize how much our possessions weigh us down. We accumulate them unthinkingly and, by their very existence, they sap our energy and limit our possibilities. When the basement was filled, leaving seemed difficult; there was so much to leave behind. When it was a bright, open, empty expanse, all we had to do was close the door and walk away.

We ended up selling our lot and selling our car and selling our previous house. We kept lots of our possessions obviously but, as we started planning it more, it just felt better and better to be able to make the decision to do whatever we wanted when we got back. Because maybe we would feel very differently about how we wanted to live our lives.

Heather

How much you feel comfortable divesting yourself of is a very individual decision. But I can tell you this. Of everything we sold or gave away, we have missed not one thing. Neither has anyone else I've spoken with.

RENTING THE HOUSE

We love our home. That may not have been entirely clear given all the emphasis I've put on leaving it, but our little green house is more than just a place to live. Peter and I purchased it shortly after we were married. It's a small, simple workman's cottage built in 1909. Nothing fancy. But, from the moment we walked in the door, we knew this was the place for us. It's our first home, and we intend it to be our last. We have no desire to trade up or move on. This is where we've put down roots, planted trees to commemorate lost friends—human and feline—made friends, made love, laughed, cried, and built our lives. We may have wanted to run away for a while, but we knew where we were returning.

Entrusting this piece of our lives to someone else for a year was not a small issue. We were not renting for investment purposes; it was a matter of finding someone to care for a good friend.

We had some experience in this department. Ten years ago, we rented the house during a two-year sojourn in Ottawa. We carefully worded a newspaper ad, making it clear that this was a much-loved family home, and setting out clear guidelines about the number of children (one) and type of pets (cat or small dog) we thought our small house could accommodate. Applicants were asked to complete an extensive rental questionnaire including financial and personal references as well as references from past and current landlords.

Then we did the obvious—at least, it seemed obvious to us. We checked every reference. And were amazed how many people provide references who have nothing good to say. After weeding out the devious, deceptive, and simply deluded, the choice came down to our comfort level. The work paid off. Our first tenants were perfect. They left our home in better shape than when they moved in. Unfortunately for us, they wanted to buy a home of their own. After a year, we were back in the rental business.

This time, we weren't on hand to interview prospective tenants, but one of our neighbours had friends moving to Victoria. What better reference could we have than good neighbours? We didn't bother to check further. Major error! The tenants lied to us about the number of people who would be living in the house. They never mentioned the dog. When we returned at the end of the year, the shower had been pulled from the wall, mould had eaten through the bathroom drywall, two windows were broken, and there were sizable holes in the bedroom and dining-room walls. (The man of the family admitted he had put his fist through the wall—"male hormones, you know.")

Renting your home, like renting a house abroad, can be perilous. And, in this instance, you have more at stake. Check out the law in your jurisdiction to find out your rights and responsibilities. If someone at home is keeping an eye on things for you, be specific about your expectations. Whatever you do, don't pay attention to stereotypes. Our perfect tenants were just folks: he was a heavy-equipment operator, she had been a bartender in a pub. The tenants from hell were a doctor and his wife who was working on a postgraduate degree. And always, always, check up on people, even if they've been referred by friends.

With all the care in the world, a lot of it is luck. But there is an upside.

It was a bit of a stress to rent the place because John and I have kind of cocooned here, plus we were renting it furnished, so it was filled with our things. I wasn't really sure I wanted people coming in here. I was a little worried. But then I thought, it's only stuff, just things. Returning and finding everything fine gave me an additional sense of freedom. Now it's not going to bother me to walk away again.

Ruth

This time round, we knew what was important. We needed enough rent to cover operating costs—taxes, insurance, etc. More important than profit was having a tenant who would care for our home and, ideally, our two cats in exchange for reduced rent. We put the word out to family, friends, and colleagues, and fortune smiled on us. My best friend, Barbara, decided she could stand to cut back on expenses and moved into the house. We probably could have made an additional $500 a month renting on the open market, but we considered it well worth the loss of income to have the security of being able to leave, knowing home, pets, and friend were well taken care of.

TAKING CARE OF BUSINESS

If you'll be in one place for a while, you can arrange for your mail and bills to be sent to you there. If you're going to be on the move, however, you need to set up systems in advance.

We left Barbara with lists of all our contacts—the plumber, electrician, veterinarian, bank manager, stockbroker—anyone she might need to contact while we were gone. We authorized her to open our mail. I trust her judgement implicitly and knew I'd be calling her regularly. She let us know if anything unusual had appeared, threw out the junk mail, forwarded personal letters to us when we had an address, and saved the rest for our return. If there's someone you trust and you know you're going to be telephoning often, have your mail forwarded to that person and ask her or him to do the same for you.

As with any move, we cancelled a number of obligations: newspaper and magazine subscriptions, telephone and cable. Some expenses, like the heating bill, passed to our tenant. We took care of other informal financial commitments in advance.

Only four financial obligations required any special arrangements: monthly payments for our furnace, the telephone credit card bill, Visa, and American Express. The last two were particularly important as we were planning to use the credit cards for on-the-road expenses. They had to be paid promptly to avoid interest charges and to keep our credit rating intact.

Finances need attention

I thought it would be a simple matter to arrange for our bank to take care of these payments and advise on other financial matters. I wanted to ensure that our bank cards would work on machines outside Canada, and I thought they might have some useful advice on handling our money while travelling, arranging emergency transfers should they be necessary, and other financial details.

Dealing with banks, I discovered, is rarely straightforward. When I asked to speak with someone who could advise me, no one seemed to have any idea what I was talking about. And reaching the manager was like trying to talk to the president of the United States. I was preparing to declare war when fate, in the form of a good friend, stepped in.

One of our friends is a vice-president of our bank. She and her husband happened to be in town one weekend. Her smile broadened as I recited the litany of inane and unhelpful suggestions I had received from bank staff. Her new job made her responsible for customer service. She wasn't particularly fond of our regional manager and relished the opportunity to point out some shortcomings in his operation. Would I mind if she raised this example with him? Mind? Be my guest.

That was Saturday night. By 10:00 a.m. Monday morning there was a message on our answering machine from the branch manager. My return call was put directly through. Later that week, the manager introduced us to the officer who would handle our account and assured us he would personally be available at any time. I do love a certain amount of grovelling.

The account officer assigned to us was efficient and helpful. She answered all our questions and changed our personal identification numbers (PINs) to four-digit codes to ensure international compatibility. (Speaking of PINs, be sure to memorize yours by both numbers and letters. Some machines abroad show only one or the other.) She provided us with forms authorizing the bank to pay the four bills mentioned above on our behalf. All arrangements were confirmed in writing. The week before we left, I phoned and confirmed once again that everything was in order. We left with a wonderful sense of certainty that we didn't have to worry about financial matters. Boy, were we wrong!

When you're travelling, everything happens on weekends or statutory holidays. It's some kind of traveller's law. On a December weekend in Singapore, we discovered that the American Express bill had not been paid since August. Our credit would be cut off if full payment were not made within forty-eight hours. (Interestingly, the Visa card affiliated with the bank was paid regularly every month.) After panicky phone calls to American Express in New York and to Barbara, a fax to the bank to authorize her involvement, three or four hours of Barbara's time, and a day of worrying on our part, payment was made in time. But just barely.

Had Peter not suggested that we visit the American Express office and see if the bills matched our records, we would have arrived in India with no functioning American Express card. We had done everything possible to avoid a problem like this, but still it happened. The bank apologized and reimbursed us for the Amex interest charges, but we never did get a satisfactory explanation.

Others have had similar experiences.

> The first time we set out, our boat was paid for but we didn't have a lot of money for trip expenses. So I went to the bank and took out a loan against the boat. The money would be made available as we needed it. We used our Visa for expenses and our accountant paid it by cheque. But I had forgotten we had overdraft protection on our chequing account. They put the overdraft on Visa. So, the next month, the Visa bill, including the overdraft, would again get paid by cheque and that would overdraw the account even more. It snowballed. One day I got this frantic call from my accountant saying, "You had better call the bank." I almost had my Visa revoked. Because the banker had forgotten the agreement!
>
> Larry

You simply cannot trust any institution to take care of business for you. This lesson was reinforced when we reviewed our bank statements on our return home. The monthly electronic transfer of Peter's deferred salary, which was to have been deposited on the fifteenth of each month, frequently didn't appear until a week later. On one occasion, it didn't show up until the third of the following month. We had enough of a cushion that this presented a problem only once. Had we been relying on the financial institutions to deliver what they promised, we might have been in serious trouble. And this was with a bank vice-president on our side! There has to be a better way.

> We ended up using an accountant to pay our bills. We prepaid
> all our credit cards so that we always had $1,000 credit. If we
> needed to, we could get cash that way. We didn't have to worry
> about paying interest. We used American Express as our bank.
> It worked out very well. We didn't have any glitches.
>
> Margaret

If I had it to do over, I'd look at a range of options. I might appoint Barbara as our designated surrogate and ask her to keep a closer eye on things for us, to phone the bank to confirm expected deposits and withdrawals and generally to track things in our absence. It's a lot easier to contact a friend on a regular basis than to deal with professionals' voice mail over thousands of miles and many time zones. I'd also look at a backup to her, just in case something happens and she's not available for a while. Alternatively, I might hire an accountant to take care of things in our absence.

I'd also recommend that you arrange for a personal line of credit before you leave. I'm not suggesting that you should intentionally go into debt to pay for your trip, but you never know what might happen. Knowing that you have easy access to additional funds if you need them might help you sleep better at night.

Even the best-laid plans don't always work. Larry's dream of circumnavigating the globe on his sailboat was cut short by a long-time business associate who took advantage of his absence. Larry and Rita thought they had taken care of every possible contingency. An accountant and a lawyer had power of attorney, as did a comptroller in their business. They were all fooled by a clever crook.

> It's an unusual situation but not uncommon. A lot of people we met who had left business or financial affairs in the hands of other people had some serious problems. We thought we were in a bad position, but the more people we talked to, the more people said we understand, we've been there.
>
> Larry

Depending on your situation, building in financial maintenance time while you're on the road may be essential. If you have a lot to lose, there is no substitute for careful monitoring.

> People have to be very, very cautious. They should not go away with the idea that they don't have to follow up or keep tabs on things. I think that people should be getting their balance sheets, reading them and checking up regularly. And they probably should have more than one person involved.
>
> Larry

Travel insurance can be tricky
When you're travelling, there's always a risk of accident or illness. You want to be sure you'll be taken care of should anything happen.

The first difficulty with travel insurance is finding a company to insure you for long-term travel outside Canada. It took a number of phone calls before we found one, affiliated with the British Columbia Automobile Association, that would sell a year-long extended travel/medical insurance policy. Between that policy, our BC medical plan (paid in advance), and the coverage provided by two gold credit cards, we assumed we were prepared for anything. Fortunately, we never had to test that theory.

Others who did discovered that extended travel presents situations that the standard insurance clauses were never designed to handle. When Suzanne and her family needed to fly back to Canada from South Africa on short notice to attend her father-in-law's funeral, their emergency backup system didn't work.

It was a logistical nightmare. We're still trying to recover money from two airlines and Visa. We thought we had travel insurance through Visa. I can remember deciding to put the tickets on Visa because we were sure we were covered. We put the card down, thinking that we were going to get reimbursed in the end. But the glitch was that we didn't buy the tickets from home. In order to be covered, we had to have purchased those tickets in Canada. It didn't make sense. If you're in a country and you have a family emergency and you have to get out of that country and come home, who could ever possibly meet that criterion of buying the tickets at home?

Suzanne

Credit card insurance coverages and services are complicated, and they vary from card to card. It's important to take the time to understand exactly what they cover.

You should also make sure that someone at home has a copy of all your important documents. Should you be robbed or lose your passport, credit cards or other documents, replacement will be a lot easier if you have photocopied them before leaving and left the copies in safe hands.

Wills/powers of attorney

I don't want to be an alarmist, but do you have a will? I'm not trying to imply that you are about to embark on a dangerous scheme. In fact, travelling intelligently can be among the safest things you can do. But, as with insurance, it never hurts to prepare for the worst.

There is no way to tell what might happen on the road. And the last thing you want to do is leave a mess at home for someone else to clean up. Tidy up your affairs before you leave. If you have a will, make sure it reflects your current circumstances and wishes. If you don't have one, make one. You may find that it gives you an added feeling of security to know that, if the worst happens, you've done everything you can to make it easier on those left behind.

You might also ask your lawyer to draw up a power of attorney so that your affairs can be handled efficiently if you are incapacitated for a time. This is particularly important if you have major assets that require management. In fact, if you are leaving significant assets, it might be wise to provide someone with a limited power of attorney for the period you'll be gone. All of us, however, would be in the same boat if we had an accident and were unable to manage our own affairs for a time. A power of attorney, in that circumstance, would make life much easier for our families.

STAYING IN TOUCH

You should decide before you leave how you'll stay in touch with the folks back home. Again, if you're going to be in one place for a while, this is less of an issue. If your plans are more fluid, however, it helps to have thought about it in advance.

These days, e-mail comes to the top of everyone's list. I can't count the number of people who assumed we would be bringing a laptop with us so that we could send and receive messages. They clearly failed to grasp that we were actively trying to escape regular contact with the familiar.

Even had that not been the case, there are good reasons to consider whether or not you should haul a laptop around. No matter how light it is, it'll weigh a lot more when you're running for a bus. Small as it looks on your desk at home, it will take up a lot of space in your one piece of luggage. You can only carry so much. If the computer comes, something else has to go.

You might also want to consider how much unnecessary aggravation you need. I hear that many people travel the world successfully with their laptops flung casually over their shoulders. I know just as many, however, who have found themselves cursing as they struggle to get their machine to work over a third-world communications system. Is this really how you want to spend your time?

A viable option for the technologically inclined is the string of cyber-cafés springing up all over the world. There were few places we visited where we could not have found a computer to use for a fairly reasonable price.

If you break into a cold sweat at the thought of being separated from your own hardware, you might want to reconsider what you're trying to accomplish with this runaway. Letters, postcards, and telephone calls are realistic, if not always easy, alternatives.

> Keeping in contact with home was a big job that we found a bit trying because of time differences and lack of access to telephones and fax machines. We didn't have a computer on board the boat so we didn't have Internet access. When we wanted to make a phone call, there were long lineups, there were time changes, and sometimes it was too much of a hassle to go to shore. We wrote. We sent postcards. But. . .it was a chore. Here we take it so much for granted—you pick up the phone and you call someone. But when you're out there, it's a big effort.
>
> Suzanne

Peter and I made a point of *not* establishing a regular pattern of phone calls. We frequently had no idea where we would be on any given day or how easy it would be to find a phone. We also lost track of time a lot. We often couldn't remember the date or day of the week. Occasionally we didn't know what month it was. We didn't want our mothers expecting a call and then worrying if it didn't come through. Instead, we surprised each of them irregularly every couple of weeks.

A non-resident telephone calling card and the services of Canada Direct were our main means of contact. Canada Direct allows you to call Canada from almost anywhere in the world at Canadian international rates. The first time we forgot and used a local international calling service, we realized what a good deal Canadian telephone rates are. There is no monthly fee for the non-resident card; you simply pay for the calls you make. We didn't hold back, and probably made ten to fifteen calls of varying length every month from all over the world. Our monthly phone bill averaged $100.

Larry and Rita established a phone network before they left. They phoned a core group of people who passed along news to others who passed it along to yet others. It's a good idea. But, once again, the best-laid plans can sometimes backfire in the execution.

> You have to be careful that everyone has their turn. I made the mistake of phoning my son more often than my daughter because

he was easier to reach. It was really tough on her and we drifted apart. She and I had long heart-to-hearts about it when we came back.

Larry

Similar problems can arise with letters. You may think that an occasional form letter to all your friends, keeping them up to date on your adventures, will be welcomed. Think again. To some people, if it's not an original addressed to them, it's not a letter. If you're planning to use a form of chain letter to keep in touch, explain what you'll be doing in advance so that nobody's feelings get hurt.

Peter and I are not the greatest letter writers at the best of times, so expectations were minimal. We did, however, regularly let people know we were alive and well with postcards. This had the added benefit of giving them an idea where we were and what we were seeing.

One of our smarter ideas for staying in touch had to do with our photographs. We knew we'd take a lot of pictures and couldn't figure out what to do with them. Would developing be a problem in various places? Did we really want to carry them around with us? We decided to mail the exposed film back to our mothers. They could have them developed and thereby get a better sense of our trip. It also forced us to sit down and write regular letters, outlining where we'd been and what was contained on each of the rolls of film, so that the pictures would make some sense. To our amazement, every single roll of film reached its destination intact. My mother really enjoyed seeing the photos and trying to figure out where they were taken. Peter's slides were less popular with his mother, but they did result in her receiving more frequent letters than might otherwise have been the case.

Communication works both ways. One of the most difficult aspects of being on the road is not having regular news from home. Phone calls are great, but there's nothing like a letter.

Everything stopped when we got mail. Even if we had guests on the boat. It didn't matter. Sorry, guys, we've got mail. You just sit there and have another drink. We've got mail.

Rita

We left behind the most comprehensive contact list we could—addresses, phone numbers, e-mail addresses of friends along the way and approximate dates we might be in the area. Other people used American Express or Canadian embassies and high commissions as mail drops.

It was a thrill to get to Sydney, call my friend Jen, and be told there was mail waiting at her house. Or, to arrive at Jennifer and Al's place in New Delhi for lunch and be invited to sit at the computer and read the dozen or so e-mail messages forwarded by friends back in Victoria. A few messages missed us as our plans shifted and changed but, in general, we managed to stay as in touch as wandering relatively footloose could permit. I guess the sign of success is that people were still talking to us when we returned home.

THINGS TO THINK ABOUT

HOME
• Take advantage of leaving to get rid of the accumulated baggage of your life. You'll feel freer for it.
• Check out the laws in your jurisdiction—know your rights and responsibilities before you rent out your house.
• Be a tough landlord. Be clear about your limits—how many people? how many pets?
• Spread the word among family, friends, and colleagues, but check all references personally.
• If you find a tenant you trust, consider being flexible on the rent. Not having to worry about your home while you're gone has a dollar value.
• Designate a trusted friend or family member as your surrogate at home.
• Leave that person a detailed contact list—plumber, electrician, veterinarian, bank manager, stockbroker, anyone you or your tenant may need to get in touch with while you're away.
• Have your mail forwarded to that person.
• Leave behind photocopies of important documents in case you lose the originals: passport, visas, airline tickets, address book, credit cards, driver's licence, health insurance card, etc.

FINANCES
• Make sure your bank card is compatible with overseas systems, i.e., no more than four digits in your personal identification number (PIN).

- Memorize your PIN by both number and letters. Some overseas machines only show one or the other.
- Ask your surrogate at home to review your monthly credit card statements. He or she won't know if every expenditure is correct, but may be able to identify if something looks seriously out of place.
- Alternatively, consider having an accountant take care of things in your absence.
- Arrange to have regular bills paid directly by your bank, accountant, or trusted friend or family member.
- If you have major assets, consider signing one-year financial management contracts.
- Don't trust your financial institution to take care of your business correctly without supervision. Build in regular checks.
- Get hold of your credit card statements as often as you can and check them for accuracy.
- Be cautious. Check your documents and have more than one person involved in handling your finances.
- Try to keep extra money in your account at all times.
- Arrange for a line of credit before you go—just in case.

INSURANCE
- Investigate and understand various travel/medical insurance coverages.
- Don't assume that your gold card will take care of everything.

LEGAL AFFAIRS
- Update your will before leaving; if you don't have one, make one.
- Consider having a lawyer draw up a power of attorney providing someone with authority to manage your affairs if you are incapacitated.
- If you have major assets to be managed, seek your lawyer's advice on providing someone with a limited power of attorney to manage your affairs while you're gone.

STAYING IN TOUCH
- Weigh the importance of taking along a laptop computer against its weight, aggravation, and the alternatives.
- Stay in touch with the folks back home, but try to avoid a regular schedule that may be difficult to adhere to when you're on the road.
- Explain in advance to family and friends how you plan on staying in touch with them and why, in order to avoid hurt feelings.

December: SINGAPORE
Administrative Interlude

DECEMBER 9

Delaying our departure from Australia has created a problem: we can't get a connecting flight from Singapore to Delhi until Saturday. We considered taking off to one of the local islands to lie around for the week but have decided instead to use the opportunity to take care of business. Singapore Airlines has come through with a good deal on an undistinguished but well-located hotel, and there really is no better place in Southeast Asia for dealing with administrative details.

Had lunch yesterday with a former colleague from BC who has been working for the Canadian government in Singapore for the past year and a half. Trading government and career gossip again was a treat, but it did bring home how little I want to go back to all that. It was great to see a familiar face, though. It's amazing how lonely you can get for a sense of your place in the universe.

Singapore has given us the chance to come to grips with planning for India. We had originally planned to stay at Jennifer and Al's in New Delhi for most of this week and to do our India planning on site. Instead, we're using the time to put something together from here. On our friend's recommendation, we met this morning with Mr. Ohri and his assistant, Fiona, of Nandas Travel, which specializes in India, to discuss what we want to do over the next five or six weeks. As if we knew! They quickly put together a tentative itinerary and faxed it to us this evening. We're in shock. $8,500 per person! This is way beyond our budget.

It seems that you can do India really cheaply—and uncomfortably—or it costs a bundle. There doesn't appear to be much in the way of middle ground. Transportation costs are relatively inexpensive given the distances involved, but it is a big country and travelling from north to south and east to west is going to cost. The real surprise for me were the hotel prices: good hotels are ridiculously expensive. Some rethinking required here.

DECEMBER 10

Back to Mr. Ohri and Fiona today with a revised plan. It may be foolish, but we're both a bit nervous about India and, for our first visit, we want to be taken care of. So we've decided to cut back on time and space. We're limiting ourselves to three and a half weeks and focusing on the north—the Golden Triangle of Delhi, Khajuraho, Varanasi, as well as Agra and Rajasthan. We've downgraded hotels in some places but held on to the palaces in Rajasthan. Some dreams are worth keeping.

We're also longing for familiar places and faces, so we're going to keep to the itinerary on our airline tickets and fly from India to England. We'll call Martin and Rosalynn and Auntie Audrey tonight or tomorrow to see if the timing works. If anyone had told me I'd voluntarily opt for England in January.... Oh well, extended travel does strange things to you.

Spoke to Bob, our friend Arlene's friend in Delhi last night. He'll be out of town when we arrive, but has kindly offered to put us up for a few days on his return. Given that he has lived in Pakistan, Bangladesh, and now India, I was somewhat embarrassed to tell him we were coming as tourists, not travellers, i.e., we wanted a level of comfort and security. He told me the first time he landed in Delhi from Bangladesh he was so intimidated he didn't even leave the airport but got straight on another plane to Italy. I suspect there's a larger story there, but it was kind of him to try to make me feel better.

DECEMBER 11

Spending time in Singapore has turned out to be an unanticipated godsend. But it hasn't been smooth. If I were to chart the emotional ups and downs, it would look like a seismic chart in Krakatoa. For example, today started with good news and then got better. We woke up to a fax from Martin, telling us that he and Rosalynn are looking forward to having us stay with them for a week on our arrival in England. Around 9:00 a.m., Barbara called to let us know she has found a job. Hurray! We headed out for breakfast, feeling great.

Then, Peter suggested we drop into the American Express office to pick up copies of our statements for the past three months. What we got was notice that our bill hadn't been paid since we left home and that we're about to be cut off! The Singapore Amex staff were remarkably blasé about it. They clearly would have been prepared to let us pile up debt almost indefinitely. Unfortunately, we were in the hands of the more tight-assed North American Amex office.

The time difference meant that we couldn't reach anyone at the New York Amex office until tonight. That gave us plenty of time to review the accounts and worry. We dashed off a quick phone call and fax to Barb asking her to work on it at the Victoria end when the bank opens tomorrow morning.

By early afternoon, we were feeling a little better. We reviewed the bills and, to my delight, my tracking system is working. There were no surprises. We're spending too much money, of course, but we were always going to spend more in the first few months. Nonetheless, I'll feel more comfortable with a bit of a cushion, so I faxed my stockbroker and asked her to transfer $5,000 into the chequing account.

Mid-afternoon, the depression line sinks to its deepest level. Fiona called with the bad news: all the palace hotels in Rajasthan are booked solid. It is, after all, the Christmas season. I had never connected the concept of Christmas with India. In fact, I remember thinking how nice it would be to spend Christmas in a country where it was not celebrated, as we would be less likely to feel homesick. I suppose I should be pleased that Fiona's news will save us some money, but I really wanted to experience the India of my dreams. However, we mustn't give up hope. Even though, at the moment, they are unable to find any hotel at all for us in Udaipur. They have us sleeping in tents, which I find sort of intriguing, but Fiona is horrified, so I know she will keep working hard to get us into a palace.

By 10:15 p.m., the emotional graph line is starting to rise a little. I had a long and difficult telephone conversation with the Amex office in New York. They are definitely more uptight than the Singaporeans. After grovelling and assuring them that payment would be made tomorrow (Monday there), they agreed to honour the large charge we would be putting through for the India trip. A good conversation with Auntie Audrey in England finished a topsy-turvy day on a good note. That is, until Linda, my stockbroker, called and woke us up at 2:00 a.m. She had forgotten about the time difference.

DECEMBER 12
A flurry of telephone calls and faxes to and from Barb confirms that all is now well. The bank has made full payment to Amex, and all the other bills have been paid as previously arranged. Our credit rating is secure. We have no idea what the trouble was and, at this point, don't really care. The fates are kind. I can't imagine how diffi-cult it might have been to try to resolve this situation from India.

DECEMBER 14
In between all the administrivia, we have been exploring Singapore. It has changed a lot since we were last here ten years ago. Not all for the better. The development on the reclaimed land down by the harbour is amazing. A whole new city of high-rise hotels and apartments has risen fully formed from the ocean. It may augur well for the economy, but they've destroyed what used to be one of the loveliest harbour entrances in the world. On the other hand, the renovations to Raffles Hotel are terrific. She was a somewhat dowdy matron when we enjoyed Singapore Slings in the Palm Court. She's now a sophisticated woman of the world. She's been pushed up and painted in all the right places and re-dressed in classic fashion. The Palm Court is off limits to non-residents these days, but the Long Bar is a great place to wile away a rainy afternoon.

Singapore has to be one of the world's most schizophrenic cities. After years of trying to eliminate its history and reinvent itself as a modern metropolis, it is now trying to cash in on the tourism potential of some of that lost heritage. Judging from Clarke Quay, where we had dinner last night, they're having trouble remembering what it was like.

Clarke Quay is a "new" old area that the Singapore government is trying to turn into a tourism focal point. On one side of the narrow inlet, the few atmospheric eighteenth-century buildings that weren't demolished years ago in their modernizing frenzy have been renovated. Across the water are modern steel-and-glass skyscrapers towering over one remaining neocolonial building. At the end of the inlet is a new hotel which would be more at home in Los Angeles.

Junks and bumboats—the low-in-the-water, broad-beamed, beaten-up old motorboats used for just about everything—prowl the water, ferrying customers to restaurants lining the wharf or on boats tied up at the quay. The smells of every imaginable food and spice fill the air.

The music competition is fierce. Céline Dion (We can't escape her!) and Bryan Adams transform one floating restaurant into a small slice of Canada. One boat over, a Sumatran performs a perfect Paul Simon imitation. Chinese opera shrieks from a stage in front of an Old West saloon, which, in turn, offers Willie Nelson to the passing parade. Around the corner, a Philippine girl group in black leather hot pants entertains the crowd with their moves as much as with their rap music.

Chinese lanterns and Christmas decorations turn the streets into a carnival. Tacky souvenir stalls inexplicably attract a crowd on one side street; a shooting gallery, pitching contest, and other games of skill and chance line another. A children's amusement park fills the centre of the square. Clarke Quay is action central. Honky-tonk, but kind of fun.

Being here in December provides an added element of lunacy to an already overpowered city. I hadn't realized what a worldwide phenomenon Christmas is. Silly me. Christmas has nothing to do with religion. It's all about shopping. And Singapore is, indisputably, the shopping capital of the world! Christmas is a big deal here.

The decorations along Orchard Road are stupendous. Not particularly tasteful, but undeniably breathtaking. Strings of lights cascade from every tree along this mile-long shopping artery. Department store fronts are covered with six-storey-high, sound-and-light extravaganzas of mechanical Santas, elves, aliens, sleighs, musicians, and slightly off-kilter fairy-tale characters. Snowmen and reindeer perform intricate aerial manoeuvres overhead. Gigantic video screens on street corners present Asian rock stars bellowing out Christmas favourites in unfamiliar languages. School choirs sing carols in the park. The nighttime street is jammed with shoppers, wide-eyed children, and the occasional gawking visitor like us.

And we came to Asia to escape the Christmas frenzy.

FIVE
WHAT TO TAKE AND WHAT TO LEAVE BEHIND

You've heard it before. I'll say it again. Less is more.

If the trip is about freedom and flexibility, packing is about discipline and control. You have to pack on the assumption that you and only you will be responsible for carrying your belongings. When you most need it, help will not be available. Inevitably, there will be more up hills than down. And you will always be staying on the third floor. You have to be able to carry your own bag upstairs.

At the same time, you need the right clothes to see you through a variety of occasions and weather systems. Like a Boy Scout, you have to be prepared for every kind of weather—sun, heat, rain, cold, snow, wind—and for every kind of activity—hiking, city sightseeing, horse-back riding, swimming, partying. You need to be both casual and elegant, as the situation demands. And it all has to fit into one bag.

Sound impossible? Believe me, if I can do it, anyone can. Exercising restraint is not one of my better-developed instincts. I am notorious for emptying my closet to go away for a weekend. I want to be prepared for anything, including an unlikely dinner invitation from the Queen. But there is no incentive like having to heft your own bags around for nine or ten months.

Not only can you fit everything you need into one bag, you will probably end up shedding like a snake as you go. The longer you're on the road, the more you realize how little you really need. You'll establish patterns of dressing that result in your wearing the same basics over and over again—because they work. Fashion takes second place to convenience. That second dress and third pair of pants will eventually find themselves into some local person's hands or into a shipment back home.

LUGGAGE TIPS
Here are some surefire luggage tips for making your wandering a little more comfortable:

- One daypack on your back and one larger bag in hand give you all the space and flexibility you need—and all you can handle.

- A well-designed and good-looking daypack can carry your toiletries, passport, tickets, money, books, etc., as your carry-on luggage. It can handle extra clothes and food for a few days' hiking trip. Flung casually over your shoulder, it becomes a purse for city sightseeing. It's versatile and easy to handle, and you'll soon wonder how you ever got along without one at home.

- Take time choosing the right piece of luggage for you. Visit luggage shops and test out various types and sizes. You'll be living with this choice for a while.

- Size is critical, and bigger is not necessarily better. Obviously, you want a bag that will hold everything you think you need. More important, however, is that you be able to manage your bag easily on your own. Fill up the suitcase in the store with telephone books, other smaller bags, anything, just to get an idea of how much it will weigh when full. Pick the size that you can handle— even if it looks small—and limit what you take to what will fit inside.

- Once you've decided which style and size suits you best, buy the sturdiest of that type you can afford. Ask about its construction. If you opt for a soft-sided bag, make sure the fabric is tough and water-resistant. This bag is going to get a real workout over the next few months, and you don't want it falling apart on you.

Luggage type is a matter of individual preference. I bonded with a standard midsize suitcase with built-in wheels and easy-to-use retractable handle. It had plenty of inside and outside pockets that made it easy to divide up my belongings so that I always knew where everything was. It also had leather handles on the top and on the side, so that I could carry it vertically or horizontally, or grasp it with both hands to heave it onto overhead shelves. It was the Cadillac of suitcases, solidly built and relatively expensive (around $400). But it proved its worth to me time and time again. Peter preferred a large open duffle bag with more interior space and the option of carrying it like a suitcase, over his shoulder or as a backpack, although he lived to regret its lack of wheels. This item was a relic of previous trips and cost him nothing. Purchase price would have been around $50.

- Always use a bag with wide, built-in wheels and a strong, solid pulling handle. Don't even consider a suitcase with a leashlike pulling strap. It will fall over or head in the wrong direction and generally give you a hard time. One solid piece of equipment gives you control and flexibility.

- Advice for men: Please don't do the macho thing and think that pulling is for girls. Pulling is almost always easier than carrying. Much though we may not like the idea, none of us is as young as we used to be and our backs are not as strong. Peter started the trip with his standard duffel bag slung rakishly over his shoulder. After a few months of heaving it around, however, image gave way to practicality. We visited a luggage store in England and purchased a similar bag, this time with wheels (approximately Cdn$150). He still had the option of backpacking it when necessary, but the wheels made his life a whole lot easier and his back a whole lot more comfortable. And I think he looked rather more attractive striding upright pulling the bag than struggling along hunched beneath it.

- Advice for women: Leave your purse at home. The daypack is all you need most of the time. You can tuck a small elegant evening bag into a corner of your luggage for special occasions.

PACKING TIPS
Once you've found the right piece of luggage, you have to pack it properly.

- The single best packing tip I know comes courtesy of my friend Barbara: bags. She suggested we put our clothes in see-through plastic bags inside our suitcases. It is a brilliant concept!

Underwear went in one bag; T-shirts in another; shorts, shirts, slacks, sweaters, dresses, bathing suits—each category had its own clear plastic bag—as did each pair of shoes.

When Barbara first mentioned this, my initial thought was, "Oh right, another Martha Stewart moment!" Why put things in a bag, only to put them in another bag? Well, Martha wins again. The bags saved an enormous amount of time, made it easy to find the clothes we wanted, took up less space in our luggage, and preserved our clothes despite the constant beating they received. You are going to be living out of your suitcase for the next little while. Think of the bags as the equivalent of hangers and drawers.

Bags also make repacking a breeze and minimize the likelihood of your leaving things behind. In a very short time, you will find the right configuration in your suitcase for all your belongings. Each bag will have its place, and you'll be able to tell at a glance if you're missing something.

Start accumulating clear plastic bags—the stronger, the better. Try to find some with zippers or closure snaps. Once you start looking for them, you'll see them everywhere: clothes come in them; linens tend to be sold in them; and stores frequently have some they're just going to throw out. As a last resort, you can always buy storage bags, but you probably won't have to.

Bags. They're a good thing!

- Think layers. You don't have much room. You'll probably run into every weather condition imaginable. Each item of clothing will have to do at least double duty. Plan your wardrobe in layers to accommodate every variety of weather you can imagine.

  For example, starting from the skin out: long underwear; jeans and T-shirt; sweatshirt or sweater; fleece liner or vest; Gortex jacket with hood. Add gloves, socks, and appropriate footwear, and you have an all-weather outfit. If it's hot, you wear nothing but the jeans and T-shirt. If it's raining, throw on the Gortex jacket. If it's chilly, put on the sweatshirt or fleece. When it's freezing, use it all. Each individual piece is relatively compact; together they can get you through a blizzard. You may resemble the Michelin man, but you'll be warm and dry.

- Consider investing in special travel clothing. A lot of firms are now making stylish clothes specifically built for travel. The clothes pack small, don't crease, wash up easily, retain their shape, and look good no matter how badly you treat them. I am very glad I swallowed my concerns about the initial price and spent the money on Tilley pants, shorts, and silks. They were worth every penny.

- I always cringe when fashion magazines go on at length about the need to coordinate your wardrobe. And here I am doing it myself. In this case, however, there's no denying that colour coordination helps. When you're dealing with a limited number of pieces, the need to mix and match is critical. Tops need to work with all the pants, shorts, and skirts. One belt has to go with everything. Working around a basic colour scheme may be dull, but it is functional. I opted for black and beige as basics and gave myself a needed colour hit with violet Tilley silks (the long- and short-sleeved tops went with everything) and a fuchsia scarf. Other scarves picked up along the way helped to provide needed variety.

- Leave your good jewellery at home. As an obvious stranger in town, you are an automatic target for thieves. Why give them something to aim for? You're also more likely to lose things when you're on the move. Substituting fun earrings for the gold hoops, and a Swatch for the Rolex, gives you fewer things to worry about.

- Bring along your own medical kit. With any luck, you'll never need to use most of it, but having it with you provides an added sense of confidence that you can deal with whatever arises. Our kit consisted of the standard items such as Band-Aids, gauze, elastic bandage, antiseptic cream, motion-sickness pills, anti-diarrhea pills, laxatives, aspirin, etc. We also obtained some good general antibiotic pills from our doctor as well as a supply of syringes. The latter might seem a little paranoid but, if one of us had needed an injection in a place like India, I would have felt much safer having the doctor use our own needles.

- Women, carry your own sanitary supplies. Outside developed countries, tampons are not universally available. And what pass for sanitary pads can be uncomfortable. An emergency supply of your preferred product will come in handy.

- If you take prescription medication, birth control pills, or are on hormone replacement therapy, bring along a good supply as well as a prescription from your doctor. Divide your supply of each medication into as many containers as you have pieces of luggage (e.g., four if there are two of you travelling). If one bag goes astray, you'll still have plenty left to see you through until you can reach a doctor to get your prescription refilled.

- Don't forget to bring along your eyeglass prescription as well. If you sit on your glasses or lose them, having the prescription will save time and money.

- A seven-day pill dispenser is indispensable if you take regular medication. Once you leave your normal routine behind, days of the week lose all significance. It's too easy to forget to take your medication or to forget if you've forgotten. At times, the pill dispenser was the only thing that told me what day of the week it was. Filling the dispenser for the week and getting in the habit of checking it every morning helps relieve a lot of anxiety.

- Substitute a cotton pareo or sarong for a towel. You'll need a towel somewhere along the way, whether camping, staying in cheap accommodation, or at the beach. Regular towels are heavy and take up a lot of room. A cotton pareo can dry you off just as well, dries itself more quickly, doubles as a beach cover-up, and disappears into a corner of your suitcase.

- Check local idiosyncrasies before you check your baggage. Every airline or airport seems to have its own rules. Our Swiss Army knives made it on to some planes, not others; matches were confiscated in a couple of places; airlines in India won't allow batteries in carry-on luggage. Ask about any local quirks before checking your luggage.

- Don't forget notebooks. Different sizes work for different func-tions—your journal, travel tips picked up along the way, daily expenditures, etc.

- If you're bringing along anything electrical (hair dryer, electric razor, etc.) don't forget an accompanying electrical adapter kit to make sure you can use the appliance wherever you are.

- When in doubt, don't take it. If you hesitate for a moment while deciding whether you're likely to want or use something, you probably won't. If you forget something or discover later that you could have used it, you will more than likely be able to buy a replacement somewhere along the way.

- There is one exception to the "forget it" rule. Bring something meaningful from home. It can be lonely out there, and it helps to have something comforting with you that reminds you of your place in the universe. For me, it was my tiny teddy bear, attached to my daypack with a small collar and leash to ensure he didn't get lost, and a small framed picture of our little green house and the two cats that was placed by my bed every night. They didn't take up much room in the bag, but they assumed a large place in my heart.

OUR PACKING LIST

Your packing list will reflect your own interests, needs, and type of trip. You might find it helpful, though, to see what we started with and what we shed as we moved along.

My biggest packing problem was shoes. They take up so much room. I finally whittled it down to five pairs: hiking boots, city walk-ing shoes, dress shoes, sandals, and a pair of thongs that doubled as slippers. I know this is ridiculous. (The only person who supported this lunacy is Barbara, who probably owns seventy-five pairs of shoes. She insists that changing shoes is better for your feet, particularly when you're doing a lot of walking.) What the heck, it worked for me. You'll undoubtedly have your own fetish. And there's no harm in it, provided you understand that you have only a limited amount of space.

GENERAL ITEMS

- Teddy
- picture of home & cats
- cameras/film/extra batteries/protective film bag
- combination radio/alarm clock
- pocket calculator
- flashlight
- binoculars
- cards/cribbage board
- bungee cord (for miscellaneous use)
- facecloth/pareos (as towels)
- universal plug
- electrical adapter kit
- writing supplies
- *art supplies
- medical kit
- sunscreen and suntan lotion
- snorkelling equipment*
- plastic bags
- packages of cold-water detergent
- picnic kit, i.e., cutting board/cold-drink carrier*
- Swiss Army knives
- address book
- passports/tickets/travellers' cheques/wallets
- guidebooks
- reading material
- notebooks

LYNDA

- toiletries
- underwear/socks—a week's worth
- long silk underwear
- hiking boots
- thongs
- sandals
- walking shoes
- dress shoes
- Gortex jacket
- fleece insert
- gloves
- T-shirts (started with 4; sent 1 home)*
- blouses (started with 2; sent 1 home)*
- flannel shirt
- sweatshirt
- sweater
- shorts (started with 3; sent 1 home)*
- Tilley pants
- jeans
- white cotton pants*
- beige pants
- corduroy pants
- dressy white pants/gold belt*
- long beach dress*
- T-shirt dress (doubled as a top over pants)
- short cotton dress
- silk jacket
- Tilley travel silks (pants, skirt, long- and short-sleeved tops)
- black dress
- scarf
- belt
- bathing suits (started with 3; sent 1 home)*
- nightgown/dressing gown
- hair dryer
- small shoulder purse
- junk jewellry
- crushable sun hat

PETER

- toiletries
- underwear/socks—a week's worth
- long underwear
- kerchief*
- belt
- Gortex jacket
- fleece vest
- gloves
- sandals
- hiking boots
- city shoes
- shirts (started with 5, sent 2 home)*
- T-/golf shirts (started with 3, sent 1 home)*
- sweater
- sweatshirt
- cotton pants
- jeans
- Tilley pants
- silk jacket
- beige pants
- shorts (2)
- ties (started with 2; sent 1 home)*
- bathing suits (started with 2; sent 1 home)*
- nightshirt/dressing gown
- hat
- money belt

discarded along the way

For every favourite thing you bring, something else has to stay behind.

There are a few things we wish we had brought. I could have used some dressy black pants but, in some misplaced mood of false economy, couldn't bring myself to buy them knowing I had some at home. I also craved a pair of high heels in order to feel more elegant occasionally, but I couldn't quite cope with the shame of carting around six pairs of shoes. Peter's needs were clearly in the comfort zone; he missed having a pair of slippers or slipper socks.

Along the way we did buy a few extras, primarily to deal with unexpected cold weather. We both bought an extra pair of heavy pants, and I added a thick sweater, a cotton galibaya (long Middle Eastern cover-up) for lounging around in, and a couple of colourful scarves to vary the look.

Awards for the most useful items go to:
Lynda: little black dress
Peter: Swiss Army knife
Both: Gortex jackets, hiking boots, Tilley pants

The booby prize for most useless item is won hands down by the snorkelling equipment. I don't know what possessed me. I guess it was because we were starting in a rented house on a Fijian out-island where I thought it might be difficult to rent equipment. Wrong! Availability of equipment was never a problem anywhere. The snorkelling bag was one piece too many and the first shipped home.

IN-TRANSIT CLOTHES
Peter and I travel better if we're dressed well. We both like to look respectable when we board an airplane. It makes us feel better and I think it results in our getting better service. There have been a few occasions when one or both of us has been upgraded to business or first-class, and I suspect being well dressed had something to do with it.

On planes, we would usually travel in a good pair of pants, shirt, and jacket (to keep them from being crushed in the suitcases). We'd carry the Gortex jackets with the fleece liners tucked inside them. When we were travelling by train or bus and our bags were with us, or if we were walking through town with the bags, we could attach the jackets and fleeces to my suitcase with a bungee cord. Normally we wore our hiking boots for travelling; they were comfortable, looked okay, and took us over all kinds of terrain. Besides, they took up too much room in the bags. Everything else fit nicely in the two daypacks, my suitcase, and Peter's duffle bag.

LESS IS MORE

We could have done with even fewer clothes. In my case, the Tilley silks, pants, and shorts would have been an adequate core. I didn't need the extra dresses and pants. The issue isn't need; it's a matter of not going insane from the boredom of wearing the same clothes day after day. By the end of our trip, despite the extras, we were royally fed up with every piece of clothing in our suitcases. I couldn't wait to get home to throw them all out.

When I look back at our photos, however, I realize how well our clothes served us. We were dressed appropriately for every situation, whether horseback riding in the Snowy Mountains, trekking in the Judean desert, shopping in Provence, or attending the theatre in London. We were always able to handle our own bags, up hills and stairs, down country lanes, on foot, bus, train, and plane. We were independent travellers.

THINGS TO THINK ABOUT

- Limit yourself to one main bag plus daypack.
- Keep it small enough to handle by yourself.
- Make sure your bag has sturdy wheels and a solid handle.
- Restrict yourself to what the suitcase will hold.
- When in doubt, leave it out.
- Organize your clothes in clear plastic bags for packing.
- Be prepared for all weather conditions—think layers.
- Consider investing in special travel clothing.
- Coordinate colours so that most clothing can do double duty.
- Leave good jewellery at home.
- Bring along a medical kit.
- Don't forget prescriptions and sanitary supplies.
- Use a seven-day pillbox to keep track of days.
- Pareos make great towels.
- Small notebooks come in handy.
- Anything electrical will need an accompanying adapter kit.
- There's always room for a small reminder of home.
- Dress well when travelling by plane—it may get you an upgrade.

December: INDIA
The Shoeshine Shit Scam
and Other Cautionary Tales

We were warned before we went: "You will love India or you will hate it. There is no in-between." I was prepared to love it. Peter was prepared to survive. So far, his approach seems more appropriate.

The overwhelming impression since arriving last night is the pollution. I've never seen anything like it and certainly didn't expect it. A blanket of smoke hangs over the city; you can feel it in the eyes and throat.

After breakfast this morning, we went out for a walk around "fashionable Connaught Place." We thought we would wander around, check out the neighbourhood, the shops, have lunch, before coming back to the hotel for a nap. A typical quiet first day before settling down to the hard slog of discovery.

Our walk lasted only an hour. Connaught Place is a rotting circle of noise and hawkers. We stumbled through potholes and broken pavement, past crumbling grey buildings, trying to avoid being hit by rickshaws, buses, cars, all honking their horns and spewing out oily fumes. We pushed our way through hordes of people wanting to sell us something, anything, to stay alive.

This stroll through the centre of the subcontinent was highlighted, if that word can be said to apply, by the infamous "shoeshine shit scam." A boy approached Peter, asking if he wanted a shoeshine. "No thanks," Peter replied, moving on. "Oh no, mister, look, look, you need one," cried the boy, running beside us and pointing down at Peter's foot. A blob of shit—perfect, round, quivering—had miraculously appeared on Peter's shoe. It was a masterpiece of surreptitious execution. Fortunately, I had just read about this particular ploy in a guidebook and knew to expect two or three other "shoeshine boys" to surround us and try to extort money. I went into immediate action. "It's a scam," I cried, pulling Peter away and running off down the street. I felt quite blasé and sophisticated to have evaded being ripped off. Peter just felt defiled.

Back at the hotel was a lunch invitation from my former colleague, Jennifer, and her partner, Al, who have been living in Delhi for a year or so. They may never know how important that invitation was. We enjoyed a couple of hours of friendly company, lively conversation, good food and, best of all, mail and e-mails from home. We may survive.

Tonight we're off to the Sound and Light Show at the Red Fort, Shah Jahan's red sandstone symbol of Mogul authority and style. Fortunately we have Prem, the driver arranged by Mr. Ohri, to drive us there. This is not a city, nor, I suspect, a country, where I would want to try to get around on my own. It is chaos on the streets. Al said it took him ten months to get his Indian driver's licence and then all they did was ask him to identify some numbers in a book—no rules, no road test. It shows.

After one relatively straightforward day, I feel tired, dirty, and disoriented.

DECEMBER 16—DELHI

Yesterday we toured New Delhi: India Gate, parliament, the government precinct, the Presidential Palace (old Viceregal Palace), as well as the Bahai Temple and the Qutab Minar, a twelfth-century stone tower. I hadn't realized that Delhi is really many Delhis, as wave after wave of conquerors put their own stamp on the city. The Moguls, who are probably the best known, created the seventh city. The British are responsible for the eighth, New Delhi. New Delhi is an incredible display of imperial pomp. It must have been spectacular at the height of British India. Now, however, you can barely distinguish shapes through the smog. The touring around became a surrealistic voyage through a gauzy netherworld.

We had Prem drop us at the Parkroyal Hotel, near the Diplomatic Enclave in the south end of the city, to meet Bob, Arlene's friend, who has offered to put us up for a couple of nights. He turned out to be a terrific guy with a great sense of humour. We spent the afternoon sitting around his apartment, chatting and sending e-mails. It was a relief to discover that even Bob, who has lived and worked in the sub-continent for most of the past decade, dislikes Delhi enormously. He far preferred living in Dacca (Bangladesh), which has to tell you something.

In the evening, Bob took us out to the Balluci Park restaurant in Hauz Khas, an old village which is being turned into a trendy area of shops, restaurants, and art galleries. It has some charm but, as the trendiest area in a city of 10 million, it leaves a lot to be desired. The restaurant was great, however, serving delicate North Indian food with a modern twist in a garden setting. It wasn't warm enough to enjoy the garden, but it was a pleasure to experience something out-side hotels and guidebooks.

Today we toured Old Delhi: the Red Fort, the Chandni Chowk market area of twisted lanes and crowded bazaars just outside the walls of the Fort, Gandhi's cremation site, the Jama Masjid—India's largest mosque, completed in the seventeenth century, and Humayun's Tomb, a classic example of elegant Mogul architecture. The latter is a lovely quiet spot but, boy, are they few and far between.

New Delhi is a lot more beaten-up-looking than I had expected. Beautiful BBC images of the Raj are clearly out of date. What you can see through the smog is pretty decrepit. The classic structural lines are still there, but that's about it. Old Delhi, in contrast, I expected to look beaten-up, and I prefer it. It's crowded and noisy and filthy, but it has life and passion. People are huddled around small fires. Life unfolds on the street. It's real and elemental. New Delhi also has filth and noise and people living on the street, but somehow it seems more sordid. It lacks any sense of warmth or com-munity. I recognize, however, that this is a highly romanticized Western impression. Being cold, poor, filthy, and living on the street is undoubtedly miserable whether in Old or New Delhi.

At noon we headed to the Canadian High Commission and the "Canada Club" for lunch with another former colleague who is now the political officer at the post. The "Club" and grounds are fine—nice pool, tennis courts, bar, and small restaurant—but if, as Ed says, this is as good as it gets in Delhi, I don't know how people stand it. If the taxpayers at home could visit Delhi for just a few days, they would never again begrudge the very few amenities that help our people make it through the day.

Neither of us will be sorry to leave Delhi. The socializing has been great, but the city itself is a pit. If this is what the world might be if we allow population and pollution to get out of control, we'd better learn the lessons fast. This place is killing itself and not all that slowly.

There is a wonderful, horrible juxtaposition in the centre of town. The World Health Organization office is directly across the street from a super-polluting hydroelectric plant. Perfect!

DECEMBER 17—DELHI AIRPORT

Waiting for the flight to Khajuraho, a small town some 450 kilometres southeast of Delhi in the heart of north-central India. We're off to see the fabled erotic temples. If we ever get there. The plane was scheduled for 10:00 a.m.—now delayed to 11:15. According to the announcements, almost all flights to anywhere are delayed "due to bad weather over (fill in the blank)." This is clearly code for something—probably "don't bug us." It's hard to imagine that all of India other than Delhi is suffering from severe weather conditions.

Flight now delayed until noon. Fortunately we have seats, and the toilet, though a stand-up, is clean. I wonder if we'll ever get out.

Bob gifted us with a copy of *City of Djinns* by William Dalrymple to wile away our airport waiting time. It's a fascinating book. Dalrymple's Delhi is only a few years old but it seems a generation away. If his description is accurate, the decay is advancing exponentially. Today, this is not a city "fraying at the edges" but one rotting at the core.

6:00 P.M.—KHAJURAHO

We took off sometime after noon, after they changed the front wheel of the aircraft! Then we landed in Agra—and sat for another hour and a half "due to bad visibility over Khajuraho." When we were finally airborne again, the pilot made numerous, presumably meant-to-be-reassuring announcements to the effect that we shouldn't really attempt to land because visibility was too poor, but he would try an instrument landing nonetheless. Do I need to know this? We made it to Khajuraho by 3:30 p.m., but it seemed longer.

On arrival, we went for a short walk to stretch our legs. This is not as simple as it sounds. We first had to run the gauntlet of 30–40 rickshaw drivers lying permanently in wait outside the hotel. Then we had to convince rickshaw driver #14, Jabra, who somehow managed to establish to his colleagues that we were his, that we really wanted to walk, weren't trying to find a cheaper rickshaw, and would be sure to use his services in future. Whew!

We were joined on our walk by two young men who parked their bikes to accompany us. Peter's companion tried to hustle him to take a tour, frequent his shop, etc. Mine, however, seemed genuinely to want to talk. Babaloo (yes, that is really his name) is 25, single, and informs me he wants to marry for love. He's well educated, has a university degree and speaks English, French, Spanish, and Italian. He is studying in Delhi to be a teacher and has dreams of opening a private school in Khajuraho.

I can't stand it anymore. We're adopting Andrew and Geoffrey (sons of our friends, Jack and Jill—yes, those really are their names). From now on when anyone asks about children, we're going to pretend Andrew and Geoffrey are ours. Everyone I've spoken with—first in Fiji, then in Singapore, and now here—is filled with pity for me when I say we have no children. Even Babaloo, despite his advanced education and liberated views, is the same. "How many children do you have?" he asked expectantly. His eyes lit up, big smile on his face, his head leaning forward for my proud response. "We haven't any," I replied. His face fell. His mouth dropped open in shock. His eyes clouded over. He didn't know where to look, what to say. We walked on. After a long pause, I heard his lowered voice murmuring sympathetically, "What a great sadness for you. All women desire children more than anything else. I grieve for you." That's it. No more. We now have two fine sons, both in university, doing very well. Andrew is academically inclined; he's going to be a doctor. Geoffrey is a good student, but he's more of a jock. Maybe a career in professional sports?

My head is filled with strange images: the incongruous dignity of an old man squatting in the field shitting; a mocking young man who thought I should take the old man's picture; a starving dog, still wagging his tail and wanting affection as well as food. Why does that last image break my heart when there are hungry people all around me? Maybe it's easier to hurt for the dog. If I think about the people, I don't know that I could take it.

DECEMBER 18—KHAJURAHO

I have finally glimpsed the India of my imagination. Here, seemingly in the middle of nowhere, the Chandella dynasty of the tenth and eleventh centuries situated a truly spectacular collection of intricately carved structures. Twenty-two temples rise above the horizon like the mountains of the Himalaya. We toured them in the company of a knowledgeable guide with the musical name of Angarad. Every inch of each temple is covered with depictions of the life and times of a wealthy, cultured, leisured, and sensual people. All of life is here—music, cooking, hunting, fighting, primping, dressing, worshipping, and loving. Particularly loving. An incredible array of erotic poses and possibilities is depicted with skill, grace, and loving care. I defy anyone to look at them without smiling. They are so lighthearted and filled with the joy of living.

In the afternoon we headed off in a Jeep through the countryside to the Ken Ghaurial (crocodile) Sanctuary. It was a wild ride on some of the worst dirt roads imaginable, but great fun. We didn't see any crocodiles but we did come face to face with huge black-faced monkeys, deer, antelope, spotted chikas (like antelope with big white spots), and wild cows. The latter are the strangest mix I've ever seen. The young look like foals; the mature cows resemble a cross between a horse and a reindeer, with an occasional camel ancestor thrown in. They're funny-looking beasts with big ears and floppy tails and, from one angle, they appear to have a hump on their backs.

At the end of an overwhelming, exhausting, and exhilarating day, we arrived back at the hotel as dark was falling and promptly fell asleep.

DECEMBER 19—KHAJURAHO

Plane delayed! So I hired our faithful friend, Jabra, to go for a rickshaw ride into town and the neighbouring village. He considers himself a fortunate man. And, in context, he is. He has five children, three boys and two girls. He lives with his two brothers and their families on a small piece of land—which they own!—near the airport. He has been cycling his rickshaw for twenty-five years.

Flight scheduled for 12:15, now looking at 4:00 p.m. We'll see.

Everything in India seems slightly off-centre. Yesterday was filled and, by the end, we were exhausted. Today we sit and wait, marooned with a group of Germans around a pool in Khajuraho. Travelling in India can be a bit surreal. Ah well, the sun is shining—life could be worse.

Indian obsequiousness is simultaneously charming and annoying. Mainly it's annoying, but occasionally I don't mind being raj-ed. Peter and I started to play ping-pong beside the pool to pass the time. A little Indian man stationed himself behind me and proceeded to cheerlead for me. "Good shot, sir" (everyone is 'sir,' including me), he would call out every time I connected with the ball—and run after every ball I missed.

DECEMBER 20—VARANASI (BENARES)

The plane finally took off around 6:15 p.m. and arrived in Varanasi, the religious capital of Hinduism some 275 kilometres northeast of Khajuraho, around 7:00 p.m. The drive into town in the dark was even more hair-raising than driving in Delhi in daylight. The streets are filled with people, animals, and vehicles of all description. It's "might makes right" on the roadways. Trucks come straight at you on "your side" and you have to pull off and hope you don't hit anything or anyone. The horns honk constantly—to tell you someone's passing, to move you out of the way, to warn you not to try to break in or just for the hell of it. Lights are minimal. The few electric lights are so dim as to be useless. Small fires dot the roadsides. Huts, stalls, and stores are lit by kerosene lamps. Everything is dirty, dusty (oh so dusty), crowded, and polluted from all the fires, but it pulsates with life. Every activity known to humankind takes place in full view.

This morning we were picked up at 6:00 a.m. by Basu, a well-educated 59-year-old, who looks twenty years older, and who claims in his youth to have guided Pierre Trudeau around Benares, as it was then called. Varanasi is the oldest continuously inhabited city on the planet. People have been living here for 4,000 years. It looks like it. We made our way through the streets of the "old city," which looks astonishingly like the "new city." Or perhaps the reverse would be more accurate. In any event, neither approximates anything we would think of as a city. We continued to the "inner old city" and the ghats, the cremation sites on the banks of the river. All devout Hindus hope to visit Varanasi at least once in a lifetime to purify themselves in the Ganges and, if possible, to die and be cremated here.

True to form, Peter and I travel in tandem with record weather extremes. The Ganges was almost overflowing its banks—the highest level at this time of year that Basu has ever seen—more typical of the monsoon season.

The boat ride along the ghats at dawn is amazing. The river is brown and filthy but that doesn't stop people from bathing, washing clothes, and brushing their teeth in it. Priests sit on the banks under umbrellas while the devout make offerings to the gods. It's a riveting site, mysterious and eternal, and it is peaceful on the water—a great blessing in this, and seemingly every, Indian city. As a religious experience, however, it leaves me cold. And this reaction surprises me. I remember being in Nepal a few years ago. Our day at the ghats in Kathmandu was a profound religious experience. Something about it touched me deeply, despite the obvious filth of the river and surroundings. Here, I remain untouched. There is something about the harshness of India that disturbs me. I find it actively un-spiritual, maybe even anti-spiritual. I cannot comprehend the Westerners who find spiritual fulfillment in India. There were a few young Western men sitting on the ghats, meditating. It seems to me they'd be closer to God in a green meadow or on a mountaintop in the Himalaya or the Rockies, or sitting on Dallas Road in Victoria looking out over the ocean to the Olympic Mountains. I can't see God through the misery. I can appreciate that Indians do—this is their history, their heritage, their culture, themselves. But what is it that Westerners find?

The streets of the old city near the river are filled with temples, shrines, beggars, holy men, shysters, pilgrims, folk. The poverty and misery of India are legendary and they are real. Being in the midst of people who have so little when you have so much places the traveller in a constant moral quandary. You know you can't support the entire country and that demonstrating any sort of charity will result in chaos.

Today, I experienced a moment of weakness. We were walking through the inner old city, Basu and Peter ahead of me. I turned a corner and came face to face with a young man who had horrible facial and physical deformities. I gasped and, in an unthinking moment of pity, reached into my pocket for a few rupees. In seconds I was swarmed. A crowd of beggars surrounded me. Lepers and amputees thrust diseased and severed limbs in my face. Scarred and mutilated children tugged at my jacket. I couldn't see Peter or Basu, and I was terrified I wouldn't get out of there without causing a riot. I pushed my way through the throng and ran.

Bob had reassured us, "India is very safe." He's right. Indians won't mug you, but they may very well pester you to death.

We are learning, of necessity, to develop the Indian isolation from fellow human beings that permits you simply to ignore their existence. We had been lectured in Delhi that our "nice" Canadian mode of smiling and saying "no thanks" or "not interested" was a serious error of judgement. What we must do, we were told, is pretend we neither see nor hear anything. To our dismay, we've discovered that it works. If you place yourself in a psychic bubble, the hawkers and beggars seem to recognize they can't penetrate and they gradually disappear. The cost to us is simply a piece of our souls.

There is a palpable sense of ethnic tension in Varanasi. In the centre of the inner old city, a mosque was demolished to put up a Hindu temple, the Kashi Vishwanath or Golden Temple. A new mosque was built nearby. That was in the eighteenth century! To this day, it is a focal point for Moslem-Hindu conflict. The army patrols all entry points to the area and no photography is allowed. Tension is also apparent in other parts of the city and country. We can't visit Benares University because of student unrest—two students were shot today. There are riots in Jaipur. Bombs have exploded on two trains in the south. The violence is hardly surprising. Life here is so schizophrenic—the extremes so extreme—there must be an enormous amount of sublimation going on just to live here from day to day. It shouldn't be startling if suppressed rage erupts occasionally into random violence.

The single most aggravating thing about India for me is its inaccessibility. I want to believe that there is a rich, vibrant culture out there, but I can't find it except in fleeting glimpses. The constant assault by hawkers and beggars makes strolling, looking, listening, and learning impossible. We are trapped on an endless sterile tourism loop of hotel, car, temples, and monuments, back to hotel, off to airport, another city, another hotel, more temples and monuments. Whenever we try to jump off, we're besieged to the point of exhaustion and find ourselves running back to self-imposed imprisonment. Occasionally we can escape to an ex-pat friend's house for dinner or to stay a few days. But never do we get to touch India.

This part of the trip is definitely more of an education than a pleasure. I'm so glad we are doing this as three-and-a-half weeks in a nine-to-ten-month journey. If this were a typical holiday trip and India our only destination, I would be feeling cheated. My head is filled to pressure point with what I'm seeing. Trying to make sense of it is exhausting. I'm suffering from an absence of Western references. I have lived in Mexico and travelled extensively in Tunisia, Central America, Indonesia, Thailand, Nepal, and other countries, but this is as alien a place as I have ever been.

DECEMBER 22—DELHI

Can you believe it? The plane yesterday actually left and arrived on time. We had the pleasure of travelling with Sir Peter Ustinov, his wife, and film crew. He looked great, dressed in a very Ustinovian coral leisure suit, scarf wrapped around his throat. His wife was even more striking, in an undoubtedly expensive but quite loud yellow checked suit (Chanel?) and gold high heels, and carrying a Christian

Dior shopping bag. Not a common sight on the streets of Varanasi, I assure you.

We made it back to Delhi in time for dinner with Jennifer and Al and their friends, Carol and Doug. The latter had just returned from Rajasthan where they had a great time—very reassuring for us. We sat and talked about travel and India and religion and politics until midnight. What a relief to get beyond the usual Indian tourist conversational mantra of: Where do you come from? What do you do? How many children do you have?

This morning we managed to get hold of Arlene's friend, Marg (thank God for Arlene's friends), and we're going to stay with her in Jaipur. That helps to make up for the disappointment of not getting into any of the palaces. Who knows? Maybe Marg's friend, the Rajput prince, can help.

5:30 P.M.—AGRA

The drive from Delhi to Agra and the Taj Mahal is almost indescribable. This is the highway to India's major tourist attraction. We set off expectantly, welcoming the opportunity to see the countryside. It turned out to be a four-and-a-half-hour journey through hell—equal parts terror and horror.

The terror comes from the peculiarly fatalistic Indian attitude toward driving. Theoretically, the road is a divided highway. In reality, the highway is largely loose gravel, dust, and potholes. And any division is purely imaginary. Yes, there is a barrier between the two sides of the road, but that's where the similarity ends. Most of the traffic is going one way when, with no warning, someone comes the wrong way—straight at you!

As in the cities, highway traffic consists of everything. Trucks, buses, cars, auto rickshaws, bicycle rickshaws, bicycles, motorbikes, horses, burros, camels pulling huge carts of grain wrapped in burlap, bullock carts, sacred cows wandering at will, people walking, limping, crawling—and all of it weaving across and around. Lanes, or even straight lines, do not exist. The noise, the smoke, and the dirt assault you. Horns honk constantly. Trucks, buses, and auto rickshaws belch black smoke and toxic fumes. Filth and dust coat your lungs with every breath. Your car jerks its way along the road, stopping constantly to avoid hitting someone or being hit. At each delay, hawkers surround the car, yelling to get your attention, tapping on the glass with water bottles or packages of gum, sticking armloads of cheap beads in the window, or simply holding out babies and upturned palms in mute despair.

Prem is calm and collected, brilliant at manoeuvring his way safely through the chaos, but even he has a few close calls. Peter's solution is to close his eyes and pretend it's all not happening. I can't tear my eyes away.

By the side of the road, things are truly obscene. Factories line the 200-kilometre route, stacks emitting thick, black, undiluted poison. The pollution is inconceivable and inexcusable. Barbed-wire fences enclose factory compounds where people live and die, enslaved to an economic system that depends on an inexhaustible supply of cheap and expendable labour. The workers who live here are basically being fed to the factories and devoured. The farmers are hardly better off; the few smog-shrouded fields left along this route produce pollution-encrusted crops.

The roadside is crowded with women of all ages, children to grandmothers, collecting firewood, cow dung, or crops. They carry their bundles on their heads, children slung on a hip or snatching at their saris, the once-brilliant colours now dulled by dust and dirt. Their eyes, in fleeting moments of contact, reflect the unreality of our existence in their world. Meanwhile, the bleak and black little townships along the way are filled with loitering men.

Thirty kilometres outside Agra, in the midst of this wretchedness, we pass a sign: Welcome to the City of the Taj. I'd like to think it's meant to be ironic, but I know it's not.

DECEMBER 23—AGRA

We visited the Taj Mahal today, primarily for my mother's sake. But, after everything we'd seen and smelled and breathed and felt, its beauty had faded by the time I saw it. It stands alone on the bank of the brown Yamuna River, coldly lovely, encased in a phony, sterile bubble. All industry has been forbidden within an 8-kilometre

radius—factories closed down—in order to preserve the tourist-dol-
lar-attracting Taj from the destructive effects of the pollution.

More honest and more beautiful to my eyes is the Agra Fort,
around a bend in the river. This is where Shah Jahan was imprisoned
by his son and from which he could gaze out upon the Taj Mahal,
the tomb he had built for his beloved wife a mile away. I'm glad he
could see it. This morning the smog was so thick we couldn't see the
river flowing at our feet.

DECEMBER 25—JAIPUR

This is definitely the weirdest Christmas Peter and I have ever spent.
We are sitting in a travel agent's office, trying to move our flight to
England up by a week. Six people—yes, count them, six—are dis-
cussing it in the next office. All we want is the phone number of
Singapore Airlines in Delhi or Bombay. Doesn't seem to be too
much to ask but. . .this is India!

It's been a helluva couple of days. I've been sick—flu or a respiratory tract infection—and I feel terrible. I was violently ill our last
night in Agra. We wondered about going on, but the urge to be with
another Canadian won out. So we set off yesterday in the car to
Fatephur Sikri and Jaipur.

Fatephur Sikri, the Ghost City, is a true monument to man's idiocy. It took fourteen years for the Emperor Akbar to complete his
new capital in the sixteenth century. It took one year after moving
there for him to realize there was insufficient water to support the
population. Now it sits lovely and quiet, deserted by all but the
birds, the mice, and the tourists, and I felt too sick to care. We had
thought of stopping at the bird sanctuary in Bharatpur but the fog
was so thick you couldn't see anything anyway. But not even the fog
could blot out the hellishness of the lives of the women and men
paving a road outside Bharatpur. Eyes blank, heads bowed under
heavy buckets of hot tar, they shuffle their lives away in ceaseless circles between the road and the fires heating the tar pots that turn
their days into endless night.

I have always dreamed of visiting India. I've read everything I
could get my hands on about this part of the world—Paul Scott's

The Jewel in the Crown quartet, Rohinton Mistry's books, V.S. Naipaul, E.M. Forster, James Cameron, the list goes on. Vikram Seth's *A Suitable Boy* is my favourite novel. But, clearly, despite all the reading, it's the BBC/Merchant and Ivory image that prevailed—an image of an India that doesn't exist, and possibly never did. In addition to the harsh reality that is at least this part of modern India, I am experiencing the demolition of a dream and reacting—overreacting?—accordingly. For whatever combination of reasons, I find myself in an almost constant state of rage.

The six-hour drive from Agra to Jaipur was the usual Indian horror story of near misses, with the added allure of dead camels by the side of the road.

I hit rock bottom at the Rajasthan border, an invisible line in the middle of nowhere, marked by a concrete block into which Prem disappeared for half an hour with a folder of papers. I was stretched out on the back seat, my head in Peter's lap, pale, aching, feverish, and nauseous. It was taking all my concentration not to be sick, when it began. Tap, tap, tap. Tap, tap, tap. It got louder. **Tap, tap, tap.** More insistent. TAP, TAP, TAP. Indian water torture—the sound of a plastic water bottle being beaten against the car window. "Lady, you buy water?" I tried to ignore it. I really did. But it just wouldn't stop. And it finally pushed me right over the edge. I gathered every last remnant of strength, sat straight up, and screamed at him at the top of my lungs to "FUCK OFF AND DIE!" The young man holding the bottle stopped. His eyes widened. He looked shocked. Then hurt. Then slowly he turned and walked away. I collapsed back onto the seat and didn't say another word until Jaipur.

We're staying with Arlene's friend, Marg, and her partner, Inder, whom she met twelve years ago when she visited India as a tourist and he was her tour guide. Theirs is a strange and very Indian household. It consists of Marg, an ex-real estate salesperson from Toronto; Inder, a Rajput prince; a scrawny seven-month-old grey spotted Great Dane; a yappy little black spitz; and an indeterminate number of "boys" from Inder's village. Inder is still very much the hereditary head of his village of 3,000 people. He pays for village boys to go to school, and he and Marg train them to get jobs in the service industry. It's somewhat feudal—the boys act as servants in exchange for the chance to advance—but the arrangement seems to work. We both found their home very warm and welcoming.

After initial greetings, I headed to bed to be sick in private. Peter was trying to read when strange, strangled sounds drew him to the kitchen. There was Inder supervising the boys as they hacked the carcass of a wild boar to pieces on the kitchen floor. Inder intended to honour us with a traditional Rajput meal. Oh no!

After dinner, we headed to our bedroom while Inder set up his *charpoy* (an Indian sleeping platform) in the dining area between our and Marg's bedroom doors. The house was freezing, as is everywhere. This is the coldest winter in Indian history, or at least the last fifty years. Our bed is rock hard—a plank with a thin felt mattress on top. Inder may have the right idea. We piled on what covers we could find, put on our long underwear, nightwear, sweatshirts and socks, and plugged in the electric heater. We cuddled and got warm together and fell swiftly asleep to the comforting noises of the house and people and streets around us.

Woke up this morning feeling better—still achy and fluey but at least not nauseous—and having reached a decision. If we can, and that remains to be seen given the production of the six travel agents in the next room, we're going to cut our losses. We don't like India, to put it mildly, and we're not going to grow to like it any better in another week. I asked Marg how long she thought it would take to get over the initial shock. "Three months," she replied without hesitation. "If you're lucky." Forget it. If we can get out a week early, we will, even if it means sitting in this damn office all day.

Peter informs me that, until today, he had thought all the "STD" signs, of which there are many on the streets, were for VD clinics. He was impressed by the Indian willingness to acknowledge the problem, but concerned about its prevalence. STD actually stands for "State Telephone Department," not "sexually transmitted disease." They are telephone boxes.

I think I'm hallucinating.

DECEMBER 26—JAIPUR—IN BED

When we got home yesterday after three-and-a-half hours at the travel agency accomplishing nothing ("Come back tomorrow. The Bombay office will be open then. Maybe."), I headed straight back to bed. I felt like hell. But I was determined to rest up enough to have Christmas dinner in a princely palace. Inder pulled some strings and made us reservations at the Rambagh Palace, a fifteen-minute walk from here. We dressed up in our best duds and stumbled our way by flashlight through the rubble of the city streets, pursued at one point by a pack of snarling dogs, and finally entered the calm and stately order of the palace grounds. The palace is glorious. Staying here would certainly give one a different, and somewhat misleading, impression of India. Dinner itself was a bit of a waste, given that I couldn't eat a thing. But it was fun to enjoy the splendour of the Maharaja's ornate dining room and to listen to the music of the sitar and tabla players, playing under an incongruous Christmas tree. Then we headed back into the night, made our way past the sleeping families by the side of the road, up the lane to Marg and Inder's house, and into bed.

Today I am in truly bad shape. Whatever I've got seems to be getting worse. Going out to dinner last night exacted a cost. I'm popping the antibiotic pills we brought with us and spending the day alternating between hallucinatory sleep in bed and sometimes equally hallucinatory conversation with Marg on the patio, while Peter struggles with the bureaucracies of India in a solitary effort to change our flight.

Marg and I have been talking about her life in India. Rajput women, including those of Inder's family, are still in *purdah*, veiled from all men, secluded from the outside world. Marg was showing me pictures of a recent wedding, including shots she'd taken in the women's room when the women had dropped their veils. As we looked at the pictures, Inder joined us. He picked up one photo and asked Marg, "Who is this?" "It's Nadja," she replied, "your sister-in-law." He's known her for more than twenty years but he didn't know what she looks like.

After Inder left for work, Marg and I talked some more. About

Marg's view of "the beauty of *purdah*" (although not for her!); how she has been accepted by Inder's wife and family in the village ("We are sisters."); and the difficulties of trying to renovate one of the ruined palaces belonging to Inder's family into a hotel.

Marg clearly loves it here. She takes pleasure in the contrast between a flower and a dung heap, side by side. But it doesn't come without a price. "The only way I can survive," she told me, "is to completely forget my Western ways. I have to immerse myself in India and its view of the world." As she was saying this, she started to butt out her cigarette on the patio railing. Suddenly, she stopped. "See," she laughed. "I've been talking to a Westerner and I was starting to get westernized." Then she threw the butt on the patio floor to be taken care of by the sweeper tomorrow.

As for me, I see the flower and the dung heap and I reach for a shovel. I don't get it—and I don't want to. India is bringing out all the worst rigidities of my being.

But Marg and Inder have been great, particularly given that we clearly loathe their country. Peter thinks Marg is a crazy person, albeit an extremely nice one. She does have a "seeing visions" look about her eyes occasionally and she certainly has chosen a strange adventure. She's put herself into a sort of voluntary *purdah*, rarely leaving the house except to go to Inder's village, a yearly visit to Canada, and an occasional trip to Delhi for "a break" (eeck!). I admire her sense of adventure, especially since I clearly don't have it.

DECEMBER 28—MUMBAI AIRPORT

Sitting in Singapore Airline's business class lounge waiting for our flight to be called, I'd like to think that India has inflicted her last indignity upon us. But she hung in there until the bitter end.

The ride to the airport was a classic. The stench of rotting bodies under a bridge. The sight of bodies—dead or alive? who knows?—by the side of the road. I'll never be able to look at a pile of rags or a burlap sack in the same way again. All those people wrapped in shrouds—the country of the living dead. I don't know what's worse—that so many people live lives of such bleak despair or that the rest of the country accepts it as normal.

The worst moment was during the usual assault by beggars at a red light. A young boy noticed Teddy peeking out of my pack and kept reaching his hand in the car for him. What to do? Thirty seconds before the light changes. Should I give him Teddy? Can I undo the leash in that time? Will the boy be allowed to keep him? How will the others react if I give to only one? Staring straight ahead, paralyzed by illness, exhaustion, and cultural dislocation, pretending not to see or hear, I feel like the coldest, cruellest person in the entire world.

This country has the ability, at the same time, to enrage you and to break your heart.

Stage II

Leaving on a Jet Plane

SIX
PICKING THE TRAVEL METHOD
THAT'S RIGHT FOR YOU

How you travel and what you decide to do are linked. The quality of your trip will be what you make of it, but the nature of your experience will be shaped by the way you choose to travel.

Marie spent most of her getaway year building a retirement home on the shores of Georgian Bay in Ontario. To her surprise, one of her most treasured experiences was the drive across Canada and back again. Taking her first solo driving trip at 50 gave her the time and opportunity to discover herself as well as Canada.

The physical activity of travelling is simple if you want to spend your time in one or two places. If sailing the world is your dream, the way you travel is already settled. Wandering the world without a sailboat takes a bit more thought. For Peter and me, the actual travelling turned out to be simply a way of getting from place to place, as comfortably as possible. That wasn't how it started, however.

The original idea was aimless wandering. A slow freighter across the Pacific seemed like a good way to get in the mood. This romantic notion was shot down fairly quickly. There are still a number of interesting freighter trips left in the world but, unfortunately, none of them matched our needs. The options for reaching New Zealand or Australia by freighter were two to three weeks at sea without touching land or a three-month wander through the South Pacific. The latter sounded wonderful, but three months was a big piece of our available time. Sadly, the freighter idea was relegated to the "nice idea but" bin.

Either of the freighter options would have been interesting travel experiences. They just weren't what we wanted at that time. There are innumerable possibilities out there. The trick is having a good sense of, if not exactly what you want, at least what doesn't feel comfortable.

If not by freighter, what then? We didn't want to admit that the practical but unromantic airplane was the best choice. Plane travel didn't seem compatible with our idea of wandering. We looked at other possibilities. But, realistically, planes offered the best chance of covering the globe and still having time to experience places along the way. Our thoughts of adventure and romance shifted from getting there (Stage II) to being there (Stage III).

ROUND-THE-WORLD AIRLINE TICKETS

One of the great travel bargains of our time is the round-the-world airline ticket. For a flat price, the ticket enables you to fly around the globe ending where you began. You can stop at a number of cities and countries en route for a far lower price than if you paid for individual tickets.

In this world, however, nothing is free. What you save in dollars, you pay in effort spent sorting out what's available and what particular scheme will work for you. Helped by Ted Woodcock of Travelworld in Victoria, I found information on sixteen separate plans, no two of which were directly comparable. The airlines do not make it easy to be an informed consumer.

Each plan has its own restrictions, rules, and supplementary charges. Each covers different destinations. Some limit the number of stops you can make, others charge for stops above a certain number. Most limit you to travel in one direction, i.e., east to west or west to east around the globe. Others permit a restricted form of backtracking. One operates on a total-mileage basis, i.e., you can fly up to a certain number of air miles for a set price. Some offer additional side trips at cut rates. The plans also differ considerably in terms of flexibility. Some charge for any change in the original reservation. Others permit free date changes, but charge if you switch destinations. The fees and prices vary enormously.

The critical issues for us were choice of destinations and degree of flexibility. No one plan went to all the places we wanted to go but, after laying out the options on a spreadsheet the size of our dining-room table, Canadian Airlines appeared to come closer than the others. This didn't narrow our options as much as you might think, however. Canadian alone offered six different round-the-world plans in cooperation with various partners. Calling the airline for help was a waste of time. Round-the-world tickets are such a small market that no staff are dedicated to them. After all my research, I knew more about the options than the airline staff.

This is where good travel agents earn their money. Ted has been our travel agent for years. He knows his business and our tastes. Many people these days are making their own travel arrangements through the Internet. I, however, remain a fan of personal, professional assistance, particularly for a trip this complicated. The Internet may provide prices and tickets, but it can't accommodate your personal style, and it won't be there for you if you get into trouble. A good travel agent can and will. Ted suggested we give him a list of places we wanted to go, and he would approach Canadian for a quote.

Talk about concentrating the mind. After two-and-a-half years of waffling, we had to make a decision. Hours of deliberation, debate, and discussion resulted in the following ideal itinerary: Victoria–Fiji–Australia–India–Eastern Mediterranean (Egypt, Israel, or Turkey)–Italy–France–England–Victoria.

Canadian Airlines, in partnership with Singapore Airlines, responded with its own proposal: Victoria–Fiji–New Zealand. Then, Australia–India–England–Victoria. (Owing to the incomprehensible complexities of various partnership arrangements, we would need a separate ticket from New Zealand to Australia.) The ticket would be good for one year. Date changes were free, but there would be a $50 charge each time we changed the itinerary.

The figures looked like this:

Cost per person, business-class:	$6,348.00
NZ–Australia ticket:	532.00
Total:	$6,880.00

For comparison purposes, we used the cost of one-way tickets from Victoria to Australia and from England back to Victoria—the portions we were sure we'd use:

Cost per person, business-class, one-way tickets: Victoria–Fiji–Australia and London–Victoria:	$7,003.00

Finally, a no-brainer. The Canadian Airlines deal didn't have everything we wanted, but it came closer than any other option. The basics were there, and we could build around them.

The only minor problem we encountered had to do with seat availability. In theory, you can change travel dates on a moment's notice. In reality, there are a limited number of seats available in this category. When illness forced us to delay our flight from Australia to India, we had to wait a week in Singapore until space onward was available. It didn't cause us any difficulty, but you should be prepared for the possibility.

TRAVEL DOESN'T HAVE TO BE PAINFUL

An economy round-the-world ticket (approximately $2,500 per person at that time) is, arguably, an even better deal. But comfort is a wonderful thing, particularly on a long trip.

Peter and I have built-in rationalizations for travelling business class. Peter is tall—6 feet 5-1/2 inches. For him, sitting in economy seats for more than a few hours is seriously uncomfortable. I have claustrophobia. I've had one panic attack on board a plane, and I don't want another.

But the bottom line is that we both love being pampered. Business class transforms travelling from an endurance test into enjoyment. We actually look forward to it: the check-in counter with no lineup; the quiet, uncrowded calm of the business-class lounge; settling into our roomy seats; figuring out how all the buttons work; selecting our personal in-flight entertainment; and toasting each journey's beginning with a glass of champagne.

Running away from home at our age should be a celebration. Go ahead—give yourself permission to be extravagant.

THE PEOPLE-ARE-LIKE-SHEEP SYNDROME

The ticket in your hand influences the way you think. New Zealand, for example (speaking of sheep), wasn't on our original list of destinations. But the Canadian Airlines flight out of Fiji went to New Zealand, not Australia. If we were touching down, why not stay awhile? It wasn't a major point of interest, but we thought we'd visit for a week before moving on. We had such a good time, we stayed a month.

Peter and I had the best of intentions. We had based our ticket purchase on using only the beginning and end portions—Victoria to Fiji/Australia; England back to Victoria. Using any of the in-between sections would be a financial bonus. Our hope, though, was to find more relaxing, more locally evocative travel alternatives along the way. We would look for a boat from northern Australia to Indonesia and then work our way up to Malaysia. We'd try to find a freighter from Bombay through the Suez Canal to Egypt, then make our way overland to Israel and Turkey, wander the Mediterranean by ferry and make our way through Europe to England to catch the flight home.

As it turned out, we used every single portion of the airline ticket. And bought more: London/Dublin return; London/Israel return; London/Naples—for which it was cheaper to buy a return ticket and use half than to buy a one-way ticket! London's "bucket shops" offer some extraordinary travel bargains. The prices were simply too good to pass up.

Maybe it's because we're used to structure in our lives. Perhaps it's because we're obedient Canadians. Possibly it has to do with some false sense of security in the midst of the unfamiliar. Whatever the reason, our thought processes tended to follow the route on the ticket.

Knowing that we had a flight to somewhere booked on a particular date subtly influenced our day-to-day plans. We regularly shifted dates of travel, but we never seriously contemplated changing destinations. Even the India/England flight, which originally seemed such an anomaly (Is there nothing between India and England in Canadian Airline's world?), turned out to be a lifeline. When I became sick and we realized how much we disliked India, a quick flight to England was like a raft to a drowning man.

Or maybe it was simply easier. Travel is tiring. Making arrangements on the road invariably turned out to be more complicated than it had appeared from the comfort of our sofa in Victoria. We found ourselves looking forward to being wrapped in the security blanket of the business-class flight to our next major stop. Unadventurous? Probably. Natural? Definitely.

Many times during the trip and since returning home I have been asked if I would change anything. Consistently the answer is: I don't know. I simply cannot make up my mind. I know that we probably missed some extraordinary experiences by taking the approach we did. I also know that we both have a limited tolerance for confusion and discomfort. And it's hard, not to say churlish, to second-guess a trip that we loved just as it was.

THINGS TO THINK ABOUT

- The experience you want will influence your choice of travel mode, and vice versa.
- If you can afford it, consider travelling business class. Comfort is important on a long trip.
- London is a great base for travel around Europe and the Mediterranean. There are some fantastic travel bargains available from "bucket shops."
- If you're interested in freighter travel possibilities, contact: TravLtips Cruise and Freighter Travel Association, P.O. Box 580188, Flushing, NY 11358, USA, phone: 800-872-8584, e-mail: info@travltips.com

ROUND-THE-WORLD AIRLINE TICKETS
- Round-the-world airline tickets are a bargain.
- Develop a relationship with a good travel agent and work closely together to get the plan that works for you.
- The options are bewildering, so consider a made-to-measure plan.
- There is a flexibility trade-off.
- Limited seat availability in this category makes changing plans more complicated than the airlines would have you believe.
- Be aware that, despite all its advantages, a ticket in hand may tempt you to limit your travel options. If this is an issue for you, you might consider spending a bit more and retaining more flexibility.

January: ENGLAND
Part 1—Strategic Withdrawal

JANUARY 3—THORGANBY

We arrived at Martin and Rosalynn's five days ago, bushed, battered, and beaten. We had called from Bombay to see if they were willing and able to take us in on two days' notice and a week ahead of schedule. Thank God for good friends.

They have given us the run of their comfortable home, Birkwood, no questions asked, and allowed us to recover at our own speed. We've spent a wonderful week, sleeping, reading in front of the fire, and taking the occasional walk. I'm still operating at only about 50%—I can't shake that bone-rattling cough and I have no energy—but, compared to the way I felt in India, this is good health.

Martin spends most of his day working on his novel in his dining-room office, and Rosalynn is busy upstairs in her study, preparing for the new university term. Peter and I have taken over the living room. The four of us come together for companionable meals but, for the most part, we go our own ways, and Peter and I have been able to get back in touch with a little part of ourselves. Our lack of interest in the local countryside is abominable—we've left the house and environs for only one trip into York to buy warm socks and a pair of cords for Peter—but this has been a necessary time for rest and recuperation.

Martin and Rosalynn are off to North America in mid-March for a month and have offered us Birkwood. We've always wanted to explore this part of the world, and both our budget and our souls could use a rest. So from March 11 to April 14, we'll be back in Yorkshire. After that, we're thinking of moving straight to the south of France for the remainder of our time. We hate to forgo Italy, but there's something awfully appealing about the prospect of moving around less. Ah well, we'll undoubtedly change our minds another five times between now and then. The more burning question at the moment is how to spend the next two months. Improbably, it seems to be coming down to Ireland and Israel.

We've been able to coordinate times with Dvora in Israel. Mid-February works for her. That leaves us with a three-to-four-week gap. Our first choice would have been to go somewhere warm—I'm dying for sun and heat—but Mother Nature has other plans. Every place that should be warm isn't. The reports from North Africa, the Canary Islands, etc., sound like England. So if we can't find warmth, we are actually contemplating throwing ourselves wholeheartedly into damp and chilly. Sounds like Ireland to me.

JANUARY 5—ON THE TRAIN FROM YORK TO OXFORD

Massive snowstorm has thrown out travel plans all over England. We're on our way to spend a week with Auntie Audrey. I'm feeling quite a bit better after our quiet sojourn in Thorganby, but it's been two weeks since this bug, or whatever it is, hit me, and I'm getting a little concerned that I haven't improved completely. Being up for more than two hours exhausts me.

JANUARY 14—MICKLETON

It keeps coming back to me how the trip's focus is shifting from external to internal. Going new places and seeing new things is losing ground to a desire to sit and consolidate. It may have something to do with the fact that I've spent most of the past week in bed doing nothing. I had my usual moment of *crise* a few days ago—tears and wondering what we were doing and why and what was the meaning of life. Simple questions like that. Peter, in his usual philosophical fashion, reminded me that this was exactly what I wanted from this year—a reexamination of basics. Well, I've had it—am having it—and it's harder than I thought it would be. Would I do this year again? Yes. The same way? No. Do I regret parts of it? Oh yes. It has cost far too much and been fairly uncomfortable, physically and emotionally, at times. Am I glad we did it? Yes. But I really wish I felt better.

Mickleton has been a lovely restful interlude for me. Auntie Audrey's friend, Anne, has given us the gift of her cottage, and she has moved in with Auntie Audrey around the corner. Between their generosity and that of Martin and Rosalynn, we have been truly blessed with refuges when we most needed them.

Peter has found it a bit stressful, though. Family, however loved, can do that to you. Auntie Audrey and Anne (AA&A) are both getting on, and their health is failing. Auntie Audrey's hearing is worse than when we last saw her, as is her eyesight, and her legs are causing problems as well. But her spirits are high, at least in front of us. Anne's arm is permanently disabled, and she's worried about a possible recurrence of cancer. Thank God they have each other, but they do rub up against each other a bit in the close quarters of Auntie Audrey's house.

So, what have we done here? Very little. We sleep in late, have breakfast in the cottage, then head over to Auntie Audrey's for a visit. Peter drives the four of us out to a pub for lunch and we wander the Cotswolds countryside, exploring the charming little villages from the car. Auntie Audrey is amazing. Eighty-nine years old and legally blind, she can still navigate us through all the back roads and country lanes of the Cotswolds. The map in her head is more accurate than any on paper. "Turn right here. There's an old stone church on the left. Then you'll hit a T-junction. Turn left…" She is never wrong. Peter lives in fear that one of these days she'll make a mistake and get us lost, and the blow to her pride will be enormous. But, so far, it hasn't happened. And I have confidence that it never will. She will navigate her way directly from the Cotswolds to heaven, with no wrong turns along the way.

We don't stop much on these excursions because AA&A find it hard to get around. We did spend one very strange afternoon in Bourton-on-the-Water. AA&A insisted that Peter and I should explore the village, so they sat in the car while we walked up one side of the High Street and down the other, waving at them occasionally and checking in on them as we passed the car. It reminded me of nothing so much as the artificial promenades of a Jane Austen novel—endearingly odd.

In the afternoons, I generally retreat to the cottage for a nap. Peter visits with his aunt, reads, or watches sports on television. In the evenings, we make a light supper, visit again briefly, maybe watch a little television, and tuck into bed early.

Days unfolding softly. I am grateful.

Still not entirely well but getting better.

JANUARY 16—LONDON

Here we are in London, paying an astronomical sum for a small but charming room and breakfast. The prices in London are unbelievable, particularly given that this is supposedly the off-season. We've decided to treat this as a week's holiday from our trip and not worry too much about cost.

Getting here was not half the fun. We had an emotional farewell from AA&A. Then we encountered a few mishaps at the train station. We needed money. But the bank machine had no letters on the buttons, only numbers. We both have name-based codes and don't have a clue what our numbers are! Then, the train departure time seemed to vary depending on whether you watched the screen, listened to the recorded announcements, or sought human advice. We ended up running for a train, not having had time or the money to eat, only to find that we were on board the local, with no food available.

We finally made it to the hotel by 4:00 p.m., having had only toast all day. Peter is not at his best when deprived of food, but a quick sandwich and a stroll soon put us right. A pizza in the room and an early night should set us up for a busy week. Seems a weird way to start a stay in London but…whatever works.

JANUARY 24—MICKLETON

What can I say? It didn't work.

London started well. We had a lovely first Saturday, checking out the shops on Oxford Street, finding a great gallery with funny, fantastic sculptures, enjoying a late, leisurely Italian lunch, and spending the evening at a stirring performance of *Cyrano de Bergerac* by the Royal Shakespeare Company. A perfect London day.

We managed to reach a friend from Victoria who was visiting relatives and arranged to meet on Sunday at Covent Garden for lunch.

We got caught up on doings at home, and I once again had that weird split sense of simultaneously missing it all and being relieved not to be there. Then Mary suggested we go to the Science Museum. This was the beginning of the end for me. Mary is a serious muse-um-goer. She walked our socks off. By mid-afternoon, I was starting to get very tired, but we had tickets for the 5:00 p.m. show of *ART*, with Nigel Havers, and I wasn't about to miss it.

I'm glad we went but, that night, I was in terrible shape. The infection, which I have never fully shaken off, returned with a vengeance. Fever, chest pains, nausea, racking cough. First thing in the morning, we headed off to a doctor recommended by the hotel. It's a serious respiratory tract infection. I returned with a prescrip-tion for stronger, more focused antibiotics, to be taken together with the general ones I've been popping since India, and instructions to get back to bed and do nothing.

With one exception, I've obeyed. What choice did I have? The double dose of antibiotics totally knocked me out. I could barely move. I did haul myself up to see Ian Richardson in *The Magistrate*, but spent the rest of the week in the hotel bed, hallucinating and feeling awful. Peter bustled about making plans to get us to Ireland and Israel and doing the tourist thing on his own. What a waste this time has been. And what an expense!

By Wednesday, it was clear I wasn't going to be able to go to Ireland on Friday as planned. This was crisis time. I clearly was inca-pable of continuing, but wasn't really capable of making a rational decision about options. At one point we seriously considered whether we shouldn't just go home and let me recover there. But we couldn't quite bring ourselves to do it. I'm not ready to throw in the towel yet. If I'm not better by the end of the month, maybe. For now, though, we decided to retreat to Mickleton, where I am ensconced once again in Anne's bed and do not intend to move until I'm better.

JANUARY 30—MICKLETON

The multiple antibiotics and four days of suspended animation, doing absolutely nothing but sleeping and reading Georgette Heyer

Regency romances, appear to have done the trick. Peter has taken advantage of this respite to spend more time with his aunt, but he's starting to go a little stir-crazy. Anne's cottage is charming, but it is much like the miniatures she collects: the ceilings are low and the rooms are small and filled with knick-knacks. At his height, he's more wearing it than staying in it.

Two days ago, I started to emerge from my cocoon. Yesterday, I was feeling well enough to get my hair cut and coloured. What intimacies this trip is imposing! Peter and I visited the hairdresser together (where Céline Dion was singing yet again!). I'm not sure I ever wanted to see him with his hair all sudsed up in public. And I know I never wanted him to see me. Somehow it seems different from at home in the shower.

This month in England has been a total blur of illness and exhaustion, suspended in space between the first and second halves of the trip. We've lost the better part of six weeks due to illness. But, tomorrow, it's off to Ireland as per Peter's revised plans (he's becoming quite expert at changing travel arrangements on the fly) and, hopefully, better days ahead.

Stage III

On the Road Again

SEVEN
SO MUCH TO DO

There's a lot to do on the road. I had assumed all the work, the planning, the administration happened before we left. While travelling, things would just flow. Trust me, it ain't so.

TRAVELLING IS DIFFERENT FROM TAKING A HOLIDAY

For many of us, a holiday means being able to forget all the mundane chores of life for a while. For two or three blessed weeks, there are no dishes to do, we can let the laundry pile up, we can lie on the beach, trek through the mountains or wander through a new city without thinking about bills or chores. Most of the arrangements have been made in advance. All we have to do is relax and enjoy. We put our regular lives on hold and immerse ourselves in the oblivion of change.

Extended travel is different. This is regular life. You still have to eat, have clean clothes to wear, sleep somewhere warm and comfortable, and get from place to place. And you have to do it in unfamiliar surroundings, with a possible language barrier. You'll be amazed—and appalled—how much of your time is eaten up just keeping yourself alive, clean, fed, housed, and travelling.

Things you do at home without thought—laundry, for example—suddenly take planning and time. Is there a laundromat nearby? Do you have the right coins for the machines? How does that soap dispenser work? Does the B&B do laundry? How much will it cost? How long will it take? Would it be simpler just to wash things in the sink?

Cooking becomes another issue. One of the joys of staying somewhere with a kitchen is that you can cruise the markets with more than mere curiosity. You can admire local produce and specialties with a practical as well as an aesthetic eye. What would I do with that strange-looking vegetable? But don't kid yourself. This type of shopping, while a pleasure, can eat up your days. And sometimes you don't want a shopping experience. You just want something for dinner. I can hear you now thinking, "What a big deal about nothing." Just wait. There will be days when, after long hours of new impressions and constant activity, you will crave familiar boredom and curse the necessity to wander through yet another local market in search of the basics for dinner.

Then, of course, there are the almost daily chores. Finding a place to stay. Figuring out how to get around town. Or on to your next stop. What road? What bus? Which track? Applying for visas for the next country on your itinerary. Solving the riddle of the local telephone system. Finding the post office. Where can I buy an envelope? And on and on and on. Nothing is straightforward. Questions and decisions, large and small, fill your days until you want to scream, "Stop! Enough already!"

There is little you can do but be prepared. When thinking about your trip and while you're on it, remember to build in time to handle chores and to recover from them.

TRAVEL IS TIRING

> I didn't realize what hard work travelling is.
>
> Mike

At one and the same time on this trip, I felt invigorated and exhausted. Travelling is tiring. You're on the go, constantly stimulated by new people, new places, new ideas. You're learning all the time. Constant travel means constantly being confronted with unfamiliarity—and it is tiring. There will be times when you are completely and utterly beat. Sometimes the great adventure seemed like simple drudgery, and we were travelling at a fairly luxurious level, in developed countries, where English was spoken. Budget travel in the third world adds its own wonders to the mix.

> There are days when you are tired. You're on a crowded bus in Central America. The ticks are dripping on Bill's head, and I have to try to take them out by a 20-watt bulb at the end of the day. And you wonder, why are we doing this?
>
> Margaret

At first, I thought it was just us. But I've now concluded that tiredness is a function of being separated from a home base. Almost everyone I spoke with who moved around, even minimally, during their time off, reported the same thing—times of absolute exhaustion.

> It's hard work. You don't go to as many museums at home as you do when you're away. And, after a while, you just can't do any more. Even the different scenery around you becomes like a museum. It gets so that all you want to do is get somewhere and read and rest.
>
> Heather

Short of staying in one place, I can't think of any way to avoid exhaustion altogether. All you can do is be aware that it will hit and develop strategies to wait it out, minimize, or overcome it.

My favourite strategy was the nap. Napping works for me, and I would try to build one in most afternoons. Thirty minutes of zzzing—preferably on a bed or couch, or on the beach or in a park when necessary—and I would feel sparky again. The occasional massage also had enormous therapeutic value. And one should never underestimate the stimulative benefits of a good haircut.

Exhaustion inevitably hits at the most inconvenient moments: the day you can't find a place to nest for a week, the one time you've made a commitment that must be met. The only consolation I can offer is that it passes. Somehow your body and your spirit respond to the pinpricks of necessity and the thrill of something new ahead. Energy and interest return. If you can ride out the moments of inertia, the time will come when you're ready to hit the road again. If it doesn't, maybe that's the time to start thinking of heading home.

COMFORT IS NECESSARY— FOR MOST OF US

Some people have an admirable tolerance for discomfort. I'm not one of them. One of our strategies to minimize exhaustion was to maximize our comfort. This option is obviously limited by your budget but, if you can afford it, being comfortable goes a long way toward keeping you relaxed and healthy.

Travelling business class meant that we arrived at our destinations feeling refreshed. Staying in comfortable accommodation provided a welcome refuge at the end of busy days in strange places where we knew no one.

Travel doesn't have to be uncomfortable. There is no adventure premium for suffering. You'll have plenty of opportunities to be miserable, so pamper yourself when you have the chance.

TAKE A HOLIDAY FROM YOUR TRIP

Take a break. Sometimes you just need to get away from your trip. I'm serious. Every now and then, you'll need a holiday from seeing and doing new things. Your version of a holiday may be tucking up in front of a fire reading or lying on a beach getting a tan. Whatever your preference, you'll want just to sit someplace calm and do nothing.

Our prerequisites for a "trip holiday" were quite different from our normal vacation needs. On a two- or three-week vacation, we usually want someone else to do the cooking, and we like having a car at our disposal. On these trip mini-breaks, however, we found ourselves craving a kitchen, and we wanted to be within walking distance of everything we needed—the beach, a local store, the pub.

Our first holiday tug occurred in Australia after we'd been on the road for slightly more than two months. We booked a cheap excursion from Sydney to Noosa on the South Queensland coast and lay around on the beach for a week (see page 84). Five or six weeks later, we did the same sort of thing again. This time it was unplanned. We had rented an apartment in Palm Cove in Northern Queensland, intending to use it as a base for exploration. Once we put our feet up, however, we realized we were explored out. All we really wanted to do was nothing. So we did (see page 98). Three months later, we took another time out in the Yorkshire countryside, house-sitting for friends (see page 241).

It sounds simple, but it's not. The pull to do something is amazingly strong. Here you are on the far side of the world, in a wonderful spot, with tons of fascinating things to see and do. It cost a lot to get here, and it's going to be a long time before you return. You feel almost obligated to take advantage of this opportunity.

> When you're working, you take a vacation where you do nothing. The same thing is necessary when you're travelling. But we also felt really guilty when we just sat somewhere for four days. You think, we've only got this much time left and this is a bad use of our time. But you have to put it in perspective. You have to recharge your batteries.
>
> Heather

Local people, like our hosts in New Zealand, are your worst enemies in this regard. They are justifiably proud of their areas, and they want you to experience it all. They are also more used to people who are on a normal vacation and want to make the most of every minute. They'll make endless suggestions of great places to visit, wonderful drives, one-of-a-kind attractions. Unless you're totally exhausted or impervious to internal and external pressures, the next thing you know, your downtime is up and you're on the move again.

Remember—this is a marathon you're in, not a sprint.

> The difference between this kind of travel and a holiday trip is the leisure not to feel rushed. You can allow the pace to set itself. That's one of the real luxuries about this kind of travel.
>
> Margaret

You have to pace yourself. Give yourself permission to let it go for awhile. Before leaving, you had to make hard decisions about where you wouldn't be able to go. On the road, you have more hard decisions to make about things you won't do. Some opportunities have to be deferred if you're going to enjoy others.

The breaks were important times for us to catch our breath and just be. In retrospect, we should have taken even more.

DOING THE ORDINARY
Ordinary things take on extraordinary meaning on the road. Things you never thought you'd miss become causes for celebration. The biggest

surprise for us was the joy of cooking. Peter and I are not cooks. We love to eat. We enjoy good food. But we'd really rather someone else made it for us. That is, until we'd been on the road for a few months.

The pleasure of eating in restaurants can fade quickly when you have to do it every day. By the end of a month of eating out, we were desperate for home cooking, even our own. Each menu started to look like every other. All the food started to taste the same. One of the few regrets I have is that we went to Italy and France at the end rather than the beginning of our trip. By months eight and nine of travelling, I was so sick of restaurant food, I couldn't properly appreciate it, no matter how delicious.

Television was another surprise. Most B&Bs offer a welcome respite from television. When we rented an apartment or were house-sitting, however, a TV was usually part of the package. After months of creating our own entertainment, it was a luxury to veg out and be entertained. Peter caught up on cricket, soccer, and rugby. I immersed myself in local culture: *Blue Heeler* in Australia (how can people who make such great movies make such terrible television shows?) and *Coronation Street* in England (while Dierdre was being sent to prison and the entire country rose to her defence—it was thrilling!). A bore at home became a treat on the road. Ah, dinner in front of the tube. How wonderful!

WHERE TO STAY

One of your most important on-the-road decisions will be where to stay—in what type of accommodation and in which particular place. Your choices, theoretically, are many: camping, hostel, basic motel, small hotel, B&B, more upscale hotel, stay with friends, rent a house or apartment, house-sit or swap. In practice, however, you'll be limited by your budget, local availability, and your mood of the moment.

Staying with friends or family along the way can be a godsend. There is nothing nicer than a familiar face after having been away from home for a while. Friends of friends can fulfill much the same function. After a while on the road, even the most tenuous connection can be important. You need to be careful not to impose too much and to understand the limitations in staying in other people's homes.

Sometimes it's better to assume the expense, stay elsewhere, and just visit. But, when it works, it can be a wonderful relief to stay in a real home with someone you already know. We were enormously fortunate, and our time spent with friends, family, and friends of friends along the way provided some of our most enjoyable interludes. But don't forget to be a good guest—take your hosts out to eat and leave behind a nice gift.

If you don't have friends along your route, B&Bs give you a great opportunity to make some. Compare the difference between a B&B and your average motel/hotel room. You can return to a plain room and blank TV. Or you can come home to a cozy room, decorated with a personal touch. You stretch out in the garden or curl up in a corner of the couch in a comfortable living room to listen to music, browse through local magazines, or read a book. The resident dog or cat will probably be available for a pat. There's a cup of tea or a drink waiting for you, along with a friendly conversation if you want it. Tiredness melts away in front of the fireplace, and a few hours later you're looking forward to dinner in the local pub.

We planned to do a lot more apartment renting than we did. Apartments were plentiful in smaller, resort communities, but harder to come by, at least at a reasonable price, in cities where we had hoped to stay longer. Sometimes we had to leave places before we were ready because the B&Bs were booked for the additional days we wanted.

Had we done more advance planning and been willing to tie ourselves down, we could have eased a lot of our fatigue from on-the-spot logistic arrangements. But we would also have missed some fabulous experiences. It helps to have some idea of what you want, but it's important to be able to roll with the punches and recognize that there's usually an upside to whatever you end up with.

Tourism bureaus can help

Generally, we were really pleased with the quality and value of the places we stayed. Much of the credit should go to travel bureaus in various towns around the world. The tourism industry has developed enormously in the last few decades, and one of the most helpful improvements has been the growth of local tourism bureaus that offer one-stop shopping for the weary traveller.

In most places, our first stop would be the tourism bureau. It would have lists of accommodation, by price range, often accompanied by pictures and brochures. In New Zealand and Australia, most offer free pamphlets on bed-and-breakfast accommodation in the region to supplement the B&B books we had purchased. Every small village in southern France had a list of local *pensions*, complete with prices and amenities. Even in small towns in southern Italy where there was no formal tourism bureau, an inquiry at the newsagent would produce a photocopied list of local hotels, government-rated from one to four stars.

Some tourism bureaus book the accommodation for you and can save you money, time, and aggravation by phoning around on your behalf. Many offer ticket services and special deals for city tours, local shows, and attractions.

Between tourism bureaus, free tourism publications, the range of guidebooks available, and the recommendations of people you'll meet, you'll have no trouble finding a place to match your budget and your tastes.

GETTING MONEY ON THE ROAD

People always ask about money: How did you get cash? Did you use traveller's cheques? Credit cards? What about exchange rates? How much cash did you carry?

Before we left, we too wondered how easy it would be to get hold of local currencies as we travelled. We had visions of spending hours in lineups at banks, trying to change traveller's cheques or get cash advances on our credit cards.

We worried without cause. Access to money was simple. Welcome to the wonderful world of ATMs—Automated Teller Machines. They are everywhere. And they are easy. With the exception of Fiji (and there only because we were on an out-island) and India, we used ATMs for all our cash needs. The machines are easy to use. You receive cash in the local currency. The exchange rates are competitive. ATMs are without doubt the simplest, quickest, and least expensive way of obtaining local currency.

ATMs solved our cash needs, but credit cards were our most treasured financial companions. We each carried two credit cards: American Express Gold Card and Visa/Canadian Plus Gold Card. Amex was useful because it has no upper limit on charges. If we had wanted to charge a $10,000 excursion to Outer Mongolia, we could have. Visa came in handy when an establishment didn't accept American Express. Between the two, we could do just about anything.

We brought traveller's cheques with us—$1,500 each. We used some in Fiji and a few in India, but returned home with $2,200 in uncashed cheques. They were reassuring, but not as necessary as they had been thirty years earlier.

> We took $10,000 and went to American Express and got traveller's cheques—three types—some for me, some for her, and some doubles. We cashed the last cheque last January—five years later. We never got around to using them.
>
> Larry

We also brought $200 in small U.S. bills—ones, fives, and tens. Everybody loves American dollars, and these came in handy for tipping or easing open a door here and there.

But plastic is, without doubt, your best friend on the road. Between your bank card and a credit card or two, you can go just about anywhere and do just about anything.

CREDIT CARDS ARE USEFUL

The credit cards were particularly useful for a variety of reasons.

- They simplify payment. Almost everybody everywhere accepts credit cards. There was no messing around with identification in order to use traveller's cheques. Present the card, sign your name, and it's done.
- There are ways to avoid interest charges. We arranged to have the bills paid by our bank immediately on receipt. Other people put large cash credits on their accounts before leaving or arranged for a regular monthly sum to be transferred to their cards.
- Merchants occasionally delay processing the charges, which can put off payment for weeks and sometimes months.
- Using the cards provides a record of expenditures.

- The exchange rates charged are competitive.
- Points, points, beautiful points. For every purchase. Between airline travel points and credit card points, we now have the equivalent of four business-class tickets anywhere in the world. Our next two holiday trips are in the bank.

KEEPING TRACK OF EXPENSES

No matter how large or small your budget, it's important to keep track of how much you're spending as you go. You'll feel more comfortable if you know that you're more or less on track. Or it will give you the chance to make adjustments if you're spending too much.

We kept track of our expenses the simplest and most unsophisticated way possible. Every expenditure, whether 30 cents for a newspaper or $30 for dinner, was marked in my little yellow notebook. At some point every day, we'd sit and review every penny we'd spent since the previous day's reckoning.

In the keenness of the early days, daily expenses were totalled. This soon gave way to more useful monthly calculations. I'd use a general exchange rate, always erring on the side of caution, to figure out roughly what we were spending in Canadian dollars. For example, when we were there, the Australian dollar was worth slightly less than the Canadian, but I treated them as equal, both to simplify matters and to give us a bit of a cushion. I preferred to think we were spending more rather than less, just in case I had forgotten something. Dividing by the number of days in that month gave us a general sense of our average daily expenditures.

TRACKING OUR SPENDING

Nov. 28—Alice Springs

Breakfast	$14.00
Lunch	25.00
Cokes	3.00
Cab to airport	12.50
Tip to porter	2.00
Snacks & paper	4.65
Hotel (1 night)	78.75

Nov. 29—Palm Cove
(week's apartment rental paid in advance)

Breakfast	12.00
Newspaper	.30
Groceries	57.43
Beer and wine	28.78

Nov. 30—Palm Cove

Newspaper	.30
Film	4.46
Groceries	12.37
Day trip to Great Barrier Reef	210.00

November – Total:	A $8,210.87
Converted to Cdn:	at par
Divided by 30 =	$273.70 daily average

Wrap-up:

Month	Budget	Expenditure	Difference	Balance
Sept.	$6,000	$5,602.83	- 397.17	397.17
Oct.	6,000	7,563.48	+1,563.48	-1,166.31
Nov.	6,000	8,210.87	+2,210.87	-3,377.18

At the end of each month, I'd compare our running totals to our budget. For the first few months, we ran seriously over budget, but we tried not to panic. We had always assumed that New Zealand and Australia would be among the most expensive places we'd visit, and extending our stays there only exacerbated the problem. Seeing the expenditures laid out before us at the end of each month enabled us to make some practical decisions, such as forgoing purchases to keep up with living expenses and cutting back on fancy restaurant meals. It also helped us make structural decisions about the trip, such as choosing to take up the house-sitting offer in England in order to even up the books a bit.

We overspent. So did almost everyone else I've spoken with. It always costs more than you think it will. But we overspent knowingly, on the basis that the additional cost was worth it to us at the time and we would be able to pay it off reasonably quickly on our return.

SAFETY CONCERNS

Before you go, someone will remind you of all the disasters that can befall you out in the big, bad world. Parents will clip newspaper accounts of random murders in far-flung corners of the globe. Friends will regale you with stories of tourist rip-offs. Everyone has a favourite anti-robbery tactic to share.

At first I thought our experience was unusual. Absolutely nothing went wrong. No one tried to rob us. No one tried to kidnap us. No one tried to shoot us. Hell, the security guards at Ben Gurion Airport didn't even bother to interrogate us.

We were prepared for the worst. We split up our cash and traveller's cheques and hid some in various places about our persons. Peter wore a money belt under his shirt. It held some cash and our passports when we weren't likely to need them. I kept a close hand and eye on my backpack, which contained most of our travel documents, and we worked out a system whereby Peter watched out for it as well. We left all our good jewellery at home and made do with a plastic Swatch and obvious costume jewellery. We assumed that, at some point, someone would steal the backpack or pick our pockets or both. It never happened. And it never happened to anyone else I spoke with either.

> The worst thing that happened to us was that four litres of juice was stolen out of a freezer in a campground. I hope they enjoyed it.
>
> Jocelyn

Obviously, there are precautions every sensible traveller should take. I'm coming to the conclusion, however, that extended travel is safer than a holiday trip. Perhaps we're more conscious about security issues when on a longer trip. Or it may just be that we're so tired at the end of a day's travelling that we fall into bed early rather than cruising the local nightlife.

Some of us may occasionally have paid too much for something, but no one I spoke with was ripped off for major amounts of money. No one held us up. And none of us ever felt threatened. We're either an inordinately lucky group or, more likely, we're adults who thought ahead, behaved sensibly, and didn't place ourselves in foolish situations.

> Any time we stopped anywhere, we made sure that we had a secure place for the motorcycles. Where we camped, we camped in an organized campground. Or, if we were camping in the wild, sort of free, we made sure that we were truly in the wild—there were no settlements.
>
> Heather

While I hate to admit it, it may also be that middle-aged people present fewer opportunities for crime. Most of us are not into the nightlife and drug scene. We tend to get to bed earlier, regardless of whether we're travelling. Most of us will probably choose to stay somewhere relatively comfortable and secure. And we've been around long enough to sense trouble and avoid it most of the time. This may be one of the very real advantages of midlife travel—less likelihood of being robbed.

TRAVELLING WITH CHILDREN
People who have travelled with their children are enthusiastic about it. But there are issues that have to be considered.

Children open doors for you.

> We met a lot of people because of Sophie. She was a draw.
>
> Helen

Travelling with a kid is really great. Instantly your problems are solved.

Patrick

But your travelling companions, regardless of age, deserve to have their needs considered. The more people involved, the more compromises required.

The kids were both a blessing and a problem....They helped us to meet people and forced us to stay in one place long enough to meet people and make relationships. On the other hand, because they were in school, they forced us to stay in one place. God, I would have left a lot sooner had they not been in the school system.

Janet

In the worst-case scenario, you may find yourself, like Suzanne and Trevor, having to make major changes in plans because of the children.

The worst was the crossing from Bora Bora to the Cook Islands—the seven-day trip from hell. The three of us were just sicker than dogs. We lost weight. We got dehydrated. The children didn't get out of their bunks. It took them three days to recover physically. The little one was only ten years old and she's small. Trevor and I agreed that it was not in the best interests of the kids to go through that again after only being on the island for 7–10 days. We made a very, very difficult decision that, on the next leg, the children and I were not going to sail. We were going to have to fly.

Suzanne

Most of the time, however, it will simply be a case of children wanting to do different things.

Seek out, conscientiously, opportunities that will keep them interested. For us, it was finding other yachties with children. Our decision to go on a particular itinerary was based on whether or not we could get together with the other boats that had kids. We adapted a lot to that. And on land, as much as we liked to go and see 600-foot kauri trees, they might not, so you have to compromise.

Suzanne

Your children's systems are operating to a different rhythm. You need to have a good sense of their limits, to be careful not to push them too far, or allow them to do it to themselves. Watch for signs of burnout because, heaven knows, they'll make your life miserable if they want to.

On the plus side, being away from your normal life and normal parent/child roles gives you a chance to form new and special relationships. You have the chance to really get to know your children. And they get to see the real you.

We went through stuff as a family. Some of it was really difficult at certain moments. We saw each other at the best and at the worst. Now we can draw on that experience. I can have discussions with them and say, "Do you remember when…? We got through that and we can get through this"—whatever "this" is.

Suzanne

The secret to successful travelling with children may be involving them in decision-making.

Let them take part in directing what you do. If they take part, they'll enjoy it. We had lots of discussions about where we wanted to stop and for how long.

Suzanne

Our parents totally loosened up when we went away. They let us do basically whatever we wanted. Well, within reason. They trusted us. Not that they don't trust us here. But they just let us go. When we were away, they let us make choices like where we were going to go and how we were going to get there. They let us read the map and say where to go. When we were in the Outback, they let us have a turn driving the car. Donny got to drive on the road and I got to drive in a parking lot. They let us do stuff we couldn't do here.

June, 13 years old

Most parents consider the time together well worth any minor difficulties that may arise. Sophie was only a year old when Patrick and Helen took her to France.

We were mumdad. Mumdad—it was one word because we were always both there. . . . She still calls me Mum because to her, at the time when her language was being formed, Mum and Dad were the same thing. I actually take that as a badge of honour. The only time it's weird is when she comes up to me in the grocery store and calls me Mum and everybody looks at me as if I'm in drag or something.

Patrick

Having concentrated time with your children may be one of the highlights of the experience—perhaps one of the highlights of your life.

That time I spent with Sophie was probably my most magical year.

Patrick

SHIFTING SENSE OF TIME

Time takes on different meaning on the road. I may not understand Einstein's Theory of Relativity, but I know for an absolute fact that time is relative.

In many ways, our experience of time was counterintuitive. Peter and I had assumed that time would pass quickly when we were travelling from place to place, doing and seeing new things. Conversely, we thought that, when we stayed in one place for a while, time would slow down. We'd have lots of time to do whatever we wanted. In fact, the opposite was true. On the road, time seemed to stretch to the infinite. In the best sense, days were long enough to accommodate any number of new experiences. They lay in front of us like the yellow brick road, inviting us to something new and exciting around every corner. We had time to do anything and everything. But, as soon as we put our feet up and stayed somewhere for a while, time evaporated. A week in Noosa felt like a couple of days; a month in Yorkshire was over before we'd begun to do half the things we had thought about.

Perhaps the best thing about being on the road for a while is that time becomes irrelevant.

> I lost track of what day of the week it was. That was dynamite. You really know you don't have a care in the world. It doesn't matter if it's Saturday or Friday. You have an idea that it's March....but that's it.
>
> Mike

We and others noticed that our sense of time changed in relation to where we were in our trip. The first few months pass languidly; you have all the time in the world. Around the halfway point, things noticeably speed up. You are halfway through. Where has the time gone? Are you going to be able to do everything you wanted? The closer you come to returning home, the faster time races by. The final few weeks disappear.

Be conscious of how time is moving for you and adjust your plans accordingly. Our decision to come home a month earlier than originally planned was directly related to realizing that, for us, time in one place sped by. If a month in Yorkshire evaporated, would our planned two months' readjustment to Victoria be enough to prepare us for "real" life again? Probably not. Three months seemed more like it. And we were right.

HOW LONG IS LONG ENOUGH?
How long should you spend in each place? The question arises in the planning stages and recurs regularly throughout your trip. There is no right answer. You can think about it generally in advance, and it's

probably helpful to do so, if for no other reason than to give you the illusion of control. But the issue will be a constant companion as you encounter unanticipated delights and unexpected problems along the way.

You'll trip over places you've never heard of, fall in love with them and want to stay a lifetime. You'll have to make hard decisions about whether to confine yourself to this newly discovered paradise or continue, possibly to find another. Places you had your heart set on will disappear in a puff of smoke (literally, in the case of our planned sailing cruise through the Straits of Malacca, see page 41) or turn out to be disappointments.

When do you decide to stay put? When do you call it quits? The only answer that matters is yours. Whatever your heart and your gut tell you is right is right.

At a B&B in New Zealand, I had a long talk with a fellow guest. Rick and his two adult sons left California, planning to spent 3–4 years sailing around the world. After seven months, Rick decided he'd had enough. It was just too long. He'd discovered he would prefer to spend his time doing something else. One of his sons was not thrilled about this change of plans, and Rick was feeling guilty and more than a little inadequate. We talked about extended travelling, about running away from home, and what we were really trying to prove to ourselves. I think he was reassured to know that I honestly admired him, for trying it in the first place, and for having the courage to accept and act on the truth of his discovery.

How can you know until you try whether it's what you want? And continuing when it's not right for you is nuts. We sure put a lot of pressure on ourselves to be perfect.

Don't allow yourself to be constrained by what you thought you wanted to do or by what you or somebody else thinks you should do. Do what feels right to you at the time. This is your moment of freedom. There are no rights or wrongs, no shoulds or musts. Whatever decision you make is the right decision. Whatever experience you have is the right experience for you. It doesn't matter what anyone else thinks of your choices. This one's for you.

THINGS TO THINK ABOUT

- Be prepared for endless administrative details on the road.
- Take care of yourself: take a nap, indulge in a massage, get your
    hair done.
- Pamper yourself now and then.
- Build regular holidays into your trip.
- Pace yourself. You've got time to take it easy every now and then.
- Stay someplace comfortable, with family or friends occasionally.
- Celebrate the ordinary.
- Use the services of local tourism bureaus. Many offer one-stop shopping
    for accommodation, tours, attractions, transit passes, etc.

FINANCES
- Bank cards are the easiest way to get local currency.
- Use credit cards to build up points, if you can ensure regular payments
    and avoid interest charges.
- U.S. cash in small bills comes in handy almost anywhere.
- Keep track of your expenses, review monthly and adjust accordingly.
    But don't panic.
- Be prepared to go over budget—almost everyone does.
- Don't worry about exchange rates. The Canadian dollar fell like a rock
    while we were away, but there was no point thinking about it.
    We weren't about to come home because the dollar was weak.

SAFETY
- Take sensible precautions. Split up money and valuables; don't flaunt
    your comparative wealth; keep an eye on your belongings; stay in safe
    places; don't do too many stupid things.
- But don't worry too much. Midlife extended travel seems to be safer than
    most holiday trips.

CHILDREN
- Take your children's needs into account.
- Involve them in decision-making.
- Enjoy your time together.

ADJUST AS YOU GO
- Time takes on new meaning on the road. Learn to recognize your
    shifting sense of time and make the most of it.
- Adjust your plans however you want whenever you want. If you find
    your paradise, stay and enjoy it; if you don't like a place, leave. This is
    your trip, and the only opinion that matters is yours.

February: IRELAND
Home Again

There is clearly something to the concepts of collective consciousness and genetic memory. All my Cronin, Hickey, and deCourcey ancestral genes have kicked in. On the basis of one and a half days' experience, I love Ireland!

How wonderful it is to feel healthy and to be able to enjoy travelling again. Dublin is a great walkable city. We've been strolling the streets by day and doing the pub music scene at night. I had never realized what nighthawks the Irish are. Dinner isn't usually until 8:30 p.m. at the earliest, and music in the pubs doesn't begin until 10:00 or 11:00. This could be a challenge.

The hours may have something to do with the fact that Dublin is without doubt the youngest place we've been. Almost 40% of the population is under 25. And it's obvious. Last night in the pub, most people were younger than we, a few were older, but there was almost no one our age. It's as if our generation has just disappeared, which, after being the dominant force in North America, is somewhat disconcerting. There's a whole new tourism marketing possibility here: Ireland—a world without baby boomers—a Generation Xer's dream.

Our hotel is a work in progress. It's well located, right by St. Stephen's Green. The staff are friendly; at 54 Irish pounds (approx. Cdn$110) including continental breakfast, it's quite a good deal for the location; and the bed is comfortable. But that's it. There's no furniture—no bureau, no bedside table, no chair, nothing. And we're on "the strip," where clubs stay open until 4:00 a.m.! Fortunately the windows are soundproof.

FEBRUARY 1—DUBLIN
Last night we headed off for another evening of traditional Irish music and found ourselves in a country-and-western bar. We had

been told that O'Shea's Merchant Pub had some of the best traditional music in Dublin. So off we went. After a long walk beside the
River Liffy, we spotted the sign on an old stone warehouse and
entered a plain working-class bar. We'd found our age group. The
eating area off to one side was filled with obvious regulars in the
40–60-year-old range. A guitar rested on a stool in front of a micro-
phone on a small stage across the dance floor. We sat at the bar,
ordered our Guinness, and waited. After a few minutes, two old
guys, one wearing a battered cowboy hat, unwound themselves from
the bar stools beside us, excused themselves, and shuffled to the
stage. A few minutes of tuning up and fiddling with the micro-
phone, then they broke into one of the more horrible but heartfelt
renditions I've ever heard of *Mama, Don't Let Your Babies Grow Up
to Be Cowboys*. The crowd went wild. This response *was* exceeded
only by the mass cheering and singing along with the next song,
Heartbeat, the theme from a popular television show. The dance
floor was quickly crowded with middle-aged groupies calling out
requests.

As the set progressed, we noticed other people coming in and
looking around with puzzled expressions that probably mirrored the
ones on our faces. It was "traditional" all right, but Irish? During a
pause between songs, we thought we heard fiddle music, so we finished our beers and headed out to the street. We walked around the
corner and, sure enough, right next door was the O'Shea's Merchant
Pub we had been looking for. "Ah, *that* O'Shea's Merchant Pub!
Why didn't you say?"

The crowd was friendly and noisy and the music fine, complete
with audience members getting up to sing and demonstrate
impromptu Irish step dances. The country-and-western influence
was thriving here as well, however. One audience member offered
"Country Roads," which was greeted with great enthusiasm by
everyone else.

Irish pubs are a stitch. People are obviously here for the music
and love it, but that doesn't stop them from chattering away at great
volume. The conversation is furious, and no one is a stranger for
long. The noise level is amazing.

We'd better get out of Dublin soon. This is a heavy pace—lots of drinking, noise, cigarette smoke, and staying up late. We may be too old for much more of this. But it sure is fun!

Today we walked, walked, and walked some more. Being Sunday, we visited two cathedrals—St. Patrick's, which has a small but wonderful choir and a very enthusiastic choirmaster, and Christchurch, which has a great crypt. I find it weird that there are two big cathedrals here and both of them are Anglican. Where are the Catholics? Then on—and on and on (we're clearly misreading the distances on our maps)—to the Modern Art Museum in the old hospital. Fortunately we found a cab waiting when we wanted to leave, because I don't think I could have walked back, and public transit seems sporadic on Sundays. Picked up some goodies at Bewley's Tea House along with a Sunday paper and headed home for tea and a liedown.

We were going to go out this evening but the Abbey Theatre is closed on Sunday nights. Second choice was a movie, but it turns out you have to reserve ahead for movies here, and anything we were interested in seeing has been sold out for ages. So this could be a quiet evening with a book. Which is not an unwelcome thought, but I'm feeling strangely at loose ends. I haven't yet regained my travel rhythm, and the situation in the Middle East is making us feel a little unsettled. The news is filled with the possibility of war, which could definitely affect our plans to visit Dvora in Israel later this month. How's that for self-centred? Please don't start a war. It will interfere with our travel plans.

FEBRUARY 3—KILKENNY

Here we are in the heartland of my maternal forebears. We're back to staying in B&Bs, and I realize once again how much I enjoy them. This time, we chose at random from the government B&B guide and found a winner, despite its name. "Dunromin" is a lovely comfortable family home. Val and Tom, their miniature Yorkshire terrier, Kizzie, and pointer, Kylie, are warm and hospitable, and the teapot is always on.

We're incapable of staying away from the music. Last night after dinner, on Val's recommendation, we headed off to Cleere's for more traditional Irish music. On entering, it seemed a pub like many others— low ceiling, dim lighting, the scent of peat fire mingling with beer and cigarette smoke. We made our way to the bar, picked up our Kilkenny beer, and headed toward the back room where the musicians were seated around a table, beers in front of them, tuning up. The music was rousing and the crowd noisy and enthusiastic. But a hush fell when one of the band called out "quiet for a traditional singer." A man at the bar turned in his seat, straightened his back and, in a pure Irish tenor voice, sang without accompaniment:

> *Once upon a time there was*
> *Irish ways and Irish laws...*

A breathless pause greeted the conclusion of his lament—years of oppression hung heavy in the air—before the crowd went wild.

But Cleere's is not your typical traditional music pub. It's gay. And I don't just mean cheerful. There was a young woman among the musicians—groundbreaking in and of itself. Even more interesting, she was gay. Her lover sat admiringly beside her, chatting softly between numbers and keeping her supplied with beer and cigarettes. The crowd contained at least six or eight other lesbians, including two at the bar in the midst of a noisy, public breakup. What was most impressive was that they were clearly an integral part of this pub community, otherwise dominated by your seemingly typical macho Irishmen. What a great country!

FEBRUARY 4—KILKENNY

Yesterday we undertook the Hickey hunt. When Mum heard we were coming to Ireland, she asked me to try to find a copy of her grandfather's birth certificate. She gave me the name of their family village, Ballyneil, and the town where he was baptized, Rosbercon, his name and date of birth and his parents' names. Fortunately for us, time stands still in Ireland and that was all we needed.

The Church of the Assumption in Rosbercon was open. The woman working in the office took my information. Then, destroying all my stereotypes of olde Ireland, she pulled out a computer print-out, looked up Hickey and, sure enough, there he was—Martin Hickey, born November 7, 1835, baptized November 8, 1835. She then reached into an old cupboard and pulled out the original 1835 baptismal record book, its dusty, yellowed parchment pages still being used for quests such as ours. This was more like it.

The parish priest arrived as we were leaving. He had just come from burying someone in Ballyneil and was able to provide us with clear directions. Which was a very good thing because we'd never have found Ballyneil otherwise. There's no sign and no village, just a crossroad at the base of a valley, with a lumberyard, a store, one house, and the cemetery. We searched for Hickey tombstones without success; most of the stones have long since fallen over, broken down, or been worn away. But there is no question that it is here that generations of my mother's family lie buried.

The old woman in the Ballyneil store informed us that the last of the Hickeys had moved up to Killeen and Inistioge (pronounced Inishteeg). She suggested we head up "past New Ross Gate" and just knock on doors. We tried to follow her directions, headed off along narrow lanes into the unspeakably beautiful hills, and were totally lost within minutes. We ended up in Inistioge, having missed New Ross Gate—which turned out to be a house, not a gate—and eventually wandered into the post office to ask if they knew of any Hickeys left in the area. There, I had the absolute pleasure of being an observer to one of those peculiarly Irish conversations between the postmistress and one of her friends:

Remember Bridgette? Now was she a Hickey?

Bridgette, married to Martin?

No, Bridgette, married to Jack Synnott. Now, was she a Hickey or was she a Bennett?

Ah sure, she was a Hickey. She was sister to Lill who married the Drae from Waterford.

No, no, Lill married the Quinn boy from over Thomastown

way. It was May married into the Draes.

Did she now? Now what ever happened to her brother, Paddy.

Well…

After about ten minutes of intensive genealogical investigation, these two women had not only outlined my family tree but had pointed us in the direction of a distant cousin still living in the neighbourhood. "Head to Thomastown and it's the second house past the housing estate and the entrance to St. Columba's Hospital. Just ask anyone for Jack Synnott's. They'll all know." And sure enough they did.

Before heading to Thomastown, however, we thought we'd explore the local possibilities a bit further. So back up the hill we headed to try once again to find New Ross Gate. This time, aided by the postmistress's directions, we were successful. There was no one home, however, so we called in at the neighbouring farm and knocked on the kitchen door. A large, friendly woman in her late sixties or early seventies answered. I explained I was trying to track my mother's family and asked if she knew of any Hickeys who used to live in the area. "Well, sure, I do," she replied. "Come on in. The Hickeys lived three houses down."

Mr. and Mrs. Diamond told us all they knew about the Hickeys who had been their neighbours when she moved to the area as a bride forty-nine years ago. They pointed toward the ruins of the old Hickey farm in a field on the upper road. By the time we'd exhausted the tea and history, the day was almost over. We postponed further exploration until the next day. We hadn't actually planned on doing any of this but, once we'd started, it was like being a detective. We couldn't resist following each clue to see where it would lead us. And we were meeting these wonderful people along the way.

Today, we headed back up the hill to see if we could find the ruins of the old house. We parked the car and were headed down a muddy country lane when we came across a farmer and his dog. We explained what we were looking for, and his eyes lit up. We were in exactly the right place. He pointed out the overgrown ruins of the old Hickey farm and took us across the road to meet his mother who had been the Hickey's neighbour for years.

There in her warm, messy kitchen, over the ever-present cup of "the tea," Bernadette Knox and her neighbour told us all about Peter Hickey and Katherine Powell who had "five beautiful daughters and one son, Paddy." We heard about Peter's "fine ways" and his work with horses. The whole family was "horse mad," and Bernadette recalled how proud Paddy looked as he rode in front of the Irish patriot, Eamon De Valera, on parade. It sounded just like the family stories my mother tells. Peter was a strict father but, as Bernadette's neighbour said, "with five beautiful daughters, he had to be." We learned about the family's love of their garden and love of life. "There was more life to them—they used to dance all over."

As we waved goodbye at the end of the day, I looked across the lane and could see the ghosts of Katherine working in her garden while May and Nellie and Lill and Bridgette and Kitty danced about, and Peter and Paddy put their horses through their paces in the paddock.

FEBRUARY 5—KINSALE

Last night, Val and Tom invited us to go to a movie with them. Once again, no luck. Half of Kilkenny was lined up outside the only theatre. Instead, we headed to the pub for beer and food and talk. Somehow, the family search, as well as a natural affinity, has made us part of the larger Irish family. We're accepted.

Today we hit the road and once again made about 100 kilometres in the course of the day. After New Zealand, Australia, and England, we are now experts at driving on the left-hand side of the road, but travelling in Ireland has its own challenges. It takes forever to get anywhere. We keep being distracted by unexpected finds and getting into long, rambling conversations with people and generally having a wonderful time never really getting anywhere or doing anything in particular.

FEBRUARY 6—KENMARE

The Irish love to chat. They're just like the Kiwis in that regard. Last night we learned all about our barmaid's family, her recent engagement, and her marriage plans. The Irish have a funny way about them—the legacy, I suspect, of years of abuse. At first meeting, they seem a little stern, somewhat wary. They don't greet you with big smiles. But, as soon as you start to talk and generally show yourself to be a friendly sort, they open right up and become downright loquacious.

From Kinsale, we set off to wander the countryside and wander we did. Almost immediately on the road out of town we saw a billboard: Welcome to deCourcey Country. "Stop the car," I screamed. My father's mother was a deCourcey. We headed down to the tip of Kinsale Peninsula and the remains of Castle deCourcey. To my dismay and Peter's delight, they're turning the grounds into a golf course! I wish now I had brought the family information from my dad's side—names, dates of birth, etc. But we never expected to be in Ireland at all. And Cronin and deCourcey are such common names in County Cork that it would be futile to attempt to trace Dad's family without them. Next trip.

We then set off to explore what has to be some of the loveliest country on earth (Glandore is a particular favourite of mine)—endless mountain, moor, and ocean views. We are now settled for the evening in an 1801 house overlooking the bay at the start of the Ring of Kerry, sitting in front of a peat fire while tea is being made. This is my idea of Ireland.

The country may be gorgeous, but the people are incredibly messy. The countryside is littered with paper and cans and plastic bags. Irish country kitchens look as if they haven't been cleaned in fifty years. They're filled with stuff, there's usually more than one old stove, and the remains of many different meals lie around on counters and tabletops. But they are uniformly warm and welcoming.

We're setting new land-speed records. After we emerged from the deCourcey lands at the Head of Kinsale, we discovered we had travelled precisely 10 kilometres in two-and-a-half hours!

The news on the radio and in the papers about the Middle East is getting worrisome. Trust us to be going there just as war is likely to break out!

FEBRUARY 8—KILLARNEY

There's something about Ireland that makes my heart sing. Yesterday we drove the Ring of Kerry. Looking out over empty miles of green rolling hills on one side and sparkling blue-grey ocean on the other. Catching tantalizing glimpses of the mysterious Skelligs, the craggy rocks erupting from the sea on which generations of monks offered their hermetic lives to God. We were blessed with a glorious day, a rarity at any time of year and a bloody miracle in February.

Today we enjoyed a nice ordinary Irish Sunday, wandering around Muckross House, a classic nineteenth-century Irish estate, and the grounds of the adjoining abbey, lunch at a comfy restaurant in front of a blazing fire in the company of multigenerational Irish families also enjoying a nice ordinary Irish Sunday.

When you're on the road for this length of time, it's the ordinary that becomes most attractive. Like the B&B we're staying at, Orchard House, in a little lane off the High Street. Not that it's ordinary but that we have it to ourselves, sitting here at the end of the afternoon, with the fire going and Peter watching soccer on TV. It's lovely.

FEBRUARY 9—ENNIS (OUTSIDE LIMERICK)

Today was mainly a driving day, although we did stop to explore Adare Manor Hotel, where we were proudly shown around by one of the staff, and Bunratty Castle, restored to its medieval state. It may be a sign of general homesickness that the clear highlight of the day was the kitty cat asleep in a cradle in one of the castle cottages who woke up and allowed herself to be patted and cuddled.

FEBRUARY 11—DOWTH, BOYNE VALLEY

Yesterday we saw the Ireland we had originally expected—shrouded in mist and rain and wind. Couldn't see much of the Cliffs of Moher or Galway, but it was certainly atmospheric. Today we decided to try to escape the weather by heading east and more or less tripped onto Clonmacnois. This was a major centre of Christianity, founded in A.D. 545 by St. Ciaran, built on by successive Christians, preached at by Pope John Paul II, filled with Celtic crosses and ruined chapels.

It's a marvellous, evocative site, redolent of the religious spirit that permeates Ireland even today. There can't be many countries in the world where, before the six o'clock news, a portrait of the Madonna and child appears on the TV screen, and a gong strikes, signifying... what? time to pray?

Then we headed into the Boyne Valley, where we had our first difficult time finding a B&B. It was worth it, however, as it led to an hilarious session with a couple of farmers as I was trying to get directions to The Glebe B&B in Knowth:

First you turn left, then left again at the next Y.

No, no, it's right at the first Y and left at the second.

No, no, he's just trying to get you lost. You'll end up back here.

Sure, it's you who'll be bringing them back here. It's definitely right...

You're an eejit. For sure it's left...

After a five-minute routine along these lines, I threatened to pound on the farm door and demand a bed for the night if they led me astray. This was greeted with great good cheer and much laughter.

We eventually found The Glebe, but there was no one home. So on we went up the road and chanced upon this incredible old pile, totally lit up, looking just like the Addams Family mansion. Netterville Manor is a Victorian almshouse with a ruined castle next door. It comes with a great family—Ann and Cormac, their kids, Claudia and Ross, Tiger the kitten, and an as-yet-unnamed female cat. There are also two ponies, but we haven't met them yet. The house is somewhat dishevelled, but our room is comfortable, there's a guest lounge with roaring fire and TV, and the atmosphere is unbeatable. All we need is a ghost.

We called Dvora in Israel and, according to her, it's business as usual. The Canadian embassy in Dublin seems to agree—no alerts—so off we go on Friday.

I've just seen my first pair of wild swans, taking off like 747s over our heads.

FEBRUARY 12—DOWTH

We keep tripping over extraordinary places I've never heard of before. Newgrange is one of the most amazing sites in the world. It's a neolithic passage grave, 5,000 years old, older than the pyramids. Presumably because it's buried and doesn't dominate the landscape like the pyramids, fewer people seem to know of its existence. In its own quiet way, however, it is every bit as impressive. A broad, grass-covered mound rises gently from the plain. Elaborately carved rocks mark the opening. Bending to enter, you make your way down a low, narrow passageway lined on either side by standing stones. Nineteen metres in is the burial chamber, a small, dark, cross-shaped room with a six-metre-high roof. The room has remained intact and waterproof for 5,000 years. At dawn on the morning of the winter solstice, and for a few days before and after, a shaft of sunlight penetrates the passage from a small opening over the door and creeps slowly to the chamber. On the solstice it touches the precise centre of the back wall. Newgrange is an absolutely magical place. The carved rocks of the inner chamber are still alive with the power of belief.

Then we returned home to explore our own private Dowth passage grave on the grounds of Netterville Manor. It's amazing to think that Anne and Cormac have their own manor, castle, chapel ruin, ceme-tery, and Stone Age passage grave. The children escorted us on an informal tour of the grounds. We climbed the castle tower to enjoy the view and found pieces of twelfth-century stone carving just lying around on the floor—one with an elephant carved on it! All of Irish history, and, judging by the elephant, some other country's history as well, is encapsulated in this one property.

Claudia and I have named the older cat Lizzie. I'm not sure why, but it seemed to fit.

Our trip has become amazingly circular. In the churchyard at Netterville Manor is a memorial to John Boyle O'Reilley, local poet, shipped as a convict to Australia. He is one of the few who ever managed to escape the penal colony, and he returned to try to help others do the same. He is a fairly significant character in Australian history; we read about him before leaving Canada and saw memorials to him in Australia. Now, here we are in his backyard!

FEBRUARY 13—HEATHROW AIRPORT

Travel day. Anyone who thinks the actual travel is fun has never done much of it. A seven-hour layover in Heathrow doesn't help.

The day started well—except for my panic attack at 5:00 a.m. worrying about whether Israel had suddenly imposed visa restrictions. This followed a nightmare about Peter's funeral. His being buried in a chef's hat seemed to upset me as much as anything else. Where does this stuff come from?

We had a leisurely breakfast and lots of cat-patting before hitting the road. It's just that the road is so long. We were awake at 7:00 a.m. (5:00 in my case). It's now 6:00 p.m., and the plane to Israel doesn't leave until 10:30. Ah well, by this time tomorrow, we'll be there.

Two weeks in Ireland have passed too quickly. But what a treat! I'm leaving with a sense of personal history, new friends, renewed health and enthusiasm for our trip, a lilt in my heart, and a dance in my step. Life looks good again.

EIGHT
SO MUCH TO THINK ABOUT

I had foolish hopes of recapturing my lost youth on this trip. The actual experience is more like rediscovering the tumultuous adolescent within. Welcome aboard an emotional roller coaster.

The confusion starts right at the beginning. You're keen to go. You've been planning this for ages. You're excited. You're thrilled. And you're saying goodbye to people you love and who love you.

> Saying goodbye and going was probably the hardest time.
>
> Larry

> I remember the day we left. My mother came down to the wharf—she was all tears—and my brother and one of his two kids. I'm very close to his two kids. My niece who would have been about eight at the time would not come down and say goodbye to us, but my nephew—he was about ten—came down. And I remember him saying to me, "Auntie Rita, are you ever coming back?".... That was difficult.
>
> Rita

From an emotional beginning, it just gets more so. Few people contemplating a time out from their regular lives have the vaguest idea of the range of emotions they will experience. We are naturally creatures of habit. By midlife, these habits are well established. They may be boring, but they offer reassuring, if occasionally misleading, proof of structure and meaning in our lives.

You hit the road and leave all that behind. Familiar routines are no longer there to comfort you. The friends and family who provide support and a sense of being needed become distant memories and occasional contacts. The job that shapes so much of your sense of self is no longer relevant.

You shed the skin of past identity and become a traveller. This is not so much a case of assuming a new identity as it is the cleansing of the old. The person you take on your trip is the essential you—the you stripped of superficialities like the house you live in, the car you drive, the clothes you wear, the job you do.

How many of you have felt that you're putting on a disguise as you dress for work in the morning? For the next few hours, you suppress one part of who you are. You put it away, to be taken out at the end of the workday. How often have you unexpectedly seen a colleague outside the business environment—coaching a kids' soccer team or singing in the chorus at the opera—and thought, "I didn't know that about him?" The traveller you, the runaway you, is who you are. Not just one part, but the whole unique blend of quirks and fears and enthusiasms and experiences that makes you distinct from every other life in the universe.

This release of the essential you may be the single most exciting part of the experience. To be yourself without fear of repercussions is an extraordinary feeling—and one cherished by almost every traveller.

> That is one of the unexpected pluses of going away and putting yourself in a circumstance and an environment where nobody knows you. They don't know who you're related to, what house you live in, what kind of car you drive, or what kind of clothes you normally wear. And they don't care. All they see is you for who you are. You run into somebody at a beach, at a swimming hole, and what do they know about you? They have no signals. They don't know if you own the biggest yacht in the bay or, as in our case, the smallest boat in the bay. And they don't care. That was very, very, very refreshing.
>
> Suzanne

It can also be terrifying, particularly if you have defined yourself primarily in terms of your job.

> What should have been an enriching experience has left me much less self-confident. You have some self-importance because of your work and the things you do, and then you have those things taken away. It made me much more humble.
>
> Janet

Whatever your reaction, the experience will not leave you unchanged. You might want to consider keeping a private journal. Not just of the places you go, the things you do, the people you meet, but a record of how you feel from day to day and week to week. Rereading it on your return, you'll be amazed at the range of your emotions. You'll never have a better or more important souvenir.

> Everybody kept a journal. Now every Sunday, we read about a week on the trip. And it's funny what each of us thought was important enough to write down....
>
> Jocelyn

> The only thing we tried to encourage the kids to do was keep a journal, which they did off and on. Now that we're sort of reliving our trip, they're really keen to get their journals out and see what they wrote. And they're kind of disappointed they didn't write more.
>
> Ian

MOOD SWINGS

Being removed from your home base shifts your centre of gravity. You're on uneven ground, and it's awfully easy to lose your balance. Be prepared for mood swings that make puberty seem like a placid summer's day.

Your highs will be higher than you ever imagined possible. Your lows will hit depths you didn't know existed. And you'll get to experience it all within a matter of moments. Some days, I went from ecstasy to agony and back again three times before noon. Anything could trigger a change. A cold, dark morning made me miserable. A chance conversation had me laughing out loud. No room at a chosen inn sank me into gloom. A short hike into the hills heard me singing to sheep. A telephone call home left me weepy with homesickness. Walking under timeless stars in an ancient village brought me tears of joy.

One moment you feel like the most fortunate human being on earth, blessed to have the opportunity to be where you are, filled with wonder at experiencing something you previously could only dream of.

A half hour later, the car breaks down in the middle of nowhere. You're tired and hungry. It's getting late and it's cold. You don't have anyplace to stay for the night. And you weep and wonder why on earth you're doing this to yourself.

These excessive reactions don't just happen to quasi manic-depressives like me, either. Even Peter, the most even-tempered man on the planet, found himself swinging to what were, for him at least, wild extremes of emotion. One minute, he was rocking along joyously with the Rolling Stones on the car radio. The next, he was driving maniacally around a full parking garage in Melbourne, determined to find a non-existent space, and cursing as I've never heard him before or since.

The emotional tumult may be a combination of lack of restraint and a sense of vulnerability. All your disguises have been left at home, but so have your defenses. The world is an exciting but potentially dangerous place. There are no barriers between you and the experience of the moment. At some unconscious level, that sense of being just a little on the edge of your comfort zone makes everything seem just a bit more real, more immediate, more profound.

If I were to pick the single most important gift I received from our trip, it would be the ability to laugh again. I don't mean the polite, restrained laughs we all know and enjoy when someone tells a joke or something funny happens. I mean the fall-down, tears-in-your-eyes, can't-stop, totally-out-of-control belly laugh that goes on and on and regurgles again and again just when you think you've got it under control. The kind of laugh that was part and parcel of being a child. The kind of laugh I hadn't laughed in years and was terribly afraid I had lost forever. As I lowered the barriers we raise to protect ourselves from life, my laugh, like the *Mary Ellen Carter*, rose again.

FLEXIBILITY CHALLENGES

Your trip will demand flexibility you never knew you had. Every day is different. There is no routine, no structure. You wake up in the morning, having very little idea what you'll encounter that day. The people are new, local attitudes different. You make one plan and have to change it because the weather has shifted. You decide on a destination but can't find a place to stay and have to move on. You'll learn to adapt—or you'll probably go home.

We all have illusions about ourselves. We create personal mythologies about the kind of person we are and how we deal with situations. And, eventually, we believe them. Running away from home strips away the pretense.

I used to think of myself as a flexible person. I thought I was pretty easygoing, that I could go with the flow, take what was thrown at me, bounce back—all the usual clichés. Where did I ever get that idea? (I've since found out that this was self-delusion on a grand scale. Very few, if any, others saw me this way.) Perhaps I was flexible within the small box of my normal life although, in retrospect, I have to wonder even about that. Certainly when the walls of the box were demolished, any vestiges of flexibility disappeared with them. I was like a kitten taken to a new home, overwhelmed by the enormity of the strange environment and desperate for a bed to hide under or a corner from which to fight off attack.

I now know that I'm a lot more rigid than I thought. Particularly in the early stages of the trip, I got frustrated and angry at the constant shifts and changes and the need to reassess and regroup. I raged at the elements, furious that the weather wouldn't respond to my needs. I whined about a geopolitical situation that could dare allow a war to interfere with my plans. I moaned about illness preventing me from doing what I wanted to do.

I can honestly say that I am now more flexible than I was when we set out. But it didn't come easily. And if it was hard on me, it must have been miserable for Peter who had to put up with my struggle to let it all go.

The following exchange between Heather and Mike reassured me that I'm not the only person who needed some personal growth in this area.

Heather: *I think I'm a bit less uptight about things....I let things slide a little more than I did before.*

Mike: *I think I'm less uptight as well, a little bit more relaxed.*

Heather: *I think you're more adaptable—you're more able to deal with the situation when things don't go the way you want them to.*

Mike: *I have a habit of planning things to death but, when you travel like this, you realize that you can't plan for everything. You have to go with it.*

Heather: *I think you learn to adjust, to make do with what you have, with things that are less than perfect. And sometimes you just don't have the choice. You have to go with what you've got. You see how the rest of the world makes do with almost nothing. They can build a shovel out of pieces of scrap.*

Mike: *I'm more aware of how fortunate we are and much more at ease with things not being as perfect as I would like them to be. Things used to have to be just so. Now I think there's no point in giving myself a heart condition over things that are not that important.*

If you are a control freak, if you are someone who is accustomed to making things happen on your own terms, if you're a Type A personality, a Virgo, or an anal-retentive pain in the butt, this kind of trip is going to be a major challenge. In fact, it will be downright painful.

The only consolation I can offer is that the rewards of learning to adapt are amazing. As the trip progressed, I could physically feel the difference. Disappointment no longer caused my stomach to clench; I knew that, if one thing went wrong, something else wonderful would happen. I became increasingly proud of myself as I started to learn to let things go. I began to appreciate the freedom of letting events unfold. I could feel that I was learning something new and developing a different aspect of my personality, something I hadn't done for a long time.

Your trip will take you from point A to point B. But the far greater and more valuable journey occurs within. Your spirit grows and your range expands and you become the person you are capable of being.

LOSS OF IDENTITY
It was a revelation to me how much of my identity and sense of self-worth was linked to my work. I have never considered myself

particularly job-oriented. I've always had interesting things to do but, given the choice between working and doing something else, I'd always choose the something else. So I was particularly stunned to find myself depressed after lunch one day with friends in Sydney. The conversation had been fun and stimulating and touched on all sorts of topics, including their jobs. When Peter and I returned to the B&B, I realized I was jealous that they had homes and jobs and responsibilities to go back to, that they had structure and purpose in their lives. Me? Jealous of people who had to go to work the next day? What I really missed was a sense of my place in the universe.

Janet's decision to take a year off was driven in part by a need to take a break from working too hard. After the first few months of that holiday feeling, however, she found herself getting bored.

> I really did miss work. I missed having a cause and a purpose and producing something. I felt like I was not a productive person in society. I am very work-focused and I should have known that, but you never know how it will play in advance. I thought, well, I'll refocus on my family. I thought that would replace everything else. But it didn't. That was the worst aspect of the trip for me—a feeling of lack of purpose. I now have confirmed that I really need a purpose and usually that will manifest itself in work.
>
> Janet

Others had the same initial reaction, but emerged with a different perspective.

> I hadn't realized how much of my ego and self-image was wrapped up in my status and my job—that I had my personal parking spot, and my business cards, and my e-mail address, and my secretary, and all the people who worked for me. When that's suddenly ripped away and you're just Joe average, there's nothing feeding your ego. It was a really good lesson to learn that my image of myself was wrapped up in a lot of stuff that had to do with my job and my career rather than who I am as

a person. I actually realized that I had gotten off track. A lot of
the things that I used to admire and respect about myself had
kind of disappeared. It gives you the opportunity to then go
back and rediscover what those things are.

Patrick

Separating ourselves from our jobs brings on a feeling of disorien-
tation that is both terrifying and liberating. As Patrick pointed out, it
gives you the chance to examine what's truly important to you. This is
one of the great gifts of a runaway, but it doesn't come easily. Arriving
at self-knowledge and self-acceptance is a painful journey. But it is one
of the reasons you set out in the first place.

MISSING FRIENDS AND FAMILY

"You don't know what you've got till it's gone." Most of us take our
support system for granted. You may be surprised how much you'll miss
the folks back home.

In my case, it wasn't just a surprise but a revelation. I was actively trying to get away from them. My family, in particular, were driving me
nuts. They were tiring me out, depending on me too much, taking
up too much of my time. I loved them, but I needed to get away. I
started to miss them on the plane leaving Canada and continued to miss
them throughout the trip.

Friends were another matter. I've always appreciated my friends,
enjoyed their company, and looked to them for support. It's strange,
then, that I and others didn't foresee how much we would miss them.

We forgot how social we are. We love entertaining. People
are an important thing in our lives, and to be suddenly cut off
from that was a bit surprising.

Patrick

I missed our friends more than I missed my family.

Rita

We met wonderful people on our travels. You will too. In fact, it's
a good idea to tell everyone you know where you're going in case they

have friends or family you can call or visit while you're there. Local contacts can provide some of the most cherished moments of your trip. You'll make new friends—some lovely but fleeting, others lasting. But it's possible to be lonely even in the midst of a crowd.

> I think the loneliest places were the bays full of other boats. And we weren't involved.
>
> Larry

And new friends are different from old friends. There are times when all you want is somebody who already knows who you are.

> There were times when we really missed our good buddies.... There was this group of women cruising and we were all very close. But there was a certain level beyond which we didn't go because we didn't know each other that well. And as much as everybody was involved with the same goal, nobody really wanted to get involved with other people's problems. I found it really hard at times not having an ear—that good buddy— on a deeper personal level.
>
> Rita

Among the best times on our trip were those with old friends. We could relax, secure in the knowledge that we were no longer alone in the universe. It was a relief to be able to take certain things for granted, to be able to build on shared experiences and common memories. It gave us a chance to stay in touch with a core part of ourselves that could then help us appreciate how we were developing on the road.

You might want to consider arranging your itinerary to touch bases with friends living along the way. It's nice to find a bit of home every now and then.

RELATIONSHIP ADJUSTMENTS

If you are travelling with a spouse or partner, you are in for the adventure of your life. Being alone, together, without the stability and supports you have at home, is an experience.

There are some risks. You can either grow or....You are each other's main companion suddenly. You don't have a family that alleviates that sort of relationship of dependency. You don't have friends that do that. You don't have the work. Suddenly you're in each other's company in a way that I don't think you ever are any other time in your relationship, except maybe when you retire. It creates a different tension.

Margaret

You've both changed. At times it's like running away with a total stranger. Which, when you think about it, is rather exciting.

Patrick only knew me as a student, so he actually didn't know the real me at all.

Helen

Running away together will either strengthen your relationship or destroy it. You will not return the same individuals or couple.

Our power positions shifted totally. I hoped going to France would put him in a position of some power, because he's from there and he speaks the language and he has people there. I wanted to balance things out a little bit. But it went way too far. And I didn't adjust very well at all. I felt like I'd gone from a situation of control and self-confidence to having very little self-confidence and very little control.

Janet

If you think leaving your jobs and spending time together in a new environment will help to patch strains in a relationship, think again.

In retrospect I can see that I knew three or four years ago that the marriage was probably going to break up. But when you're in a marriage, especially with children, I think you try to do what you can to make it work. But the year away sped things up. Had I stayed at work, we would probably have limped along for another four or five years...maybe even made it until the kids were grown up...maybe.

Janet

Even the healthiest of relationships will have to cope with some bumps along the way. Isolated together in your travel cocoon, small ticks and quirks have a tendency to loom large.

All those little habits that you may see in a normal life maybe once or twice a week, you see all those habits all the time.

Rita

Well, the marriage survived, but I think it was a strain in a way. Little things that bothered each other became more important. On a boat, you're in a smaller area than this room, sometimes for three weeks at a stretch, and you don't have space for yourselves. Sometimes you just need someplace to go and burp and fart and do just what you want to do without having to answer to anybody.

Larry

Time together can also bring out the best in your relationship. Peter and I have always loved being together and, not having children, we've probably had more time together than many couples. We felt pretty confident that our relationship could withstand the strain of constant companionship. What we didn't anticipate was how much we would enjoy it.

We had acknowledged in advance that we would need breaks from each other. We discussed the possibility of one of us saying, "Look, I need a break, I want to spend next week at the beach by myself," or "I'm going to spend the day at the art gallery, so why don't you do something else." The advance discussion was a good idea. It just wasn't needed. The first week we experimented with going our separate ways we were so lonely that we both independently returned early on day four.

We did spend hours pursuing different interests: I would go horseback riding, go for a walk, or take a nap; Peter would read, watch sports on television, or go to a cricket match. But we also cheerfully shared an intimacy that neither of us had anticipated. We adjusted to resting our sudsed-up heads in adjacent wash basins at the hairdressers and spending weeks in accommodation with no distinction between bedroom and bathroom.

We got to see each other at our best and at our worst, coping with alien environments and new roles. And we discovered all over again how much we loved each other. It got stronger and stronger and better and better. Just being outside our normal routine made us discover, after sixteen years of marriage, new and exciting things about each other. Our experience wasn't unique.

> What we realized most when we were away was how much we enjoy each other's company. We spent all day, every day together. There weren't friends to lean on. We learned that we really like each other.
>
> Patrick

Being dependent on each other for so much can also lead to a whole new level of respect. Travelling together opens your eyes to the fact that your partner is pretty competent at things you may not be. When you return home and are faced with difficult situations, that appreciation of each other's strengths can add a powerful dimension to your relationship.

One of the wonderful things that happens is that you see your partner through other people's eyes. I saw Peter who, at home, can sometimes be shy and somewhat withdrawn, relating wholeheartedly and openly to total strangers. And I saw them responding with a warmth and acceptance that made me appreciate all over again his humour and intellect. It makes you realize what you saw in this person in the first place.

> At home, everybody knows you and it's boring. Here, people kept asking us how we met. I looked at him and said, "I don't think we've talked about this for twelve years. How did we meet?" We related a lot of stories that we hadn't talked about for a long time.
>
> Suzanne

It may occasionally be painful to rediscover yourself, but it is pure pleasure to rediscover the person you love.

SEX AND THE MARRIED TRAVELLER

Those of you who have been married for ten or twelve or fifteen or more years will understand. As much as you and your partner love each another, your sex life can occasionally get a bit mundane. There may be long-time couples out there who can still light each other's spark every night, but I haven't met them. Most of us fall into a comforting, loving but, if we're honest, sometimes boring routine. We run around all day. We work too hard. We come home tired. The kids, if you have them, always need something. There's no time.

Let me introduce you to the pleasures of a runaway. Suddenly all you have is time and each other.

> We realized that the most valuable, the most important thing we have is time.
>
> Patrick

Routine does not exist. You're in new places, sharing new experiences, relying on each other for emotional and physical support. You see each other through new eyes. You feel younger, more exciting, more adventurous. It does wonders for your sex life, at least if you're travelling without children.

> We were very happy with each other's company. The only drawback was we did not have much privacy. That certainly was an issue and needed to be planned. The odd time we were invited to stay in homes, and Ian and I would take a bedroom in the home and the kids would sleep in the van. But normally they were just off doing their thing, so that gave us a chance to do our thing. We'd say, "We'll all meet back at the van at eight o'clock." You have to plan more just to have a little privacy.
>
> Jocelyn

Bonded babysitting services are available in most large Western cities. B&B hosts may know a reliable teenager willing to stay with the kids. Many large hotels offer babysitting services. There are ways to give yourselves privacy, but it's probably not quite the same.

For middle-aged couples travelling without children, however, I could recommend a runaway if for no other reason than the sex. Assuming that your relationship is a good one to begin with, this experience will perk up your marriage like no other therapy I can think of. You have time to luxuriate in bed in the morning or take a nap together in the afternoon. Even after a busy day of sightseeing or adventuring, your tiredness is somehow exhilarating as opposed to the empty exhaustion after a day at the office. You have time to give each other long, sensuous massages and the emotional freedom to try something new and potentially exciting. After all, the whole idea of the year away was to try new things. Why shouldn't that extend to your sex life?

You remodel yourself on a trip like this and you can remodel your relationship as well.

HEALTH AND THE MIDLIFE TRAVELLER

When travellers talk about their worst experiences, illness is a common topic. For some people, it is their own illness; for Peter, it was mine.

Anyone, at any age, is vulnerable to getting sick when travelling. If you're in a strange environment for any length of time, at some point you're bound to have food poisoning, the flu, or worse. But the middle-aged traveller has perhaps more to worry about than the teenager. Our bodies are not as strong as they once were. We tire more easily and are perhaps more susceptible to various bugs.

We do, however, have some built-in advantages. We are smart enough to take care of ourselves. We can recognize and acknowledge our limitations. We understand what works for us—what type of food or drink we will react badly to. And we can probably afford to pamper ourselves a bit.

There are obvious things you can do to better your chances of staying healthy. Take along multivitamins and remember to take them every day. Pace yourself. You don't need to see everything. When you're tired, take a break. Have a nap. Build in downtime. Eat and drink sensibly. Use mosquito repellent or netting where necessary. Indulge in the occasional massage.

With all the precautions in the world, however, there are times when nothing works. At some time in the course of your trip, you should expect to be sick—maybe very sick. You need a fallback plan.

> I missed structure in my life. Not having a home made me feel quite rootless and adrift. And, when I got sick, I wanted to be with my family. My recommendation to anybody who is going to do this is that it's nice to keep some ties, to have some-place to go if you get into trouble.
>
> Marie

Our fallback plan was Auntie Audrey. We knew that, if we needed help, she would take us in, no questions asked. And, together with her friend Anne, she did. (See page 161.) You need to think about what you'll do if you're in an accident or seriously ill and discuss it with the other people concerned.

In some cases, you have no choice. If you have a serious accident, you need to get home. Most of the time, however, it's a question of making a very personal decision about how much you can take, what options are available, and how much you want to continue the trip.

When I became sick in India, I knew I couldn't cope with that par-ticularly challenging environment in my debilitated state, but I wasn't ready to throw in the towel on the trip as a whole. I made the assessment that, if I could find a refuge, I could get better and we could continue. It took longer than anticipated but, fundamentally, I made the right decision for me.

Others have had to make more difficult choices. As mentioned earlier, Suzanne and Trevor had to consider a major change in plan when she and their two daughters became seriously seasick. They decided they couldn't put the girls through another harrowing sea journey right away.

> It was a very, very difficult decision. We knew that Trevor was going to head into some really nasty snarly weather. It felt like letting your husband go off to war because you don't

know what's going to happen out there. But you don't have a
choice. We waved goodbye, not really knowing when we
would meet up.

Suzanne

Try to think ahead to what you will do if disaster occurs. Plan your
medical kit with a view to handling minor emergencies (see page 128).
With any luck, you will never need most of these supplies—our antiseptic bandages and syringes never left their plastic covers. It would
be miraculous, however, if you emerged untouched by any health problems. Expect them, have a backup system in place, accept them, survive
them, and move on.

If things are serious, the Canadian embassy or consulate will be
able to provide the name of a doctor who speaks English. Good hotels
have doctors on call, and B&B hosts can recommend their own family physicians.

When you return home, it's a good idea to have a complete
physical to make sure you haven't brought any unwanted souvenirs
back with you. Peter is still dealing with a skin infection, a reaction to
mefloquine, the antimalarial drug we took in preparation for India. The
condition may take two years to clear up.

There is, however, a positive aspect to health on the road, which I
suspect is as much psychological as physical. Some chronic health
problems seem to disappear. I didn't have a serious headache from the
time we left Fiji until we returned to Victoria. Which just confirms
what I've always thought: doing what you want is good for you.

50 IS NOT 20
The older we get, the more we appreciate learning something new.
But it's harder than it was when we were younger.

The differences are both physical and emotional. I remember myself
as a 21-year-old flower child wandering through Europe. While I
recognize in her the seeds of the 50-year-old compulsive, there is no
doubt that she was more open, more flexible, and braver than I am, even
at the end of this eye-opening trip. Courage came more easily then. I
knew less, and cared less, about consequences. I had time, seemingly

unlimited time, to correct any mistakes, to retrieve any losses.

At 50, it's a different story. We take with us an accumulation of fears, constraints, knowledge, and experiences. We sense the boundaries of time. We are inherently more cautious, more cowardly. As it sometimes takes longer to get your joints functioning normally in the mornings, so too does it take time and effort to get your spirit functioning as it should.

Give yourself time to adjust. Some people recommend that you spend a month before you leave home, decompressing and taking care of last-minute details. At the very least, don't just take off and expect to hit the ground running.

> We worked until three days before we left. I would never advise anyone to do that. The month before we left was just frantic.
>
> Margaret

Be kind to yourself. Don't assume you can do it all and enjoy everything all at once. Be patient. Rereading my journal, I am astonished how hard I was on myself in the first few months of the trip. I interpreted every setback as a personal weakness, as a failure of courage or lack of imagination. In retrospect, I feel exactly the opposite. I feel courageous. Not for the way I always responded to situations, but for the fact that I was willing to try, to put myself in a position where courage might be required.

While travelling in midlife is very different from doing it when you're young, it can be even more rewarding. A lot of my youthful trip is now a blur. I know I had a great time. I made one lasting friendship. I remember a number of individual places and experiences. But there are huge blanks where I was simply partying my way through Europe. A lot of what I saw and heard washed over me. I had no experience against which to measure it, few standards against which to judge it.

As an older traveller, you bring along a lifetime of education, experiences, values, and moral assessments.

I remember Helen coming home from the Musée d'Orsay in
Paris and saying how much more meaningful the paintings
were than when she had first seen them. As a kid, you wander
through and you like it, but you don't know why. As an adult,
you wander through and you're educated on art and history.
You know why you like it, and you have more of an emotional reaction to the things that you see.

Patrick

As it is with art, so it is with life. You've lived more, you've seen
more. When you go someplace new, you have informed reactions to
enrich your experience.

It will not always be easy, but it will always be rewarding.

THINGS TO THINK ABOUT

• Be prepared for emotional highs and lows.
• Consider keeping a private journal. It will give you a chance to
  explore what's happening to you, and it will be the best possible
  souvenir of your experience.
• Your limits will be challenged, and not always comfortably, but you
  will be a more flexible person by the end of your trip.
• Don't be panicked by self-doubts and a sense of loss. Turn them into a
  new sense of self.
• You'll probably miss your family and friends more than you anticipate.
• Before leaving, ask if friends can provide you with contacts in places
  you'll be visiting.
• Plan your route to visit friends along the way.
• Constant companionship under unusual circumstances places enormous stress on a relationship. If there are cracks, don't fool yourself
  into thinking that running away together will patch them over. If
  your relationship is basically sound, chances are this will make it
  even better.
• Take care of your health. Eat well, take vitamins, get rest. Take along a
  good medical kit.
• Despite your best efforts, you'll probably be ill at some point in your
  trip. Have a fallback plan for dealing with it.
• For every physical and emotional drawback of being an older traveller,
  there is a compensatory blessing. Give yourself time to adjust, be
  kind to yourself and enjoy the emotional richness of mature travel.

February/March: ISRAEL
Non-Hotel Tourists

FEBRUARY 17—JERUSALEM

Arrived here four days ago at dawn. Dvora picked us up at a disappointingly ordinary airport—where were all the guns and security people we'd been warned to expect?—and drove us through a Shabbat-deserted Jerusalem to her tiny, perfect apartment. The three of us are living in two rooms which, together, are probably no more than twelve by eighteen feet. We're having a ball. It's an ongoing pajama party.

It is, however, somewhat strange to be staying with Dvora so soon after visiting with Martin and Rosalynn in England. We first knew and loved Martin and Dvora as a couple, travelled with them, laughed with them and thought them perfect together. Only to watch from a distance, stunned, as a one-year visit to Israel drove them apart: Martin, the rabbinically trained Jew, couldn't tolerate the violence and the general atmosphere; Dvora, the convert, found her heart's home and didn't want to leave. That was ten years ago.

After adjusting to the loss of a night's sleep, we have begun to take in a bit of what's going on around us. It's not all good. The calming report we received from the Canadian embassy in Dublin has clearly not made it to the rest of the world. We appear to be the only tourists in Jerusalem. Everyone else, more wisely perhaps, has decided to wait and see what happens. The situation is undeniably tense. The Americans are threatening to attack Iraq this week or next if Iraq doesn't comply with the weapons inspections agreed upon after the Gulf War. The Iraqis don't appear to be backing down, and the Israeli media are filled with speculation about a retaliatory chemical attack against Israel. Much of the time, we can ignore it—not understanding Hebrew is a definite advantage—but occasionally it hits home that we are sitting on a powder keg.

Last night, we were visiting with Nomi (Martin's very pregnant daughter, Dvora's stepdaughter) and taking advantage of the opportunity to watch the Olympic figure-skating competition in the company of another Canadian. After the skating, the news came on and Nomi translated for us. The government is directing everyone to buy blackout material, seal one room, and pick up gas masks. For the Israelis, this is old hat. They lived through this during the Gulf War. For us, however, it was seriously weird to be discussing how long plastic wrap will keep out gas and how to handle gas-mask-induced claustrophobia, in the same ho-hum way Canadians discuss the weather.

Gas mask distribution began a few days ago. Israeli citizens can pick them up at designated outlets. Hotels received their supply yesterday. We, however, are the lowest of the low, officially designated as "non-hotel tourists." In a few days we should be able, if we wish, to go to a department store and pay the equivalent of Cdn$280 each for a mask. Assuming we survive, we can turn the masks in when we leave Israel and get half our money back. Nice to know where we sit in the scheme of things. We've decided just to take our chances.

Balancing the ugly reality of war, however, is Jerusalem. The city dazzles the eye—warm, brown stone, shining gold and orange in the sun. My image of Jerusalem, to the extent I had one, was of a cold, stark, somewhat forbidding place. I guess it was shaped by nothing more than news reports of clashes between Israelis and Palestinians, and it couldn't have been further from the truth. The Old City, like Ayers Rock and Newgrange, pulsates with ancient life. It keeps drawing us back to wander more of its narrow alleyways.

All our other preconceptions have also been proved wrong so far. Contrary to popular mythology, the Israelis have been pleasant and helpful. One fellow almost drove off the road in his enthusiasm to help us find our way around the city. I love their quirky sense of humour that manifests itself in weird and wonderful sculpture and architecture. The military presence, which I had expected to find intrusive and threatening, is hardly noticeable. The atmosphere, which I had thought would be religious, is actually sacrilegious. The place is swamped by the religious fervour of too many fanatics.

We're exploring the city at leisure. In the absence of crowds, everything is relatively calm and quiet, and we can take our time wandering through the museums and the streets. It is somewhat disconcerting, however, to be told repeatedly by shopkeepers how "brave" we are to be here.

FEBRUARY 18—TEL AVIV

Dvora had a meeting in Tel Aviv today and we've tagged along to sightsee. It's amazing how tiny this country is. A one-hour drive separates the two major cities. Tel Aviv is disappointing. I was expecting a Middle Eastern New York or Riviera. In fact, it's just a city and looking somewhat shabby. But the beach makes up for a lot.

On the other hand, Jaffa, the old city at the north end of the bay, is stunning and, at the moment, poignant. We picked up Dvora after her meeting and headed into this old town of golden stone buildings, lovingly restored, filled with shops, cafés, and restaurants. And there was no one there. I mean no one. Other than the mournful-looking shopkeepers, we were it. The squares look made for crowds of people, singing, talking, dancing, having a great time—and they are all empty. The threat of war keeps everyone at home.

FEBRUARY 20—JERUSALEM

Rolls of plastic to seal off rooms from chemical attack are being sold conspicuously in the streets. The anxiety is definitely increasing. The military presence was considerably heavier today but, strangely, there were also more people around, both Israelis and tourists. I'm not sure if this is a demonstration of strength in numbers or solidarity in the face of adversity.

The tensions building around the prospect of war are mirrored in the internal relationships between Jews and Arabs and between orthodox and secular Jews. We spent a morning on the Temple Mount, visiting the Dome of the Rock and the Al Aksa Mosque. The latter is by far the most impressive, most beautiful (on the inside), and most spiritual site I've seen in Israel. It actually feels like a place of worship, unlike the Church of the Holy Sepulchre, which is a jolting combination of rival camps and a carnival. There are actually money-changers in the courtyard of the church.

The Temple Mount, in contrast, is a large, lovely, open space. Its serenity is somewhat undermined, however, by the grim-faced, Uzi-armed Israeli soldiers one has to pass before entering and knowing that plainclothes Muslim security people are watching everything you do. The day we visited, they decided, for some unknown reason, to close to visitors earlier than scheduled. Peter and I were wandering around, unaware of the change, admiring the buildings, observing the different robes and headdresses being worn by the faithful. Gradually, we sensed a chill in the atmosphere. We looked around. There were a lot fewer tourists in sight. In fact, we were among the last of the visitors. In place of the welcoming smiles that had greeted us a half hour earlier, we were now on the receiving end of noticeably hostile stares. We moved quickly to the gates.

FEBRUARY 21—JERUSALEM
Today we headed off to Masada and the Dead Sea with Dvora and her friend, Chaim. He is in a mild panic at the moment as his family in Tel Aviv is threatening to descend on him next week to get beyond the range of Iraqi missiles.

Masada, the last Jewish fortress in the war against the Romans, is situated on a high granite plateau in the Judean desert overlooking the Dead Sea. It is a spectacular site with a compelling history; it is the spot where the Jewish Zealots resisted the Roman legions for more than two years and finally committed mass suicide rather than surrender to slavery. I've always been fascinated by the story but, for some reason, I didn't get caught in Masada's spell. Maybe it was all the tourists. For days we haven't seen any other visitors at all. Suddenly, Masada is filled with them, and most seem to be German. Like the presence of all the middle-aged Japanese tourists at Pearl Harbor, the effect is somewhat jarring. I find myself wondering what impact the site has on them.

The Dead Sea on the other hand was a blast. We posed for the ritual picture, bobbing unsinkably in the salt-filled water while read- ing newspapers. Then it was off for a mud wrap, a gift from Dvora. Advertisements for mud wraps always imply a sensual experience—a slow massaging with a warm solution, more a cream than mud, followed by a quiet interlude for contemplation, from which you emerge soothed in body and soul. Not in Israel! Instead, a tall, brusque woman with a full mouth of those extraordinary metal Russian teeth ushered me into a bare concrete-walled, tile-floored room. A plastic chair and a plastic-covered bed were the only furnishings. A shower stall took up one corner. Ludmilla, as her name tag identified her, indicated—there being no common language—I should take off all my clothes (Peter in his room was instructed to keep his underwear on) and then she left.

I was standing there naked when she returned, carrying a large plastic margarine bucket filled with brown goop. She motioned me to sit on the bed, scooped a handful of hot mud out of the bucket and spread it over my shoulders and back. Then she pushed me down on my back and slapped it on my front. Slip, slap, slop. No gentle, soothing rubbing here. Large handfuls of mud were plopped down on various body parts, squished between my fingers and toes. In a flash, she flung the plastic bed cover up over my body and wrapped it tightly around me, pinning my arms to my sides. Towels were tucked around my neck and shoulders, the heat turned on, the light turned out. Totally mummified in mud and plastic, I was left to the soothing tones of Doris Day singing *Que sera sera*.

Twenty-five minutes later, Ludmilla returned. The bare overhead lightbulb was abruptly switched on. She whipped off the plastic, pulled me up, and pushed me into the shower. As I was scrubbing myself, the shower curtain was flung open. There stood Ludmilla with a hose. A blast of water spun me around to get rid of any stubborn clinging mud. I felt like an actor in a 1930s southern women's prison movie. Ludmilla left out a towel and a glass of water and motioned me to get dressed. As I staggered out the door, she flashed me a wide metal smile—goodbye.

The whole thing had a sort of "welcome to Bulgaria" feel about it. I was left totally dazed—relaxed, but stunned.

Driving back to town through East Jerusalem, the Palestinian part of town, was an eye-opener. It is much more third-worldly than the rest of Jerusalem. The problems here are enormous and far beyond my ability to comprehend, much less suggest solutions. The concept of Arab neighbourhood, Jewish neighbourhood and never the twain shall meet sounds horrible to a Canadian ear, but it may be the only practical solution here and now. The constantly evident inequities between Jews and Palestinians are more difficult to accept. I appreciate that the distinctions are based on a very real sense of fear, but they're not easy to excuse. The people searching through garbage bins are always Palestinian.

FEBRUARY 22—KFAR BLUM KIBBUTZ
We're on a whirlwind weekend tour through northern Israel with our friend, Norman, who used to be the Canadian ambassador to Israel and recently returned as publisher of the *Jerusalem Post*. Our first stop yesterday was a Druse village to meet some of his friends who own an art gallery. Norman had hoped to lunch with them, but the crowd of Jews fleeing a boring Jerusalem Shabbat meant that business was too good to close the gallery. Although Norman did wonder if his no longer being an ambassador might also have had something to do with his friends' decision. On to Akko, to see the old city and Crusader fort, then west to Galilee—getting lost on the way, of course—continuing on Naot Mordechai Kibbutz and other friends. This time, an invitation to dinner was forthcoming!

As with all Israelis we've met, Yehuda and Zvi were enormously hospitable. On three hours' notice, Yehuda whipped up a delicious maza (the Israeli selection of different dishes) for two total strangers. Zvi is from Argentina. He arrived on the kibbutz thirty-five years ago when he was 19. He's a big bear of a man with the blackest hair I've ever seen. If it weren't for the occasional strands of grey and grey sideburns, I'd swear it came out of a bottle, but I doubt kibbutzim men colour their hair! Yehuda is a little older, originally from Iran, and has been on the kibbutz even longer. He's solid like the rocks—not tall, but strong and dependable-looking.

The two of them reminisced about their years on the kibbutz. When they arrived, it was very much a communal agricultural endeavour as well as a philosophical and emotional commitment to building the State of Israel. Over the years, they have witnessed the evolution of a cooperative, socialist experiment in rural living into a Cdn$55 million shoemaking and plastics business. (The main business of the neighbouring kibbutz is now running the hotel where we're staying.) Yehuda and Zvi accept the changes and are adapting extremely well, but there was no hiding their disappointment in the passing of a dream.

The kibbutz makes Naot sandals and exports them worldwide. The kibbutzim are management, with hired staff to fill the orders. The old communal lifestyle is becoming a distant memory—witness our dining in Yehuda's home rather than in the dining hall. The kibbutz's latest venture is manufacturing the plastic sheeting used to seal rooms against chemical attack. Business is booming. They have just finalized a big sale to Jordan and, while they obviously don't want the Iraqis to attack, they wouldn't mind tensions continuing for a while. People whose kibbutz includes bomb shelters to protect them from regular Syrian rocket attacks don't get too excited about threats.

We ate and chatted, mainly about travel and politics, and chatted and ate. Not surprisingly, Yehuda and Zvi are strong Labour supporters. They're a little concerned about Iraq, but think Iran and Syria pose a greater threat in the long run. It surprises me the extent to which Israelis do not take the survival of the State of Israel for granted. In conversations with Yehuda, Zvi, Norman, Dvora, and others, "if" is a word often heard. Phrases like "If Israel survives…" "If Israel still exists in ten years…" regularly preface speculation about the future.

Bumbling around Israel with Norman is an experience not to be missed. He's not quite used yet to travelling without an executive assistant to lay things out for him and a driver to get him around. Add to that, he's a quick, on-the-go kind of person. I've been the navigator, sitting in the back seat with the map, calling out directions—"Turn right," "Left here," "Straight through"—all of which Norman questions—"Are you sure?" "That can't be right"—and usually ignores.

As a result, we get lost a lot, miss major sites (like the subterranean crusader's city in Akko), and don't spend long in one place. Peter has expressed admiration for the fact that I've refrained from hitting Norman with the map, but I keep reminding him I've gained many virtues from this trip, patience being one of them. In fact, I've found the whole experience a thorough pleasure.

The funniest time was last night, heading to the kibbutz for dinner. Norman wasn't clear if the invitation was to dinner in the communal dining room or in Yehuda's home, or where either of those was. So we drove onto the kibbutz and wandered aimlessly around in the dark, not having a clue where we were or where we were going, Norman mumbling throughout. We finally sat in the darkened parking lot of the closed sandal shop and waited for someone to find us. Sure enough, eventually Yehuda came slowly bicycling out of the black night to lead us to his home for dinner. I was convulsed with laughter in the back seat.

FEBRUARY 24—BEERSHEVA BUS STATION— WAITING FOR BUS TO EILAT

War preparations are continuing. The latest idiocy is a government proposal to distribute antibacterial vaccines door-to-door. Can't you just see us all sitting in sealed rooms with our gas masks on, shooting up!

I was primed to accept war in Israel, but I've been surprised by the extent of petty crime. After dinner last night we dropped in on Dvora's friend, Hannah, a 70-year-old sculptor who lives in an exotic apartment in an old Arab house overlooking the Old City. Unfortunately, it's located on the edge of an Arab neighbourhood, and neighbouring Arab and Jewish areas tend to rub each other the wrong way. Hannah has been mugged a couple of times by young Arab thugs and is now nervous about living there. So the place is on the market for a cool Cdn$1,120,000. Chaim's new car (not even one week old) was broken into, radio and speakers stolen. Apparently, it's an everyday occurrence.

I'm also astounded by how hard people work here. Everyone seems to have more than one job. Dvora is basically doing three and making just enough to support herself. She's employed at the Jerusalem Mediation Institute, is doing a project for the government trying to clarify funding for mediation services, and is working with a colleague to try to establish a new delivery method for mediation services. Everything overlaps, but is separate. Business seems to be conducted at an intense pace with major emotional involvement by all parties. The possibilities for conflicts of interest are huge, and the ground is constantly shifting. One day something's a done deal; the next, it's fallen through and you start again. The stresses of everyday life here are enormous. Living is expensive, salaries are low, change is constant, anxiety is ever-present. Yet Dvora loves it—is thriving on it, in fact. It's exciting. And, as a Jew, she feels connected to a larger purpose. It's not a lifestyle I could take for long, but I do understand its appeal.

FEBRUARY 25—EILAT

The Lonely Planet guide said it and it's true: Israel occasionally feels like one long camp-out. From Beersheva south, we appeared to be in the middle of a Scout jamboree. It was us, one other civilian, and the Israeli army on the bus. We stopped at just about every army base in the Negev to drop off and pick up troops, all of whom look about 16 years old. No wonder most people thought we were crazy when we insisted on going to Eilat via Beersheva and Mitzpe Ramon rather than taking the direct route. But Dvora's advice was right. It was worth it. We've travelled through wonderful, vast lunar land-scapes. The three largest craters on earth are in Israel—and we drove right through the middle of the largest of those. Occasionally we'd pass Bedouin encampments. Forget the romantic image; these are shabby black oilskin tents, a flock of goats, and a goatherd. Only briefly, at Avdat, an ancient hilltop city, did a line of camels outlined on the brow of the hill provide the stirring tableau my soul craves. For the most part, it was stony desert covered with the tracks of army vehicles.

The arrival into Eilat, with the soft folded mountains of Jordan gleaming purple and blue in the sunset, was spectacular. My knowl-edge of geography is pitiful, and I hadn't realized that Aqaba is right next door. Eilat is just a tiny Israeli toehold on the Red Sea. Jordan is cuddled up east, Egypt is 6 kilometres to the west, and Saudi Arabia begins just 25 kilometres south. Having travelled from the Golan in the north to the Red Sea in the south, I now truly understand the Israeli sense of vulnerability.

MARCH 4—EILAT

Eilat would not normally be my choice of vacation destination. The town is a totally artificial tourism invention and a little honky-tonk to boot—a cross between Coney Island and a minor league Miami Beach. Here we've encountered our first, supposedly typical, surly Israeli service. By Australian standards, the beaches are pathetic; even by Canadian standards, they're pretty puny. But we've had a great time anyway. We're clearly getting easier to please.

We indulged in one excursion on Friday—a day trip to Petra. As usual when we do a quick trip, I find myself wishing we'd taken more time, gone on our own, and stayed for a while. Petra is an extraordinary place, a pink jewel of a city carved out of the desert hills of Jordan. The city and surrounding country are worthy of long, quiet contemplation, but we're feeling travelled out at the moment. The thought of more day-to-day decisions, more buses, more lugging of bags seems more trouble than it's worth. We want it easy or we don't want it. We'll come back to Jordan and Petra another time.

Aside from its stunning physical beauty, the highlight of our day in Petra was finding Marguerite Orthman. She is a New Zealand woman who visited Jordan, met and married a Bedouin, and whom our friends, Nery and Michael in Queenstown, suggested we look up. When they first mentioned the idea, I wondered how on earth we would find her, but it was dead simple. On the main walk through Petra was a sign saying Bookstore, and there she was. We stopped and chatted for a while and were introduced to her husband, Mohammed, but couldn't stay as long as we would have wished. Next trip. (In one of those weird coincidences, when we returned to Victoria, we were talking to a friend of a friend and mentioned locating this New Zealand woman married to a Bedouin and living in Petra. "Oh," she said. "Marguerite. Is she still there? I thought they had split up and she had headed back to New Zealand." We were able to fill each other in on all the gossip and latest goings-on of Marguerite whom she had known years before in New Zealand.)

The trip to Petra was also notable for the police presence. A police officer joined our bus at the Jordanian border and police cars escorted us fore and aft. It seemed a little excessive, but we tried not to pay too much attention. At one point, in the middle of the desert, our little caravan stopped dead. Furious negotiations ensued. After a lot of yelling and arm waving, we set off again, leaving the police escort cars behind. Apparently on the previous Friday, there had been a major riot in Ma'an, a city close to Petra. We were later told that Fridays are volatile days at the best of times, as people emerge from the mosques all stirred up and ready for action. Funny how no one ever mentions these things to you when you're booking a trip.

Otherwise, we've spent our days in Eilat lolling about on the beach, snorkelling, horseback riding into the hills, taking a cruise along the coast, spending a day in Taba just over the Egyptian border with a new friend met on the trip to Petra, and just generally taking it easy. It's remarkable how relaxing it is being on holiday as opposed to travelling.

Once again, the trip dilemma strikes. Having made plans, I'd now prefer to change them, although I'll not tell Peter that. Now that we're in the sun, I'd rather stay here, go to Sinai and Egypt, Turkey, Italy, than return to England. Outweighing that, however, is a commitment to Rosalynn and Martin to house-sit for them, as well as the practical financial reality that we could stand to spend less, not to mention that we're tired of moving around. I just hate to give up the sun. And I love the exoticism of this part of the world.

MARCH 5—JERUSALEM

I did, of course, talk to Peter. (Have I ever been able to keep my mouth shut?) The reality is that, on a trip like this, you simply can't know in advance what you're going to want. In January, when we made our plans, I was sick and tired and desperately wanted just to feel comfortable. Now I'm well and rested and ready to keep going. Peter, on the other hand, is ready for some contemplative time and really looking forward to Yorkshire, despite the likely weather.

We took the direct bus route back to Jerusalem yesterday via the Dead Sea. Comparatively speaking, this area is considerably more built up, but it's still very strange to see people getting on and off the bus in the middle of seeming nowhere. The trip also included the unexpected thrill of being confronted with the desalination plant at the south end of the Dead Sea. How can you not love a country that is in a constant state of high tension or suppressed hysteria, which prides itself on its warlike reputation, but which transforms a practical necessity like a desalination plant into a work of art? A fairground erupts upon the calm beige desert. Giant red and yellow roller-coaster tubes channel the waters of the Dead Sea through orange and green Ferris wheel sorters into blue and purple funhouse storage blocks. You gotta love it!

Today we were drawn back once again to the Old City. We wandered the *souqs*, the old markets, looking for gifts for the folks back home. What a difference a week makes. The Jerusalem we're seeing now is a totally different city from the one we first experienced. The threat of war has receded. It looks as if at least a temporary diplomatic compromise has been reached. People are flooding back into the streets. The city is noisy, people are rushing everywhere, the *souqs* are crowded, the shopkeepers are smiling. What we saw our first week was a nation in shock. This feels more like the real thing.

MARCH 6—JERUSALEM

The ethnic and religious craziness here is discouraging. We were at Damascas Gate this morning, watching the Arabs pouring through on their way to the Temple Mount and the mosque for midday prayers. Colours and costumes straight from the Bible with faces to match. And overlooking it all from a window above the gate, a lone Israeli soldier with rifle at the ready.

After enjoying the colour and chaos at Damascas Gate (soldier notwithstanding), we set off on a walking tour of Mea Sharim, the ultraorthodox Jewish part of the city. What a gruesome expedition. Dour, unhealthy, unhappy-looking people, crammed into eighteenth-century Polish-ghetto-like conditions. Litter everywhere. Children pale and undernourished. The atmosphere was claustrophobic and totally unwelcoming. I had asked in advance about clothing and was told just to ensure I was modestly dressed. I was covered neck to wrists and ankles but that didn't prevent one passing woman from hissing at me for not wearing a skirt. The difference between these folk and the Tel Avivi crowd of miniskirted, high-heeled young people on Ben Yehuda and Ben Hillel Streets is light-years greater than that between the Jews and Arabs.

We had coffee this afternoon with Dvora's friends Irela and Moralie. Moralie is a retired general, a former aide to David Ben-Gurion. Meeting them brought home once again how short the history of Israel is—and how complicated its problems. Irela and Moralie are secular Jews, as are most of the people we've met. One of their daughters, however, is married to an ultraorthodox Jew. If they want their grandchildren to be able to visit and eat in their home, they have to keep a kosher household. To make things even more complicated, a second daughter is married to a Palestinian. (And we heard from Dvora after returning home that the third daughter has married a black Muslim from the Sudan.) Israel is not a country with a high tolerance for diversity. This is not an easy situation.

This trip is making me downright antireligious. The extremists we've encountered—Hindus and Muslims in India, Catholics and Protestants in Ireland, fundamentalist Jews and Arabs in Israel, not to mention the Christian sects here—are enough to convert you to atheism. At least you'll do less harm.

MARCH 8—JERUSALEM

Yesterday being Shabbat, Dvora suggested we get out of town on an excursion to the Judean desert with her friend Lorna. Lorna is a sculptor who has lived in Israel for twenty years. She is South African by birth but true to the spirit of the *sabra,* the cactus fruit Israeli-born Jews have proudly assumed as their symbol, she is one of the prickliest people you'll ever meet, at least on the outside. There were moments when I thought it was going to be a long day, and Peter thought we were going to come to blows. In the end, I rather liked her, but only in small doses.

The Judean desert is magnificent—but full. We sat to enjoy the view, the silence, and the seeming emptiness. After a few minutes, a Bedouin boy with a radio tucked under his arm appeared around the hill on his burro, followed by his dog. He joined us. The five of us sat in companionable silence, gazing across the *wadi*, the dry river valley, to the distant hills. Something seemed to be moving. Gradually movement took shape. The Israeli army was conducting manoeuvres on the hill across from us. The boy's goats appeared on the hillside behind. All-terrain vehicles were spotted in the distance. This country is too small for solitude.

We visited St. George's Greek Orthodox Monastery, a quiet oasis, built into the side of a *wadi*—seemingly inaccessible but very welcoming. Greek Orthodox monks have lived and worshipped here for hundreds of years. In Israel you're always tripping over the unexpected and inexplicable. Then we drove on to Jericho in the Palestinian Territory. I know it drives some Israelis nuts (Lorna included), but I found it stirring to see Palestinians flying their own flag. It may just have been my imagination, but I thought they walked a little straighter and prouder here. (Although passing the compound of the Palestinian Society of Martyrs does give one pause.)

We enjoyed a leisurely lunch under orange blossom trees, listening to the music of the legendary Egyptian singer Oum Khaltoum, before heading back to the Old City and tea at Lorna's apartment in the Jewish Quarter. Once home, she explained that she had been anticipating trouble driving around the Palestinian Territory in a car with Israeli licence plates. No wonder she had seemed so uptight. What had been a lovely, relaxed day's outing for us was a traumatic experience for her.

In the evening, we set off to provide Nomi with some relief from her mother who is visiting in anticipation of the baby's birth. There we were, having dinner in Jerusalem, in a spaghetti restaurant (listening to—who else?—Céline Dion) with Martin's first wife, Shani, his second wife, Dvora, his daughter, grandson and son-in-law. In a few days' time we'll be having dinner with him and Rosalynn. I'm not sure if this feels cozy or crazy.

MARCH 10—JERUSALEM
Yesterday, we headed to the beach south of Jaffa with Dvora and Chaim. We had a lovely lunch at Turquoise overlooking the sea, then lay out on the sand, reading and snoozing the afternoon away.

I love the chaos of Israeli beaches. There were the four of us: Chaim, a large and imposing presence, with his curly greying beard, booming voice, and eyes glowering like an Old Testament prophet; Dvora in a charmingly ludicrous flowered hat that made her look like Minnie Pearl; and Peter and I in full tourist regalia. Beside us was an Arab family—mother in traditional Muslim gown and head covering, her daughter in modern business suit, and a mentally challenged teenage son being introduced to the water by two older brothers. At various times, a car, motorcycle, or all-terrain vehicle would race along the beach in front of us. A young man on a wild-looking Arabian horse with different-coloured eyes cantered back and forth while a motorized light aircraft flew low overhead. A fisherman stood out on the reef, gracefully casting his rod repeatedly, while a middle-aged man to our left pursued a bizarre chicken-like form of Tai Chi, totally oblivious to everything going on around him. And this is the low season! If Australians have turned the beach into art, Israelis have transformed it into circus.

Today we experienced the surreal contrast of Yad Vashem, the Holocaust Memorial, and Purim celebrations. We kept putting off going to Yad Vashem, but it wouldn't have felt right to leave Israel without seeing it. It's thought-provoking, enormously sad, moving, and surprisingly beautiful. We exited, however, into full Purim preparations. Purim seems to be some kind of Jewish combination of Halloween and *Carnivale*. We shared the bus leaving Yad Vashem with four young women dressed as cats—tight black bodysuits, white velvetine ears, neckties and tails, and painted faces. They looked as if they were about to serve cocktails in the Kit Kat Klub. Downtown it was more of the same. Devils, sheiks and their harems, scantily clad bunnies and witches wandered the streets. This must be a nation of orphans—these girls can't have mothers.

Our last night in Israel was enlivened by Nomi's giving birth to a little girl, Ella. We didn't get much sleep, but we can bring news of his first granddaughter to Martin.

We have dearly, and unexpectedly, loved Israel and felt amazingly at home here. It's largely due to Dvora who has wrapped us in warmth and welcome, but it's also something about the place. For all its lunacy and paranoia, in the face of innumerable constant fears, there is something nonetheless comforting about Israel. Jerusalem, in particular, feels like everyone's beginnings. A friend of Dvora's captured something of the essence: "In America," he said, "I used to be a fat, cigar-smoking, middle-aged Jew. Here, I'm just a fat, cigar-smoking, middle-aged guy."

Stage IV

Homeward Bound

NINE
IT'S TIME TO COME HOME

It may come on you slowly. It may hit in a blinding moment of clarity. It may be forced upon you. You may fight it off. You may welcome it with open arms. But at some point, you will realize it's time to come home.

With luck, your homing instinct, time, money, and energy will all be in sync, and homecoming will be as positive a part of your experience as the leaving. But it doesn't always work that way.

SOMETIMES YOU HAVE NO CHOICE

The decision to come home may be taken out of your hands. Things happen while you're away, and some of them may dictate when you call it quits.

I heard through a friend about a couple who had the worst possible homecoming. Their year-long exploration ended suddenly at the six-month mark in a car accident in South Africa. The man was badly injured and needed to be transferred back to Canada for extensive medical treatment. The person who told me about this couple reported that, a year and a half after the accident, their major regret is not the accident per se, but the fact that it interrupted their travels.

Janet made the decision to cut her year short by four months not for physical reasons but for emotional ones. It was clear that her marriage was over, and there were things that needed to be done at home.

> I had to get out of France. For real practical reasons like needing to get some legal assistance. I'd run out of money. I just had to get out of the situation I was in. It was horrendous. Coming back here was better than staying there.
>
> Janet

In Suzanne and Trevor's case, it was the death of Trevor's father that brought them back three months ahead of schedule.

There is no fighting these kinds of signals. Reality rears its head, and there is no decision to be made. You do what you need to do and you adapt. The only thing to be hoped for is that your time away has prepared you to deal better with the realities of "normal" life.

Larry and Rita's sail around the world came to an abrupt halt when word reached them of financial mismanagement at home. They will never recover financially, but they have come to emotional grips with what happened. "I think the time away really strengthened us personally as individuals and as a couple," Rita told me. "I handled it a lot better than I would have if we had just been away for a short time. You develop a sort of fatalistic attitude. This has happened. We can't change it. It's not going to undo. We just have to deal with it." They likened it to being on their sailboat and hit by a gale in the middle of the night. There's no point sitting and crying about what's happening. You just deal with it. "It was just an afge," said Larry. "An afge?" I asked. "Yeah," said Larry, "just another fucking growth experience."

Grow you will. And a good thing too because coming home early presents its own challenges. Chances are you have rented out your house. You may have no place to stay.

> We had planned to be gone for a year and had rented out the house. I guess as a landlord I could have been an asshole and evicted the tenants, but they were on a year's sabbatical from Missouri and they had their house rented out. And they were being good tenants. I wasn't going to mess them up. So I and the kids ended up living with my mother, and my husband was sleeping on a couch in the basement because I couldn't get rid of him yet. He refused to leave. He didn't want to be separated from the children. My poor mother ended up putting up with all of us. She lives in a townhouse on a golf course where kids aren't allowed, so there are no facilities for children. She had a room for the kids and they had their own bathroom, but I slept on one couch and my husband slept on another couch for three months. It was a real nightmare.
>
> Janet

It doesn't have to be that bad. Thankfully, it rarely is. But coming back early can present logistical problems that call on the reservoirs of flexibility you developed during the trip.

> We didn't move into our house because we were a couple of months early. So we ended up renting a little townhouse on Beacon Hill Park. It felt like we were in somebody else's life. We splashed down in Victoria but they got our lives mixed up with someone else. The transition was awkward, very, very awkward. The girls went back to school for the last month. Can you imagine! It was strange for them. The pattern was all mixed up. But we made the best of it. We just kind of hung out. spent a lot of time outside in the park, and went for a lot of walks, kind of looking around.
>
> Suzanne

SOMETIMES YOU'RE JUST NOT READY

The opposite can also happen. Sometimes you set a date for coming home, or you have one imposed upon you, and then you realize you're simply not ready.

> We were in the airport in Los Angeles on our way back home, and Ian was wildly doing numbers and figures. Looking at the figures, I saw that they didn't have anything to do with our holiday budget. I asked him what he was doing. He replied that, if we sold all our assets at home, we could travel for another six years.
>
> Jocelyn

You can't always act on your instincts, no matter how much you'd like to. But, sometimes, you can stretch your break a bit. Marie knew from the start that she needed a long break from work. She had requested an eighteen-month leave of absence but was given a year. Nearing the end of the twelve months, she knew she wasn't ready to go back and, fortunately, was able to negotiate an additional three months.

I knew from the beginning that I wanted more time—that I would need more to do what I wanted to do. But the problem was, I was starting to run out of money and so there was a trade-off there. I decided to opt for three months instead of six. I really wish that I had gone for six. I built my home and I didn't have enough time to live in it. I would have liked to have had three more months just to live by myself in that house doing nothing.

Marie

On her return, she encountered a problem of a different type. Her condominium council presented her with a bill for $6,000 for renting her condo for a longer time than permitted by the bylaws. She's still arguing this one in small-claims court.

AND SOMETIMES YOU JUST CHANGE YOUR MIND

Peter and I simply changed our minds, numerous times, as we went. We had set off with the idea of travelling for ten months and spending the final two enjoying a Victoria summer. We left open the option of extending our time away if we found a place we didn't want to leave.

By January, we were a little homesick—undoubtedly helped along by Christmas and illness—and we started considering the possibility of returning not later but earlier than planned. By April, that possibility had begun to solidify. After spending a month in Yorkshire, it was clear that time was taking on a whole new meaning. We couldn't believe that a month could disappear so quickly. Our planned two-month re-entry in Victoria was going to evaporate. It wasn't going to be anywhere near long enough to give us the decompression period we thought we needed.

We still weren't ready to make a final decision. We talked to Barbara, who was renting our house, to see how flexible she could be. With her blessing, we decided to hold off a final decision until we had hit the road again and discovered how we felt. But, in our hearts, I think we knew.

HOW TO DECIDE

At many points in the trip, we felt down and homesick and tired and frustrated, and we thought to ourselves, "Oh God, I wish I were home right now." This appears to be a fairly common reaction. Most people have had moments, usually at about the three- or four-month mark, when they desperately wanted to touch base with the folks at home.

> It wasn't so much homesickness as wanting a break. I want to be back where I know. I even had dreams where I went home for a week just to say hi to everybody and then left. I didn't want to come home from the trip; I just wanted to visit.
>
> Mike

It was the same with us. We didn't want to give up on the trip. We just wanted a break. But it wasn't possible. So, we swallowed the home-sickness or the frustration or whatever it was and we moved on.

There is a qualitative difference between those momentary, deep-felt bouts of depression and the quiet but insistent tug of the homing instinct. One is sudden, dramatic, painful, and over quickly. The other is a gentler, simmering reminder. You'll recognize it when it happens. Whether it comes upon you gradually or you wake one moment with certainty, the day will come when you realize you are looking forward to being home with even more joy than you are anticipating the next new experience.

It's not that you're not having a good time. In fact, you really know you're ready to come home when you're having a fabulous time, but you still feel the tug that says "ah, home" and brings a smile to your face.

Our homing magnet had a geographical element to it. From the time we left southern Italy, we felt headed toward home. The farther north we went, the stronger the pull became, the more we wanted to be home, the sooner we wanted to be there.

> As we got closer to home, you get this kind of destination direction. It wasn't that I was tired of travelling but I just thought it's time to go home.
>
> Margaret

For us, this was proof positive that the decision to head home a month early was the right one. Italy and France are among our favourite places on earth. We love the food, the sun, the people, the passion. Our time there was close to perfect. Still, softly underlying our enjoyment was the pleasurable sense that we were headed homeward. Rather than thinking, "Isn't this wonderful? Why don't we rent a house and stay for another month?," we thought, "This is wonderful. Won't it be great to return for a longer stay some other time?" If we could be in Italy and France and still looking forward to home, it was time to return.

Home is a powerful force. It will call to you when the time is right. There will be no misunderstanding the message. The trick is to leave yourself open to respond. You shouldn't feel bound by earlier decisions or plans. Those were made under different circumstances, perhaps by a different you. That was then; this is now. You'll know when it's time, and you have to do what your heart tells you is right.

READJUSTMENT TIME

Keep your timing flexible, but make sure you build in time for a quiet period at home before you start working again. Coming home is a pleasure, but it is also a shock, no matter what the circumstances. I can't conceive of anything more difficult than returning home and going back to work the next week.

It can be done. Ian arrived home on a Wednesday and went to work the following Monday. He says it was okay for him. Margaret had a job interview three days after her return.

> It was real culture shock. It was harder coming back than going. Especially the way we did it—landing smack into a job interview. That was horrendous. I would never do that again. You adopt a different time schedule. Different issues are important to you. You need time to switch back. Coming back was hard.
>
> Margaret

Most people don't recommend this approach.

Everyone needs a slightly different readjustment time. We're probably at the excessive end of the scale, but we did love our three months at home. In talking to others, a month appears to be the recommended minimum to handle the transition back to real life with any degree of composure.

THINGS TO THINK ABOUT

- Don't consider yourself bound by earlier decisions or plans. Trust your instincts and come home when it feels right to you.
- The real homing instinct is a softer, more insistent pull than the depression- or frustration-induced "I want to go home" primal scream. You'll learn to recognize the difference.
- If the decision is taken out of your hands by forces beyond your control, what choice do you have? Adapt and make the best of a bad situation.
- Give yourself some quiet time at home before going back to work or looking for new work.

March/April:ENGLAND
Part 2—Aga Rules

MARCH 19—THORGANBY

We've been in England a week, but it feels like years—and worlds—away.

Drove up from London and arrived on Martin and Rosalynn's doorstep in considerably better shape than the last time they saw us in our guise as refugees from India. I'm pleased to have had the opportunity to demonstrate to Rosalynn that I am a functioning human being. Before Martin and Rosalynn left for North America we had one day of overlap to become reacquainted with Birkwood (I've never lived in a house with its own name before), introduced to the neighbours, shown where to buy a paper, the best place for groceries and, most importantly, to be inducted into the mysteries of the Aga.

The Aga is the traditional coal-burning stove of the English countryside, reincarnated in recent years in gas and electrical versions as the trendy stove of choice for real cooks. Our Aga has more to do with religious ritual than anything to do with housekeeping. It sits against one wall in the kitchen—a big, shiny, bright, blue, enamel monarch presiding over the house, quietly warming the kitchen, drying our clothes hanging from the ceiling rack, and keeping us supplied with hot water. Provided, of course, we feed it regularly and demonstrate proper respect. The Aga rules our lives. It must be fed at twelve-hour intervals. First thing in the morning I head downstairs to start the day's obeisance. I "riddle" the tray at the bottom to loosen the ash and take the night's deposit out to a pile in the yard. Then I head to the coal room outside the kitchen door, push my large tin feeder into the mountain of coal, and carry it into the house as the morning offering. I wait expectantly for the hiss and crackle that will reassure me my gift has been found worthy. Then I or Peter repeat the service in the early evening.

At first, I saw the Aga as some form of benevolent deity. If we provided appropriate care and attention, it would take care of us and keep our days warm and cozy. After a week of living with it, however, I'm beginning to understand the true nature of the beast. It's an unforgiving tyrant demanding constant attention or it goes into a sulk.

It took a few days to get used to the change of pace—staying in one place, in the country, by ourselves. But we're starting to find our rhythm. We are doing very little and loving it. Lots of sitting and reading and tending the fire (which is a great deal more cooperative than the evil Aga). The house sits in the middle of the countryside. From every room, we look out on farm fields and small woods.

Springtime in Yorkshire is a scene out of *Watership Down*. Thousands of daffodils brighten our yard. Rabbits and their bunnies are furiously digging burrows everywhere. Pheasants, filled with spring fever, chase each other all over the countryside including, unfortunately, onto the road, which is littered with dead pheasant bodies. Our bird feeders attract a constant stream of unfamiliar, beautifully coloured little birds that send us poring over the bird book. An occasional hare races madly across the neighbouring field. Yesterday I saw a stag in the field, although where it came from or went to I have no idea. Our surroundings are soul-restoring, but it's not quiet. In fact, the pheasants' croak is like shifting gears without the clutch in. It sounds like we're living in the middle of a race car-driver training school.

MARCH 22—THORGANBY

Charles and Dulcie, our neighbours and Martin and Rosalynn's land-lords, invited us over for dinner last night. So much for the stereotype of the standoffish Brit. These are nice, warm, outgoing, friendly folk and, in Dulcie's case, thrilled to indulge in a good gossip if the occasion arises. Our stock increased considerably when they found out that we actually know some of the real people fictionalized in Martin's novel. Sorry, Martin, we offered your life up on the altar of settling into the neighbourhood.

Martin and Rosalynn are vegetarians and keep a kosher house-hold, so we're using the local pubs for our meat hits. We're almost equidistant from The Jefferson Arms in Thorganby and The Drover's Arms in Skipwith. The food is better at the Jefferson but Julian, the bartender at the Drover's, has a way with words. He has already informed us that Charleton Heston, whom he dealt with at a hotel in York, was a "pillock," Twiggy, the skinny '60s model, was a "sweetie," and Tuesday night "the place would be heaving with young farmers."

We're starting to get out and see a bit of the countryside, which reminds me constantly of nineteenth-century novels and BBC costume dramas. It's as if nothing has changed in hundreds of years. I can't figure out if it's a tribute to the staying power of the earth or testimony to the inertia of the Brits.

Mum and Barbara have phoned on successive nights. Not only is it nice to be able to receive calls, Barbara had some good news for us—Mr. Ohri of Nandas Travel has come through and there's a refund cheque on the way for the unused parts of our India trip. We were also able to talk to Barbara about our coming-home date. One day, we're homesick and want to get back by the end of May. Another day, we think of the joys of Italy and France and are sure we'll need an extra month to savour them fully. We simply can't make up our minds. Fortunately, Barbara's flexible.

So far, the only problem I can see with staying put is that I'm going to gain weight. We go cheerily from meal to meal to tea to meal, and the fact that they're almost all vegetarian doesn't seem to make them any less fattening.

MARCH 23—THORGANBY

We've been exploring York, little by little, and in the best way possible—not by being tourists but simply by living here. The centuries-old buildings, the small winding lanes, the thick stone walls encircling the city—everything seems so familiar. All those hours spent reading historical novels have not been in vain.

Every shopping trip brings another discovery. Today's was the engraver. We bought a garden chair for Auntie Audrey's birthday and want to put a little plaque on it. We were directed to a tiny nondescript door with no sign beside a newsagent's. Up two exceedingly steep flights of rickety stairs we climbed to a tiny landing. There was barely room for the two of us to stand together. On the landing was another door—the bottom solid, the top barred—with a wizened little man seated behind the bars and a video camera recording all comings and goings. There were no goods on display and no sign of what might go on in the backroom. We outlined our needs in hushed tones more suitable to purchasing illegal substances, and headed back down the dark stairwell. But he took our order and presumably a few days from now we'll end up with a plaque—or something.

Yorkminster Cathedral is becoming a favourite haunt. We have wandered it by ourselves and with a volunteer guide. You could spend a lifetime there and never exhaust its supply of wonders. I was particularly struck by the heartfelt memorial placed by a grief-stricken husband in memory of his beloved wife who died at the age of 35 after having given birth to eighteen children! Perhaps if he had loved her more, he would have loved her less.

After a concert in the cathedral one night, they threw open the central doors for the audience to exit. It was a spectacular sensation, walking under those extraordinary ancient arches. I am not a religious person, but I am in awe of the religious impulse that drove artists and artisans to devote their lives to the creation of temples to their god. I've never understood why so many grand buildings don't allow the common folk to use the central doors. They always seem to be reserved for the Queen or someone equally exalted, and the rest of us normally have to make do with entering and exiting by side doors. What are they saving them for?

Yesterday was the most beautiful spring day imaginable, and we braved the Mothering Sunday crowds to head to Ilkley for lunch with an old school friend of Peter's father and his wife. Today, in contrast, is overcast, damp, and dull, and I think we will celebrate it by staying tucked up in front of the fire.

The Stupid Aga, as it has come to be known, has just done it again! That makes three times it has gone out in ten days. Must be some sort of record. I'm getting very tired of this. We plan our days around Aga-feeding—it's worse than keeping cattle—and then it dies anyway, for reasons I can't figure out. We're doing everything we're supposed to do, and it still keeps going out. Arg!

MARCH 29—THORGANBY

Just got back from Mickleton where we celebrated Auntie Audrey's ninetieth birthday in fine style. Lunch with a few close friends at her favourite restaurant, then home for an open house and tea with more friends and neighbours. There was lots of laughter and love and funny reminiscences. She had a great time, and so did we. The garden chair, with plaque, was a great success. She liked it so much she originally wanted to keep it in the house, but I think we've managed to convince her it was built for the outdoors. It thrills me that a few years ago we promised to be here to celebrate this day with her, and things have fallen into our laps to enable us to do it so easily.

We've declared defeat. The Aga wins. We decided not even to try to get back in time to feed it and, instead, flipped on the hot-water heater. Ah, freedom!

APRIL 6—THORGANBY

I thought that staying in one place in the country for a month would be conducive to serious thought and journal writing. In fact, it's been primarily conducive to lazing around and doing nothing. Our days have developed a lovely rhythm. After a leisurely breakfast, we head out for a morning explore, a visit to a stately home, a walk over the moors, a drive through the Dales, whatever strikes our fancy. Usually we head out for one place and end up sidetracked to another.

One day we set off to see Whitby (about 80 kilometres away) and never got farther than Pickering (30 kilometres). We wandered into a little church on the top of a hill where the walls were filled with extraordinary medieval murals. They had been covered during the Reformation and disappeared from public view and memory until the church was renovated in the early 1800s. For a few glorious years, the people of Pickering were able to celebrate their religion surrounded by these colourful, funny, bawdy vignettes until the local rector decided they were paying too much attention to the murals and not enough to his sermons and had them plastered over once again! Fortunately, they resurfaced in the twentieth century.

By the time we could tear ourselves away, it was time for our daily pub lunch. Then our usual day takes us back to beautiful Birkwood to read in front of the fireplace, take a nap, have tea, more reading, feed the Stupid Aga, prepare supper, cuddle up in front of the TV and fire in the evenings, and then off to bed. Quiet, wonderful days.

The best part of being at Birkwood has been getting to know Charles and Dulcie. We never expected to be so fortunate as to inherit friends with the house. This Saturday we took them out to The Jefferson Arms where we're becoming part of the scenery. (Céline Dion insists on following us.) It's easy to understand how Martin and Rosalynn have ended up staying here for so many years.

The only drawback of staying in one place is that you remember what it's like to have a home and miss yours all the more.

APRIL 8—THORGANBY
Yesterday was hair day. Peter and me at Toni & Guy's, York's newest and poshest hair salon, getting set to assault the continent. We're actually getting used to getting our hair done together.

The Irish peace talks are all over the news. It's been fascinating to have major political or philosophical debates taking place in many of the places we've visited. What's bizarre about this one is how much the process is like the endless Canadian constitutional debate. The consequences are more serious—they can be deadly, in fact—but the way of it is all too familiar – the phony deadlines, the posturing, the chatting up the media, the building of a sense of doom and gloom, the intervention of the P.M. You can watch it like a stage play. You know there will be a last-minute deal. That's the way these scripts are written. What's impossible to know is whether they can make it work.

APRIL 9—THORGANBY
It has finally hit me that we are coming to the last stage of our travels and looking at the final phase of our year off. I find myself wondering if I've made the most of my time. I've loved our trip, the sense of freedom, the people we've met, the opportunity to see how others live. But I'm coming back more or less the same person I left—or so,

at least, it seems to me—when I had hoped to grow and develop more, or at least more noticeably. My instinctive reaction is still to go into Type A mode when there are things to be done, and I still get frazzled when things don't go right, although my definition of "things to be done" and "things going right" is a lot broader than it used to be. I am both anxious to be home and sad to be nearing the end. In fact, I am the same mass of contradictions I have always been.

Shock! Evelyn, our accountant, faxed us the news that we owe approximately $5,000 in taxes—each (later revised to $5,000 for both of us). What happened? This puts us squarely on the overdraft side of our year's budget. Peter's upset and questioning the amount of money we've gone through this year. He's talking about heading home early. I'm upset too, but I can let it go more easily. I keep reminding myself that we would have been spending most of this money even if we had stayed home. Now that we're tracking it, however, it looks as if we're spending so much more. At least that's what I keep telling myself.

APRIL 10—THORGANBY
A perfect Good Friday. Weather abominable. Cold, rain, sleet, snow, and flooding in some parts of Great Britain. Worst Easter weekend in fifty years! Fortunately, we were able to spend it tucked up by the fire, watching *Ben Hur*, then off to The Jefferson Arms for beer and a burger, and home to watch the Master's.

APRIL 12—THORGANBY
Spent part of Easter weekend with English friends we met on their holiday in British Columbia a few years ago. Dave and Sue live in Cheshire, which appears to be enjoying the only good weather in England this weekend. It was sunny and lovely, and we wandered the green hills and dales as Dave took us on one of his famous "loops," which consist of driving aimlessly through the countryside at high speed.

To heck with history being made in Northern Ireland. All of England appears to be focused on Dierdre, a soap opera character from *Coronation Street*. She has just been wrongfully convicted of theft and thrown in the slammer. At one point on our "loop," we were talking about her when we rounded a corner and there on the side of a hill in huge letters written in lime was Free Deirdre—Justice Now. These people take their soaps seriously.

This afternoon, Easter afternoon, we are back at Birkwood. I'm looking out the window at bunnies of all sizes, frolicking and silflaying on the lawn, male pheasants with their gorgeous red faces chasing dusty little peahens. I feel blessed.

APRIL 14—AMBLESIDE, THE LAKE DISTRICT

Today we left Birkwood. Very sadly. I felt as if we were leaving our own home. And this is the woman who, in Israel, considered not coming here at all. I would never have imagined I would find it so difficult to leave. I really bonded with the place. It must have been the bunnies. Dulcie and her daughter, Rachel, dropped by yesterday to say goodbye, and Charles came by today. The teapot has been working overtime.

Martin and Rosalynn arrive home this afternoon, and we wanted to allow them to settle into their home without having to be sociable. Yesterday we did a mad round of housecleaning so that Birkwood would sparkle for them. This morning, we fired up the Aga for the last time before we left. I really hope Martin has trouble with it too. I'd hate to think it was just us.

Once we could tear ourselves away, we drove over the Yorkshire Dales to the Lake District. Initial impression: overbuilt, overcrowded, overcommercialized. After checking and rejecting a number of blah B&Bs—they seem to come from the same mould, slightly seedy with somewhat surly keepers—we found a lovely old farmhouse outside Ambleside. Our room is tiny but comfortable and there's a big sitting room overlooking a sheep pasture where lambs are gamboling in the twilight. This might be okay after all.

APRIL 17—MICKLETON

Things looked up considerably immediately following the last entry. We walked into town that night and found it enormously improved once all the crowds had disappeared. The only people left appeared to be hikers. I've never seen so many hiking boots in one place.

The next day, while the rest of England was hit with rain, hail, or snow, the Lake District was filled with sunshine and blue sky. After chatting over breakfast with the other two couples at the B&B, we decided to leave the car in the driveway and try a local hike they had done the previous day. It started with a hard climb straight uphill for three-quarters of a mile—strange how people never remember to tell you about those parts—but it was worth it. From the top, we looked out on one side over Ambleside and a distant lake; on the other, over Windemere and back to the Yorkshire Dales.

We returned to the B&B around 4:00 p.m., threw ourselves on the bed, and immediately fell asleep. By 7:00 we had recovered sufficiently to follow our host Paul's advice and drive around the Langdales (Langdale and Little Langdale), stopping at The Three Squires pub for dinner. What an extraordinary drive! The terrain becomes much more rugged, filled with jagged peaks. The road is unbelievably narrow—and I say that as someone who has now driven in New Zealand and Ireland—although Paul assures us that a connecting road over the passes is narrower still. It was staggeringly beautiful and gives me some idea why people are so crazy about the Lake District.

Today, we drove down to the Cotswolds for an overnight stop on our way to the airport. We have just had a lovely dinner with Auntie Audrey, Anne and their friend, Jean. They're all in great form. Auntie Audrey was cracking jokes. Her body may be falling apart, but her spirit dances on.

TEN
RE-ENTRY

Welcome home! But be prepared. Stuff happens while you're gone.

There is something enormously powerful about returning to the place you call home after being away for a while. At first, the comfort and familiarity envelop you. You can let everything go, safe and secure in your normal environment. Or so it seems.

After the initial euphoria of seeing family and friends, patting the cats, wearing different clothes, sleeping in your own familiar bed, things start to get a little out of focus. The bed's lumpy. The cats won't eat. The furniture looks awfully tatty. The rose bushes are scraggly. The basement seemed so empty when we left, and now it appears to be full. Did we ever actually wear all those clothes? Family and friends have their own lives. Is my niece ever going to have time to visit? How could my sister have broken the computer?

THE HOME FRONT
Coming back is harder than you might think. And some of your reactions may surprise you.

> I took ten months and I wish I'd taken a year. It would have been a better way to do it than just to plunge back into work.... I like to do things, so I thought I would hate it when I came back and wasn't working. But, in fact, by the time you take a year off, not having anything to do is quite natural to you. I didn't know that was possible. I loved not working. Now I know...
>
> Margaret

In contrast to Margaret's relaxed mode, my first six weeks back were a blur of frenetic activity. I couldn't slow my system down. I had imagined languid afternoons, swaying in the hammock, reading a book, napping. But I couldn't sit still. Ten minutes of hammock time and, whoops, the rose garden needs to be weeded. Five minutes of reading and, oh no, I forgot to clean out the kitty litter. Ten more minutes in the hammock and, my goodness, I'd better rush right out and buy that rope to tie up the bushes. There was always something to be done, at least in my mind. My system was so used to new stimuli that it couldn't adapt to just relaxing. I got a lot done, but it just about killed me—and Peter.

This activity level can also be expensive. Your new eyes see your old home in a different light. After nine months spent in a variety of exquisitely furnished bed and breakfasts, I couldn't stand our ragged living-room furniture. And our bed! Heaven knows we'd slept on a variety of different beds, from the plank in India to the sink-into-the-middle-and-never-emerge softness of Anne's Cotswolds cottage. You'd think we'd be used to anything. But our bed felt old and worn out and lumpy in all the wrong places.

I was overwhelmed by a nesting instinct. This was Home, with a capital H, and I was going to burrow in, fix it up, and never leave. There may also have been an element of subconscious guilt. After all, I had walked out on my beautiful home; I needed now to demonstrate how much I really cared. After years of buying nothing but essentials, I went into spending overdrive. Thousands of dollars' worth of new furniture later, we were more comfortable but deeply in debt.

Fortunately for Peter's sanity and our credit rating, this fit passed at about the month-to-six-week mark. I've since discovered I'm not alone in this madness. Marie decided her entire apartment needed to be repainted before she could unpack. Four months after arriving home, she was still living in the middle of boxes and paint cans.

VALUE SHIFT

A seemingly contradictory impulse kicks in at the same time. Almost everyone I've spoken with has experienced a heightened awareness of the meaninglessness of possessions and the freedom that not worrying about them brings.

> You have this preconceived idea about a whole bunch of things that you need in your life that you don't really need. I was so

shocked when I came back and started unpacking my clothes. I was appalled at how many clothes I had. You don't need all that stuff. When you're working, you get on this spending wheel and, I don't know, maybe it compensates for how bad you feel about work. But when you stop working and you come back and you look at the stuff you've accumulated.... It almost made me sick.

Marie

We realized how materialistic society is. How crazy and big this house seems. I still have problems with that. We lived in very small dwellings in France and I liked that. It's ridiculous the space we have.

Helen

I realized that you don't need very much.... I came back and wondered what we were doing with this huge house. We don't need all this space.

Margaret

Every traveller in a developing country returns with a similar reaction.

It's almost a cleansing experience to be travelling. You see people who are so happy in mud huts, so happy that they caught a fish that they can feed their family with. Simple things.

Larry

On the beach in Tahiti we found this old carved wooden paddle. It was half gone—half a paddle and a handle. I brought it back to the boat and we were going to chuck it over the side when I thought, Let's just hang on to this, you never know. So we strapped it to the back of the boat and carried it all the way to Tonga. One day we're anchored in a bay and this Tongan fellow comes by, rowing a little outrigger with a palm frond. I chatted with him for a few minutes and I gave him the paddle. Well, honest to God, you would have thought we'd given him the moon.

Rita

A shift in values is inevitable after experiences of this sort. This idea may be a little hard to reconcile with my fetish for new furniture, but the two actually do coexist. Along with the desire for the house to be fresh and clean comes an urge to purge it of non-essentials. After getting along just fine with one suitcase each for nine months, it was clear we didn't need all the stuff stored in the basement for our return. We thought we had cleaned house before we left, but it was nothing compared to the garage-sale pile we put together on our return. Nothing moved from the basement to the house proper unless we were absolutely convinced it was essential to our happiness. Very little was.

You always wonder whether the changes you feel immediately after returning will stay with you over time.

> I think a lot of the values gained from the trip are core values. I hope they are.... I think that we appreciate what we have, but I don't think that it has made us take it for granted. We are very aware of how fortunate we are.
>
> Rita

Ruth received a care package after they'd been in Bolivia for a while. When she came home, the friend who sent it asked how it had felt to be sitting in a fancy hotel, drinking champagne and eating smoked salmon, knowing how poor the people were right below her. Her answer: "Lucky."

Whatever your experiences, you too will come home feeling fortunate. And that feeling will last.

EMOTIONAL DISCONNECTION

My period of frenzied activity eventually came to an end, to be replaced by soft summer days of quiet contemplation. What continued even longer, however, was an unexpected sense of apartness.

> When we came home, it wasn't our friends who had changed, it was us.
>
> Rita

I knew it was unrealistic to expect to return home and immediately assume my old place in people's lives. In fact, there was nothing I wanted less. A desire to change old patterns of behaviour and relationships was one of the reasons for the time away. Nonetheless, I was surprised how long it took—has taken—is still taking—to reconnect to the lives around me. For the first few months, some part of me felt as if I were standing aside, looking on, being an observer rather than a participant.

Part of the reaction I had to being back was simply cultural dislocation. It takes a while to adjust to the fact that you're home and you're staying and this is your life again. Another more important aspect, I think, has to do with an unconscious desire not to rush too quickly into behaviour and relationship patterns that will shape your life for the foreseeable future.

I have found myself, not always consciously, reassessing relationships, and taking time to decide which I value and in which I want to invest time. I've made choices about who I called to say we're back and who I waited to run into. I recognize more explicitly than ever before in my life the value of time, and I want to spend it cautiously, wisely, and richly. This seems to be a fairly common reaction.

> The people who weren't really our friends, we've drifted away from. And the people we're solid with, we're even more solid. We don't have a lot of hangers-on in our lives anymore.
>
> Ruth

> It shifted some of our relationships a bit. People who could dream of having such an experience could understand where we were coming from. Then there are people who think that it's bizarre—why would anyone do this to themselves? It's really hard. You can maintain a friendship, but it's not the same kind of closeness.
>
> Margaret

You will probably discover some of your relationships changing. I find myself closer to some people and putting more distance between myself and others. I have a crystal-clear sense of who my solid, enduring, cherished friends are, and which people I like, sometimes very much, but with whom I am simply friendly. Your emotional life becomes simpler, clearer, and more enriching.

ATTITUDES TO WORK

You probably shouldn't do this type of trip too much before midlife, because your attitude to work may never be the same. Re-entry to the labour force after a period of freedom is not easy. This is particularly true if it's not what you had planned. For Larry who had to return to clean up a financial mess, "Work was a four-letter word." When I asked how he dealt with it, he was frank. "I burst into tears."

Even if you were always planning to return to work, your definition of what's important may never be the same.

> I think I'm dealing with things differently. I have a much broader perspective on work now. I don't think it is as important as I thought it was. The first day back, I laughed a lot because it just struck me as so funny some of the things that were happening. It was so ridiculous really, what people were getting all exercised about. They were small things. We spend a tremendous amount of time at work, worrying and fussing over things that are not important.
>
> Marie

> When I came back, I felt that I was in a little bubble watching the world go by.... All of a sudden, all that stuff that was so vitally important that you worked nights and Sundays and evenings and got up at 4:00 a.m. to do seem unimportant. It's not that I won't be a hard worker again or give less than 110%, but I think I will have a much different way of establishing priorities and deciding what I can let go and what I don't need to control or do.
>
> Janet

> It was hard for me to get back into work and probably hard for my co-workers as well since I refused to get back into the rat race....There's so much triviality.... So I really work very hard

at just trying to appreciate what I'm doing at the moment and not get into that total push and pull toward next week or next month or freaking out because I haven't got a project finished. It was so precious to be able to actually just sit and just be. I don't want to lose that. The world would be a saner place if more people could just be.

Rita

It's not only adults who feel the difference.

I feel more relaxed. The routine before was just too plain and straight. But now, every time I get up, it's different. Also, my attitude is more laid-back than it was before. Before I was worrying about where I kept my pencils— must have everything perfect. Now my pencils will be where my pencils will be.

June, 13 years old

Some things assume even more importance. Things like taking pride in what you do and wanting work that is worthwhile. Peter was clear that he wanted to try a different area of government work, one that gave him more personal satisfaction. He was willing to exchange status for interest. He accepted a lower-level position in order to do work he felt was meaningful and gave him the opportunity to learn something new.

The time off gives you the chance to take stock of what you want to do with your life. For many of us, that means having a clearer sense of the things we want to accomplish while we have the chance. You may find yourself heading in an entirely different direction workwise. Returning home was the perfect time for me to try writing for myself for a change. I cut my consulting business back to the bare minimum needed to support writing this book.

John decided to find a new line of work that would enable him to indulge a newfound passion.

I could have gone back to the government. I decided not to because we want to do more and more volunteer work and I wanted to have more flexibility.

John

Helen and Suzanne made the decision to spend more time with their children.

> The trip gave me the courage to do what I have been saying I
> wanted to do for many years. While I was away I just decided. I've
> been talking about staying home with the kids for years. I've
> been trying to break away. This is the perfect opportunity. Do it.
>
> Suzanne

> Before we went to Europe, I wanted to work for the Ministry
> of Health like you wouldn't believe. I wanted to be a policy
> analyst. I wanted my own little cubbyhole and to have my
> job and my job description. Now, it's not important.
>
> Helen

Whatever you return to, you'll approach your work with a healthier attitude, a broader perspective and a happier frame of mind. It may be the effect of your travel experiences or it may just be a result of getting a much-needed break.

> Until I was able to get away for an extended period of time, I
> didn't understand how very burnt out I was—emotionally,
> physically, spiritually, every possible way. I think just getting over
> many years of burnout has made me able to come back and
> have a different perspective about my work. It's that simple.
>
> Marie

Whatever the reason, your attitude to work will never be the same.

JOB DISLOCATION

Your attitude may be better, but chances are your job won't be. Taking time off hurts your career. It's the one almost universal negative about taking a midlife break. This seems to be particularly true the more senior a position you had prior to leaving. It's understandable, but it's a shame, for the individuals and for their organizations.

You return home filled with energy and new enthusiasm. Peter was looking forward to starting a new job to which he could bring renewed vigour and broader experience and perspective. Instead, he was shuffled into a holding position—interesting, but not particularly challenging—and spent the next three months seeking out a permanent spot for himself.

People forget you while you're gone. "Out of sight, out of mind" has seldom applied so well. It's a shock to come back, raring to go, and find there's nothing for you to do. Even the program specifically designed to help Peter and others take the break appears to have neglected the re-entry component. People who are supposed to be guiding your career avoid direct eye contact:

Oh, you're back. What are you going to be doing?

I don't know. I thought you might have some idea.

Self-employed people have it easier. But almost everyone who has attempted to re-enter a large organization, whether the public or private sector, has been disappointed by the lack of enthusiasm for their return. Structures have been reorganized; old contacts have moved on. Responsibility for finding a new position falls squarely on the shoulders of the person returning, regardless of any previous commitments.

> The expectation I had was that, within the system as a whole, there would be some effort made by somebody somewhere to assist me to try to find a place. I had value before I left, so I presumed that there was still some value in me. I've been back in a position as a special adviser to the CEO, one of those death titles which means that they created a spot that I presume will disappear shortly. And I'm left on my own to look around for things, which I've been trying to do but have not as yet been successful. I am finding it quite challenging to figure out how and where to fit in.
>
> Janet

In some cases, the career damage starts even before you leave, either because of others' perceptions or your own actions. Patrick found himself out of line for promotion from the moment he applied for Deferred Salary Leave. "My deputy minister took me aside when they were

creating a new assistant deputy minister position and told me I would-
n't be considered for it because I was on the program." Rita did the
damage to herself. She decided not to pursue a master's degree because
she would be heading off on the trip. She started slowly easing out of
her job by not taking on management duties and choosing to stay in
familiar areas. It was her choice, but it meant that, when she came
back, she had given up the ability to work full-time in her profession.

The career damage is real, but the situation isn't all doom and
gloom. Your trip experience may have changed your perspective on
what's important and given you the emotional strength to adapt.

> A lot of people who used to work for me are now leaping
> ahead and I'm stuck…. In some ways, I'm now able to say
> that's good. Before, I might have pushed really hard to get
> myself into one of those positions and wouldn't have been
> happy about it. I remember perceiving myself as being on the
> fast track or whatever, and now I'm quite happy to be at the
> level I am, where I'm still in control of my life.
>
> Patrick

REACTIONS OF OTHERS
Organizational inertia contributes to work re-entry problems. Few
organizations devote much attention to employee career development.
But there's more to it than that. I am convinced that part of the difficulty lies in some deep-seated, if rarely expressed or even acknowledged,
emotions. You may be surprised how much suppressed anger you
encounter on your return.

> I remember people treating me as if it was almost disloyal to
> have taken this year off while they were sitting there minding
> the fort and going through the hard grind of cutbacks and
> layoffs and I was prancing through Europe…. I remember
> somebody coming up to me, contempt in his eyes, saying,
> "You don't know what we've had to go through here. We've
> been laying people off. It's been tough." Well, look, you can
> do it too if you want.
>
> Patrick

On the personal front as well, reactions of friends and family can come as a surprise. It starts even before you set out. People talk about how "lucky" you are to be able to do this. The implication is that somehow it just fell into your lap.

> To a couple of people I said, "You know, I want to tell you something. Luck has nothing to do with this. It's a decision. We made a decision." The same person would make fun of me because, in the year and a half prior to leaving, we were on the ultimate penny-pinching budget. So every day at work, there I am with my little brown paper bag, and I got ridiculed to death about that. One person would say, "Eating out of a bag again, eh?" I would just smile because I knew that one day I'd be eating my lunch on the beach in Bora Bora.
>
> Suzanne

When you return, you may assume that people will be thrilled to hear about your trip. I spent much of my first month back going through mountains of photographs, selecting the best and putting them in books for easy reference. I can count on the fingers of one hand the people who have asked to see them. I don't push them on anybody. I wait for others to raise the subject. But very, very few people do.

> One thing I was disappointed in was that I felt that my parents didn't display a whole lot of interest in what we'd just done. It was very strange…. My dad seemed pretty excited before we left but, when we got back, it was like he didn't seem all that interested. It didn't seem like all that big a deal.
>
> Mike

> I can't believe the number of people who have said, "Tell me all about it," and within seconds, they are off describing the most mundane aspect of their job and their life.
>
> Patrick

Family and friends have their own lives. However mundane they may seem to you in your post-adventure bubble, their experiences are more important to them than anything you've done.

> We were actually inserting ourselves back into their lives. And I think it was just simply that we had forgotten what it was like to be totally involved in the stresses. There isn't a whole heck of a lot of energy to put out into different things, especially things that you don't understand. And so people would ask us about the trip and after about five minutes their eyes would start glazing over because they simply could not relate.
>
> Rita

By grabbing your dream and running with it, you force others to question their own dreams and how much they're willing to risk for them. These are not easy issues. It's hardly surprising that a lot of conflicted emotions come to the fore.

Retaining the goodwill of family, friends, and colleagues requires a fair amount of sensitivity on your part. The trip is your private experience. You have to refrain from talking about your experiences and showing your pictures and generally proselytizing about the wonders of a year away. You need to remember that other people's lives have been going on as well. They have stories of their own to tell. And, as one friend told me frankly, they may not want to hear about the glorious time you've had while they've been dealing with flooding basements and leaking oil tanks.

Fortunately, there will be a few core friends who are genuinely interested. They will welcome the opportunity to live vicariously through your adventures. You won't have to go entirely cold turkey. But do be prepared for the vast majority of your acquaintances simply carrying on as if you had never been gone. Like the spectre at the wake, you have to sit and watch and wait. Eventually someone will see you, understand that you've been through a life-altering experience, and ask you about it. But, unless you want to alienate everyone you know, contain the wonder of it all inside you until you're sure your audience is a willing one.

THINGS TO THINK ABOUT

- Expect things to look and feel different when you return.
- Watch your wallet. The temptation to spend may be extreme.
- Take advantage of a new perspective on possessions to get rid of a lot of accumulated junk that you previously thought was essential.
- Recognize that family and friends have gotten along just fine without you. You can't expect to waltz back into their lives.
- In fact, you may not want to. Take advantage of the opportunity to assess what and who is really important to you and adjust your life accordingly.
- Don't expect to walk back into work and find a spot waiting. Chances are you'll have to start job-hunting, regardless of what promises were made before you left.
- Your attitude to work will likely change for the better. Priorities will be different. Balance may be easier to find.
- Your career may suffer. Be sure you're prepared to accept a stall or a step backward.
- Don't be surprised if you're greeted with a mixture of anger, resentment, and envy. You've done something a lot of people think they would like to do but can't find the means or the courage to try. You may find yourself on the receiving end of a lot of mixed emotions.
- Try not to be overly evangelical about the benefits of a runaway. It's not for everyone.
- Exercise restraint in telling stories and showing pictures. It's been a year in other people's lives as well.

April/May: ITALY/FRANCE
Southern Comfort

APRIL 18—NAPLES

As always, arriving in a new city was a bit stressful. The hotel, which we arranged from York together with the flight, is great—perched at the top of a hill on the outskirts of Naples, complete with dynamite view (pun intended) of Vesuvius and the Bay of Naples. But the first evening got off to a bit of a rough start when we discovered that the tobacconist had closed for the night. This doesn't sound earth-shattering; however, it meant that we couldn't buy a ticket for the funicular to get to the Mergullina waterfront below us. Did I mention our hotel is at the top of a hill? A very high and steep hill. The closest restaurant is at the bottom.

After staggering and grumbling (on Peter's part—hungry again) our way down, Ciro's saved the day. Fabulous food in a setting worthy of an Italian movie. The place was full when we arrived at 9:00 p.m. and just kept getting busier. People were still arriving when we left around 11:30. Much to our delight, every corny Italian stereotype was present and accounted for: exquisitely tailored aristocrats waving cigarette holders; noisy three- and four-generation family groups; wealthy older men with stunning younger women; beautiful young lovers; and Ciro himself, who hissed something at our waiter in a pure Marlon Brando *Godfather* voice. The noise was pumping, the waiters hustled. God, I love Italy.

Today we set off to discover Naples. We bought transit passes for today and tomorrow, Sunday (no more missing the funicular for us), and headed off to the National Archaeological Museum (good collection, terrible display). Then we wandered our way on foot and by bus through the shopping district to the Piazza Municipal, saw some sights, found a bank machine, headed down to the Santa Lucia waterfront, and eventually found the restaurant we were looking for. After another wonderful Italian meal, we managed to miss a torrential downpour and found the right bus home in time for a siesta.

The small successes of travel.

It's such a relief that, despite the McDonaldization of the world, distinctiveness survives. This could be nowhere but Italy. The people here are clearly Italian, with incredibly strong, distinctive faces. Somehow they make North Americans look homogenized. Here, a nose is a nose and something to be proud of. Attitude is everything. It looks, smells, sounds, feels Italian.

APRIL 19—NAPOLI (you can see I'm becoming more Italian by the minute)

Today we mastered the intricacies of the Neapolitan transit system. Made it to Pompeii via funicular, *metropolitana*, and *circumvesuviana* ("trains" to the uninitiated). The latter got interesting when it simply stopped a couple of towns before Pompeii and everyone got out. There was an announcement in which the words "Pompeii" and "*autobus*" were discernible. A group of people, including an older Italian couple we had been chatting with, went running off to catch the bus. (Actually, they did most of the chatting. We smiled and nodded a lot and occasionally added a heartfelt "*sì*" or "*no*" as seemed appropriate.) We were persuaded by some locals to stay put and await the arrival of a "poolman" in five or ten minutes. All of this was in Italian, of course, which meant that we were never entirely sure what was going on. (My niece's Italian lessons, coupled with my Spanish, have given me just enough knowledge to think I know what people are talking about, but not enough to be certain—a potentially dangerous combination.) Sure enough, in a few minutes, the older couple came running back to catch the "poolman," short of breath, shamefaced, and muttering about "*solo in Italia.*" Apparently the bus was to Pompeii town, which is different from Pompeii historical site. We assured them these mix-ups happen everywhere, while internally preening ourselves on our superior travel skills.

Pompeii was fascinating. It's much larger than I had expected, although everyone who's ever been there says that, so I don't know why I wasn't expecting it. It provides a very clear idea of what an Italian city in the first or second century looked like. The houses are filled with colour—murals on the walls, mosaics on the floors. The streets are lined with amazingly well-preserved remains of bars and restaurants, reminiscent of a twentieth-century Italian city. In truth, the whole thing looked more like a modern Western city than anything we saw in India.

APRIL 24—CAPRI

Five days on the Isle of Capri have melded into one soft, languorous interlude. Capri bursts from the ocean, all mountains and crags and rocks and shadows, crowned by a sunny blue sky. After struggling up the funicular from the harbour to Capri town, I deposited Peter with the bags at a café in the *piazzetta*, Capri's tiny, perfect town square, and set off in search of reasonably priced accommodation, not a readily available commodity in Capri. But, with the help of the friendly owner of the Hotel Tosca, I was directed to the Casa Luisa.

Maria and her brother, both in their seventies I would guess, rent out five bedrooms in their home. For 80,000 lire (Cdn$64) a night, we have the find of Capri—a comfortable double room with spacious balcony complete with table and chairs for dining *al fresco*. We overlook the ocean and the Faraglioni, the offshore rock formations that are the symbol of Capri. The entry to the house is through a colonnade of wisteria, which leads to a rose- and cat-filled garden tended lovingly by Maria's brother. From the *parfumeria* on the main floor beneath our room waft the sweet scents of perfume and flowers.

Southern Italy really is about leisurely walks and long lunches, siesta and food again. Our Capri days are soft and slow. Morning strolls in the countryside to escape the crowds, a visit to the sleepy town of Anacapri high in the hills, wandering down unknown lanes to quiet delights. The greatest joy of extended travel is surely the luxury simply to *be* somewhere—no schedule, no rush, no hassle. What a marvellous place! In some previous life, I just know I was Italian.

But Capri, to be honest, though exquisite, is seriously overcrowded, particularly at this time of year by these damn school groups. Spring is the season for Italian students, the *ragazzi*, to be in *giro*, on school field trips. I wouldn't have thought it possible, but Italian kids are even noisier than Australian ones. And they are everywhere. What is it they pretend to be learning as they sweep at full voice through the lanes? We return home each day from our quiet explorations to be serenaded beneath our balcony by the shrieks of *ragazzi* calling out to every passerby, "Do you speek Engleesh? Do you speek Engleesh?" Over and over and over again.

Fortunately, by late afternoon, tourist noises are replaced by bird-song. Most of the visitors are day trippers who bail out around 3:30 to 4:00 p.m. Capri is ours!

It didn't take long to stake out not only our bar in the *piazzetta*, but our seats. The waiter knows us, and the number and type of nib-blies proffered with our Cinzanos increases daily.

In the evenings after dinner, we stroll through town, one evening to the highest lookout, the Belvedere Cannone beneath the castle. The lights of Capri were just coming on; the stars were emerging softly from the dimming sky. This has to be as romantic as anyplace on earth.

Yesterday we circled the island by boat and made the requisite visit to the Blue Grotto. As our boat entered the small bay fronted by an imposing cliff face, a school of tiny rowboats surrounded it like minnows. We scrambled into one. Our rower, Gino, headed toward a larger rowboat in which two older gentlemen sat solemnly. This was the ticket office. Gino asked us for 7 lire each. He handed the money to one of the gentlemen. The other carefully tore two tickets from a large roll and handed them to Gino, who conspicu-ously presented them to us. He then rowed a further 15 metres to another anchored boat and two more solemn older gentlemen wear-ing official caps. This was the tax office. Eight lire each was requested and received. (This may be the first time I've encountered tax greater than the price—at least so blatantly.) A receipt was issued. I'm convinced that something astonishingly corrupt is going on here, but I can't figure out what it is.

Business completed, the little boats lined up in front of a low opening in the cliff face. As our turn approached, Gino called out, "Lie back. Ready? Watch your heads." He pulled on a chain attached to the cliff wall and, swoosh, we're in. The blue water, caused by light entering from below, is beautifully blue. The rest is black—totally black. Just as we were starting to get oriented, it's "Watch your head. Ready?" And swoosh, we're out. That's it, folks. Ten minutes and about Cdn$20. Not too bad considering the laughs we got out of it, but not exactly a romantic experience.

APRIL 25—POSITANO

I wasn't sure anyplace could be as gorgeous as Capri. Then we came to Positano. It was a cover of *Travel & Leisure* magazine that prompted it. I took one look at that stunning photo of craggy mountainside terraced with organic buildings of pink, white, saffron and coral, all wrapped in clear blue sky and even bluer ocean, and I just knew there could be no more beautiful place on earth. I was right. The good ship *Uregano* slowly rounded the corner into the bay, and there was Positano gleaming in the sun, even more gorgeous than the picture.

After disembarking, we struggled across the sand with our bags, and I once again left them with Peter and went in search of a room. Up, up, up. Up steps and alleyways, past tourist shops and art galleries, past restaurants and grocery stores, past La Sireneuse, the town's famous five-star hotel, in search of the first place we might be able to afford. Only to stumble across the Albergo California. A couple we met at Wendy's B&B in Melbourne had told us wistfully about their stay here. It was meant to be.

Frank greeted me on the patio with a warm *"buona sera"* and an endearing tolerance of my wretched Italian. It was somewhat embarrassing to discover later that he speaks perfect colloquial English with a strong New Yawk accent. He led me to a large, spotless room and flung open the floor-to-ceiling shuttered windows to display the balcony and full panoramic view of ocean and Positano. This was the *Travel & Leisure* cover, and it was ours. Price ceased to matter. As it turns out, we can have all this for 160,000 lire including breakfast (about Cdn$125). Some might say I should have kept looking for something cheaper, but those would be people without souls.

Frank sent a porter down for our bags and I backtracked to rave to Peter about my find. Returning to the hotel, we were introduced to Maria, Frank's sister-in-law, who took one look at Peter's six feet, five-and-a-half inches ("God blessed us with more of you.") and upgraded us to her king-bedded room for the same price. We're now in the seventeenth century part of the Albergo, in a bigger room with a higher ceiling, complete with *trompe l'oeil* ceiling cherub, and the same extraordinary view.

Positano has a very different feel from Capri. While even more spectacularly beautiful, it doesn't feel as exclusive. The shops are not as ritzy, the hotels not as flashy. It feels more like a real community. It's noisier—we have a road below us—and people bellow. But no *ragazzi*, thank God.

Italians really do bellow, especially the young women. It's a hoot. They look so perfect and then they open their mouths and sound like longshoremen. They remind me so much of my niece, Michaela, and even my sister. I'm starting to understand better how difficult the transition must be for them from LIFE in Italy to the calmer attractions of Canada. Everything here seems brighter, louder, more dramatic, passionate. The simple ordering of a drink becomes a production filled with hand-waving enthusiasm. I had forgotten just how full Italy is.

I seem to have developed a perverse interest in plumbing. What do you suppose it says about national psyches that New Zealanders have teeny tiny little sinks and Italians have huge ones? And given that Italians are frequently people of ample build, why do you suppose they have such long skinny bathtubs? How do they ever get in—or out—of them?

APRIL 30—POSITANO

Yesterday we visited Ravello, which must be really beautiful because we saw it under horrible conditions and still loved it. The day started out well. The sun was out, the sky was blue, the air was warm. So we decided to explore the Amalfi Coast and, like idiots, left our jackets behind.

A light rain had already started by the time the bus along the winding coastline south from Positano to Amalfi arrived. What a drive! Standing in the exit stairwell by a floor-to-ceiling glass door on the Amalfi Coast bus route is no place for someone who's afraid of heights. At various turns, we seemed to be hanging out over the ocean with no net. It was terrifying for me and nauseating for Peter, who did his stoic routine and refused to sit in the one available seat even though he admitted he would feel better sitting down. (Does anyone really understand male behaviour?) In Amalfi, we switched to the little bus that climbs the mountains up to Ravello. Up, up, up. Still standing up. This one gets my nomination for nausea-inducement.

After reaching Ravello—and seriously considering taking up permanent residence in order to avoid the return trip—we set off walking to the Villa Cimbrone, former haunt of Greta Garbo. We caught only a brief glimpse of the famous view along the entire Amalfi Coast from the Belvedere dell' Infiniti, before the temperature plummeted and the skies broke. Within seconds, it was freezing and we were soaking. We raced for cover and stood huddling with a half-dozen other poor souls while the rain pelted down and at one point turned to hail. There we were, the seasoned travellers, in sweatshirts and me in bare feet and sandals!

The weather cleared up in the afternoon, and we decided to try the boat back. After a brief visit to Amalfi Cathedral (filled with the requisite noisy *ragazzi*) and a quick look at downtown Amalfi (a little honky-tonk but with a certain quirky charm), we waited in the sunshine on the wharf for the boat to Positano. We were tired and somewhat incoherent (Peter kept looking at his watch and mumbling, "My clock is long, my clock is long." It turned out he was trying to say, "My watch is fast.") but we were very happy.

This morning, it is raining again. "*Pazzo, pazzo*," as Maria says. I think a rough translation might be "It's crazy, but what can you do?" It must be time to leave.

It's clear to me now that the trip has changed character. Most of our contacts and real conversations here tend to be with other visitors rather than residents. Part of it is language, of course. My Italian is pretty rudimentary and Peter's is non-existent. But it's more than that. I sense that we have started on the road home. We are tourists here, not travellers. The distinction is primarily in our own minds, but it is real. Our time is no longer unlimited. We have a return date and everything now is shifted, however subtly, by that fact.

MAY 2—ROMA

A Fellini interlude. My niece asked me to look in on her father. So there we were, in my ex-brother-in-law Renato's tiny, dark, dismal apartment atop a veritable slum dwelling, listening to his neighbour, Miradona, a transsexual and self-proclaimed astral traveller, go endlessly on in Italian about parallel realities, spiritual healing, the properties of stones, etc. Looking on skeptically were Renato and his friend, Loredana, whom we met at dinner last night. Hanging on to every word was Mirella, Renato's 30ish, plump, pleasant, vacant, and possibly clinically mad girlfriend. Hanging in the background, trying to look invisible and succeeding only in looking visibly uncomfortable, was Peter.

Even Loredana, the only seemingly normal person in the room—excepting ourselves, of course—was weird today. She walked in and immediately went into this bizarre routine about smelling eggs. "I smell eggs," she said accusingly, before even saying hello. "I'm very sensible (read: sensitive) to eggs." We assured her repeatedly that none of us had been anywhere near eggs and eventually, reluctantly, she left the subject. When Miradona left, however, Loredana leaned over to me and whispered knowingly, "It was her. I can't smell eggs anymore." Under the circumstances, I thought smelling of eggs was the least of Miradona's problems.

The past twenty-four hours have felt like a lifetime. It's sad to think of a well educated, sophisticated man from the Italian upper classes, used to the best things in life, living like this. This apartment is the end of the line. Almost everything is gone, the result of a life-time of bad choices. In true Renato fashion, however, there may be nothing in the kitchen but one glass, three mugs, and four bowls, but he still has one remaining Pierre Cardin suit in the closet. He may not be my favourite person but, I have to admit, he has style.

After we left Renato sitting at his typewriter in his underwear, tapping out the pornography which now provides his only source of income, I could only rid myself of a raging headache by walking aimlessly for hours through the streets of Rome. We ate meagrely in a Chinese restaurant and are now sitting in the Café Peru—I kid you not—outside the train station, waiting for midnight to board the overnight train to Nice. Not a moment too soon!

MAY 3—ST. JEAN CAP FERRAT

We pulled into Nice yesterday morning, filthy and somewhat rumpled, but cheered by sunshine.

The night train from Rome was a pit, covered in graffiti, no showers, two toilets for the whole car. And this was first-class! We were made even more comfortable by Italian media reports of women being murdered in train toilets. Not to mention the admonitions of Renato and his friends not only to lock the compartment door but to erect a barricade to wake us up when, not if, someone tried to break in.

Refreshed by *un chocolat et un croissant* on the boulevard des Anglais, we picked up our rental car and attempted to make our way to Cap Ferrat. This is a task more easily contemplated than accomplished, particularly on Sunday when Nice closes half its streets to cars. We were also aided by our helpful Gallic car rental clerk who insisted on speaking to us in his abysmal English (far worse than our French) and who gave clear directions to turn left, then left again. What he really meant, of course, was right and right again. Aha!

Finally, we made it. Neither one of us knows exactly why we chose St. Jean Cap Ferrat, but we're glad we did. It's an upscale, quiet Riviera community. There are three beaches within walking distance, three pedestrian walkways of varying lengths (20 minutes, 1 hour, 2 hours), flashy yachts in the harbour, and great people-watching from our corner bar. We found a charming little two-star hotel, L'oursin, on the main street. Very French and, at 450 francs a night (less than Cdn$100) including breakfast, it's a perfect spot from which to explore this part of the Riviera.

MAY 4—ST. JEAN CAP FERRAT

Yesterday, we had a quiet day wandering around town, lying on the beach, and generally recovering from Rome. Today, it clouded over a bit, so we decided to start exploring a little further afield. First stop, Eze, a medieval hilltop town—touristy, but with great winding narrow streets and a collection of seriously good artisans. We were fortunate to visit it without hordes of other tourists. I suspect it's a zoo in the summer.

Our hostess at L'oursin suggested that we visit nearby La Turbie. We weren't sure why, but one thing we've learned is to pay attention to the suggestions of locals. La Turbie, which doesn't appear in any of the major guidebooks, is the site of one of the most spectacular monuments on the Riviera. Towering over the countryside is a huge 2,000-year-old memorial to the Roman conquest of the Gallic tribes—the Trophée des Alpes. This is a major historic site, a monument to the linking of the Roman Empire from Italy across France into Spain. It also boasts an expansive view of Monte Carlo, Monaco, and the coast. Why are they keeping it a secret?

We had a simple, perfect French lunch in a café in the square, where the owner was rightly proud of his homegrown gherkins and olives. "The best you'll ever taste," he whispered softly in French. He was right.

From La Turbie, we continued over narrow, twisty mountain roads, trying to find Reillons, which we had been told was an untouristed version of Eze. It's probably untouristed because it's almost impossible to find. Fortunately, we happened upon a friendly woman who was heading that way and volunteered to lead us. At the end of the road was an isolated, quiet, medieval hilltop town, soft brown and grey stone buildings piled haphazardly on top of one another. We were guided through the cobblestoned lanes by a big old shaggy dog, seemingly the only living soul about, except for the unseen man singing *La Marseillaise* as he swept his house. They really do this sort of thing! I've actually heard two people say "oo-la-la."

MAY 8—CAP D'ANTIBES

A succession of quiet days, exploring the countryside, lying on postage stamp-size Riviera beaches, and just generally hanging out. A highlight was our day in Monaco where we had lunch on the terrace of the Café de Paris in Monte Carlo beside James Bond's original Dr. No girl, Ursula Andress. Ursula was ravishing—but short, very short. Our waiter indiscreetly informed us that her plastic surgeon had done an excellent job. When he waited on her a few years ago, "She was all wrinkly," he reported. "But she looks lovely now."

We drove yesterday to Antibes, expecting a village and finding the second largest city on the Riviera. We quickly moved on to Cap d'Antibes, a quieter and less intimidating suburb. The people here have been lovely, totally destroying the stereotype of the aloof and snobbish French, but the peninsula that includes Antibes, Cap d'Antibes, and Juan-les-Pins just doesn't do it for me. Our original idea of using this as a centre from which to see Vence, St. Paul de Vence, and area isn't really workable. Distances look short on the map but it takes forever to get anywhere. So tomorrow, we'll head on.

MAY 12—ST. PAUL DE VENCE

Unfortunately, this is our fourth and final night at the Hostellerie des Messugues, a little piece of heaven in the hills above the Mediterranean. I would never have anticipated that we would so prefer the hill towns to the coast, but so it is.

In the mornings, we wander the countryside, tripping over extraordinary places that are almost commonplace here. We spend the hot, sunny afternoons in and beside the pool. After our siesta, we make our way into town for a drink on the terrace at the Café de la Place, where we watch the village *boules* players and eavesdrop on the incredibly salacious goings-on of the locals. (There is a real advantage to being in a country where you can understand the language.) Another marvellous French meal and home for a cognac on the balcony with the light of the full moon shining on the vineyard below, before falling into bed, as contented as it is possible to be.

Our pace since hitting the Riviera has seemed incredibly leisurely, but we've seen an enormous amount. To my surprise, a lot of it has been religious. We were the only visitors in the Cocteau Chapel in Villefranche (the village where Cary Grant's grandmother lived in *An Affair to Remember*). The chapel was specifically designed for local fishermen and Gypsies and is as vibrant, earthy, and true to their spirit as could be imagined. The Chagall Museum in Nice is filled with colour and a set of Biblical tableaus that present religion as a wonderful, joyous experience. The Renoir house and gardens, contentedly overlooking Cagnes-sur-Mer, may not be religious but they are definitely spiritual—a touch of old Provence, with an overgrown garden and the house left as if Renoir himself were likely to return at any moment. My favourite spot, though, may be the Matisse Chapel in Vence, a white, open, airy jewel of a place of worship, every detail planned with love.

I had always associated the Riviera with hedonism; I now find myself thinking of it as both a sensual and a spiritual destination. Overwhelming everything is the sheer beauty of the natural light and landscape. It is no mystery why so many extraordinary artists chose to live and paint here, and why so many noted sensualists chose religious themes for their art.

MAY 14—ST. TROPEZ

Now *this* is my idea of the Riviera. Head-turningly dressed people strolling along a café-fronted harbour filled with yachts. To my disappointment, the Riviera, with the exception of Monaco, hasn't been as chic as I had expected. There's lots of money in evidence. Rolls-Royces, Mercedes, BMWs, Ferraris, and Jaguars rule the roads. Yachts cram the harbours. Villas fill the hillsides. But the stores are not extraordinary and, for the most part, folks are folks. The one exception is the women. They are undeniably elegant. Our female taxi driver in Nice wore a stunning designer suit. The bag person at the grocery store in St. Jean Cap Ferrat put the customers to shame—slim, totally made-up, wearing fashionable pedal-pushers, and high heels. I thought she was just being friendly, when she started putting our groceries in the bag.

One thing that has impressed me on the Riviera is the size of the yachts. They are truly remarkable. In Victoria we may think we know something about yachts, but we don't. Yesterday afternoon, we sat on the port having a drink, watching a head-to-head yacht competition. The three-storey *Iroquois* was already docked, blocking out the sun, attracting a large crowd, when the *Louisianna* pulled in alongside. It was wonderful to watch the crew and passengers surreptitiously checking each other out to see which boat was bigger and better.

MAY 18—CASSIS

Once again, our trip circles in on us. We would never have come to
Cassis were it not for the recommendation of Martin and Rosalynn
who spent three months here last year. Cassis is perfect—a tiny port
lined with cafés and restaurants, two nice (by Riviera standards)
public beaches, beautiful countryside, and all of it small and accessi-
ble. We found the perfect little hotel, Le Golfe, where I sit now on
our balcony overlooking the port. We've decided to stay for a week,
then head up into the heart of Provence and on to Paris.

Yesterday we headed off to the unpronounceable Ollioules for
lunch with Peter's cousins, Jeanette and Bob. After an amazing drive
over the Route des Cretans, the highest seacliffs in Europe, we made
our way into the hills to their perfect Provençal home surrounded by
olive trees, overlooking a swimming pool and valley filled with vineyards. As we experienced on a previous visit with them in Paris,
Jeanette performed her usual magic in the kitchen and produced a
totally exquisite meal. For our parts, we looked good, brought the
right present (irises), and spoke stilted but acceptable French. All in
all a successful outing, although we couldn't eat another thing for
twenty-four hours.

Today we took a boat trip along the coast, exploring the *calanques*
(inlets, almost fjords) for which this area is renowned. We picnicked
on pâté sandwiches and wine and lazed on the beach. We are now
sitting in a bar on the port, enjoying our pastis and beer. The sun is
setting to my right. The last postcards have been written. We are
definitely on our way home.

MAY 19—BONNIEUX

Our luck is holding. We arrived in Bonnieux looking for five days'
accommodation, only to discover that this is Ascension weekend and
all of France seems to be heading to Provence. We followed a sign for
a small *pension d'hôte* (B&B) and found *Le Clos du Buis*, a small
treasure. There are, of course, complications (we'll have to move out
for one night) but nothing insurmountable.

The extent of French ingenuity when it comes to plumbing, particularly toilets, is a continuing source of amusement for me. In this

entire country, there appear to be no two toilet-flush mechanisms alike. Some you push, some you pull, some you press. Some are on top, some on the floor, some on a wall. Today I encountered an automatic one that flushes as you open the door to leave. (Only discoverable, of course, after you give up.)

MAY 20—BONNIEUX

From Les Terrasses du Luberon, our temporary B&B, we have a full panoramic view of the Luberon valley, vineyards, and hills. It's amazing that there are two such wonderful, inexpensive places to stay in this town. I sit here enjoying my ritual cognac after another great meal and marvel at the number of extraordinary views we have enjoyed from the most reasonably priced places. Sitting in the soft night, looking up at the star-filled sky, with the frogs snoring up a storm below, I find my heart swelling with gratitude to a God I don't believe in for the privilege of being alive and in the here and now.

A donkey just joined the frog chorus. It doesn't get any better than this.

MAY 23—BONNIEUX

Provence has been a succession of mornings spent exploring villages and afternoons lounging by the pool. Each town has its own distinctive feel: Bonnieux is bleak and black—closed. Ghosts haunt the abandoned cathedral at the top of the hill. The villagers are not yet resigned to the presence of tourists in their midst. Lacoste is silent, seemingly deserted under the shadow of the crumbling château of the Marquis de Sade. You know people live here—you can see the signs—the occasional car, laundry on the line, flower pots filled with bright red geraniums—but you never see the people. Menerbes has been changed forever by Peter Mayle and the popularity of his book, *A Year in Provence*. The *routier* is now a thriving restaurant. The tourists have arrived and the town will never be the same. Gordes has been used to tourists for ages, and its restaurants, shops, and wonderful town square welcome them with open arms. Apt's market is justly famous, filled with all the life and colour of Provence. Aix is gorgeous but feels a bit big and busy for us this trip. Avignon is filled with spirit. We *dansed sur le pont* and *baised* under it. Rousillon, awash in soft colour, is our favourite, I think. It has just enough tourist amenities, but remains a real place.

There's an eternal element to Provence, a dark side under the bright sun and vibrant colours. It's a seductive place, but I suspect no outsiders should ever delude themselves into thinking they'll be accepted.

MAY 28—HEATHROW AIRPORT
We're going home!

The trip up from the south of France was uneventful, but too long. We were anxious to get home. At some point, we had switched from holiday to in-transit mode and, in retrospect, we would have been better off to push it and reach Paris in one day. We splurged on first-class tickets on the Eurostar train through the Chunnel to London. I wouldn't do it again—economy would be just fine next time—but it was fun being waited on hand and foot, served an excellent four-course lunch with champagne, fine wine and cognac, while racing across the French countryside to the twenty-minute tunnel under the Channel.

Then it was on to Mickleton and a wonderful last day with Auntie Audrey and Anne. We said goodbye this morning and feel quite sad. Auntie Audrey looks great, but every time we've left her in the past few years, we wonder if this will be the last time. I suspect she is wondering the same thing, although, being a proper English family, neither she nor Peter would ever acknowledge it, of course.

What mixed feelings we have about going home. We're ready and anxious to be there and see everyone again. And we're a little apprehensive too. What will have changed? Us? Them? God forbid, nothing. What's ahead? Who knows? But we're ready to face it, whatever it is. It's true, you know. There's no place like home!

Stage V

There Are Places I Remember

ELEVEN
THE BEST OF TIMES/
THE WORST OF TIMES

The hardest question to answer is the one most people ask: What place did you like best?

How can you pick a best out of so many different, individually spectacular places? I try to answer because someone's waiting expectantly. I wrack my brain, trying to find something specific to say that will still be fair to all the places I can't mention.

> Best:
> Being with the family from France for two weeks in Bora Bora. We anchored in the bays, got together every evening to talk and share stories.
>
> Worst:
> Seasickness. The storms. Fear.
>
> Suzanne

I guess what stands out in my mind are the unexpected places. I didn't particularly expect to like Australia and Israel. We went primarily to visit friends, but ended up loving the countries. Or, I discovered I love deserts. I found a calm, a sense of peace, in the centre of Australia and in the Judean desert that has stayed with me.

Then I start to feel guilty because I've left out all the other wonderful places. I find myself rambling on: Ireland was another unexpected treasure. We hadn't planned on going there at all. Now we can't wait to go back. Or, Southern Italy, the Riviera, Provence were all spectacular. And, the people in Fiji and New Zealand were unbelievably warm and wonderful. We felt so welcome and at home. And, I still dream about our quiet month at Birkwood—the bunnies, the pheasants, the daffodils, the fireplace. . . . I end up running through the litany of places we've been (with the glaring exception of India) and notice eyes starting to glaze over.

Best:
The exhilaration of standing on the edge of Cape Horn and
seeing the Straits of Magellan—places I had only ever read
about...Meeting new people—people who are doing something totally different from you.... New adventures.

Ruth

Worst:
Being sick in Sancta at Christmas. Being sick away from home
is really bad.

John

What most people really want is a traditional travel story: Where did
you go? What did you see? What did you eat? Only one person,
Norman, understood that the real travel story is the internal journey.
It's the emotions that surge through you, the changes that overcome you,
that make the experience special. At first, I actively sought revelations
and, of course, they didn't come on demand. Instead, quiet changes,
subtle shifts in emotions occurred without my even being aware of
them. By the end of our journey, my spirit had developed in ways I
could never have imagined and still have difficulty articulating. But I
can recognize and feel the growth. Norman asked the right questions
when we saw him in Israel in February: What's been the best part of it
all so far? What's been the worst?

Best:
It was a really valuable and wonderful experience for the kids
to go to a foreign culture.

Worst:
A feeling of isolation. A feeling of lack of purpose.

Janet

The single best thing about the trip for me was the total absence of
responsibility. I found the freedom I was seeking. I had a totally self-

indulgent time. I did what I wanted to do, when I wanted to do it, without having to worry about anybody other than myself and Peter. (And taking Peter's needs into account now feels the same as considering my own.)

Best:
Waking up each morning and not knowing what I was going to do.

Larry

Worst:
Being very vulnerable, really. We had a lot of problems with the boat. One of the worst things for me was not knowing what was in the process of being broken. Not that I fretted and worried, but it was always in the back of my mind, especially if we were embarking on a long trip somewhere.

Rita

It was fabulous. A ton of worry levitated off my shoulders, broke into small clouds of concern, and drifted away. There was no work to worry about in the middle of the night. There was no point being anxious about Mum's health, Barbara's job prospects, my sister's leg, my niece's life. There wasn't a single thing I could do about any of them. I let it all go and breathed more deeply and easily than I have in years.

The worst part was the opposite side of the same coin. The price I paid for freedom was missing my friends. And I did—more than I ever would have imagined. I wanted to be able to trot over to Barbara's for a glass of wine and a yatter. I wished that Bob and Mary were trekking through the hills with us. I thought how comfortable it would be over at Jack and Jill's, watching Jill cook, catching up on the boys' latest sports results, and listening to Peter and Jack chatting happily about golf like bigger boys.

Best:
I built my house. I don't know what that represents in my psyche, but building that house was very important. I was

driven to build it and I built it and I like it and I'm not sorry
I did it. It was a very satisfying experience.

Worst:
I can't think of anything negative about the time away. I really
can't. I was very fortunate. I'm back and I'm working. I'm
doing something that I feel enthusiastic about. Some of the
problems that I was trying to escape have disappeared. I'm
financially okay. I can't think of one negative thing.

Marie

Peter's favourite part of the trip was uniquely his own. He revelled
in the people we met. Throughout the world, he found himself in a continuing series of conversations about local politics, customs, art, sport,
history, you name it, with people we met in B&Bs, in restaurants and
shops, on the beach and on the streets. This seemingly quiet man let
loose the wacky and weird persona that usually only his close friends
know and love. He rediscovered the charming extrovert within and
pushed himself to take advantage of this opportunity to know how
other people live, think, and feel.

Best:
The best part is the freedom from responsibilities. And that's
the difference, I think, between staying home and going away.
And the Galapagos.

Worst:
When we were both quite sick away from home, and you're in
a foreign country, and you can't do anything.

Margaret

On the downside, Peter found it very hard to deal with our ill-
nesses away from home. Peter's not a good sickie at the best of times and,
the few times he was ill on the road, he was truly miserable. He wanted
to be home. Even harder for him was my illness. All his protective
instincts perked up. He simply hated my being unwell in a strange

country, having to shuffle from place to place, barely aware of what was going on around me. Even when we found refuge at Anne's cottage in England, it bothered him enormously that he couldn't just transport me home to recover in my own bed with my cats curled up around me.

Best:
One of the best things for me was losing track of what day of the week it was. Another was actually going to Tierra del Fuego and looking across the Beagle Channel. It's as far south as you can drive any place in the world. The next stop is Antarctica basically. That felt very special to me.

Mike

Worst:
The poverty.... In Quito [Ecuador], there were a bunch of little kids sleeping on the street. It was almost at the end of the trip, and I just started crying. I think it's because they had their little-kid drawings for sale. They're just like little kids anywhere in the world. They'd done their little drawings of dreams that they have, and you realize none of them will happen.

Heather

As individual as different people's high and low points are, they often touch related themes. Some things are primal. The despair of being sick away from home is a recurring motif, as is a sense of isolation or alienation. We are a species that balances creativity and a need to explore with a craving for familiarity and routine. When we wilfully separate ourselves from the known and the comfortable, we are bound to feel a little lost.

Best:
The realization that we really love each other. And we wanted to spend time together. That feeling is really neat.

Helen

Worst:
Food poisoning. And being dumped off in the middle of the night in this weird place, not knowing if the person who was going to pick you up would show up.

Patrick

In every case, people discovered truths about themselves, whether as individuals or as couples. Adrift alone or together, you can't avoid coming to grips with issues of who you are and how you relate to each other and the world around you.

Best:
To see the different cultures, the different animals, different way of living. You see how many materialistic things you've got that you don't really need.

June, 13 years old

It stimulates your imagination and your appreciation of life. You get bombarded with things here at home, on television, in the media, or whatever, but it's not real. When you're on the trip, it may not be as spectacular or as violent as the media images, but it's more tangible, more real.

Ian

I learned that, no matter what is, it will be okay. Our lives are complicated because we make them complicated. If anybody tells me their life is too rushed, too busy, whatever, I feel like saying, "Well, change it. It's you that makes it like that." I know that I'm responsible for my own stress, my own busyness, my own boredom, whatever. Change it. And you can do it.

Jocelyn

Worst:
Ian: Were there any worsts?
June: It was unsettling when we had to break into that motel.

Ian: Rain. A car breaking down.
Jocelyn: Fear when I was caught in a tide. Fog and not knowing
where we were going.
Ian: At worst, just very minor inconvenience.

Peter and I each set out to achieve a particular objective. I actively
sought freedom from responsibility. He unconsciously was looking for
freedom from constraint. And we succeeded. At the same time, we
craved a lost sense of the familiar and the comforting.

Other people's choices reflect a similar need for connection with
something intrinsic—a knowledge of themselves, an opportunity for
growth, a sense of sharing. And most acknowledge at some level an
element of fear that must be faced and faced down.

The memories of your trip will last a lifetime. You'll see places
you've dreamed of, others you didn't know existed. You'll do strange and
wonderful things. But the lasting value is not in the places you are
drawn to but in the feelings that are drawn forth. The next time someone asks about the place I liked best, I may answer truthfully, "Myself."

THINGS TO THINK ABOUT

- The best part of your trip will be what you feel, not where you go.
- The worst will tell you a lot about your needs and your fears.
- Be prepared for the worst. Expect the best. You won't be disappointed.

June/July/August: VICTORIA
Home Strange Sweet Home

JUNE 2

Everyone looks exactly the same. We walked into the reception area of the airport four nights ago and there they were—Mum, Yvonne, Barbara, Liz, Michaela and her boyfriend, Al—all looking just as we had left them nine months ago. I feel like a totally different person. I wonder if it shows or if I, too, look just the same to them?

It was wonderful to get home and find the little green house waiting for us. Popping open the corks to toast our return, it could have been nine days or nine weeks since we had all been together. There was a lot of babbling and trying to catch up on everything all at once but, to be honest, I don't recall a word that was said. We were just tired and happy and contented to be home.

After everyone but Barbara had left, the cats felt it safe to emerge from the basement. Georgia was first up the stairs and surveyed us rather uncertainly. She went to Barbara for reassurance, but eventually allowed herself to be won over. Jerome, on the other hand, flashed a look that clearly said, "So, where have you been? I've been waiting," and came instantly over for a cuddle. Within two hours, they had both totally deserted Barbara who has taken such loving care of them for the past nine months. They hopped on our bed and slept with us that first night and never looked back. When Barbara moved out yesterday, they never even said goodbye. Selfish beasts.

Everything is so familiar and yet somehow foreign. The house obviously hasn't changed, the cats are their same old selves, the plants in the garden are in the same places as when we left. So why do I find myself looking quizzically at everything, trying to figure out just what's different? We go for walks and find ourselves staring silently at street scenes and landscapes, heads slightly tilted, eyes somewhat narrowed, trying to assimilate what we're seeing. There are recognizable landmarks, but everything looks slightly out of focus. It's as if we had lived here in some previous lives.

There hasn't been a lot of time for contemplation, though. We had expected to be camping in with Barbara for a couple of weeks or a month until she found a place of her own, but she's been a marvel of efficiency and wonderfully considerate. She rented a perfect apartment for June 1 and we helped her move in yesterday. Our house is ours again. And there's so much to do.

The mail alone is staggering. We had notes waiting for us from Dvora, Martin and Rosalynn, Sally and Jerry in Auckland, and other people we had met along the way, along with the usual assortment of junk mail and housekeeping items. Nine months of bank and credit card statements to review. Think we'll leave those for a while. Mum has handed over a two-foot-tall stack of photos. It's so exciting actually to see our trip. We'd forgotten what pictures we had taken—and how many!

Our first and most welcome chore was to unpack our bags and get rid of most of our clothes. Salvation Army, here they come. Oh, the joy of wearing something different. But, good grief, what a lot we've got to choose from. I own nineteen pairs of slacks. Nineteen! This is nuts. We've also been unpacking the boxes in the basement and moving things upstairs. Where did it all come from? It's overwhelming. I thought we had shed everything before we left. What did the dishes do? Multiply in our absence? The contrast between what we have been happily used to living with and what we own is shocking. I'm embarrassed and made uncomfortable by our accumulation of objects. Most of it will just have to stay in the basement. We'll move up what we need for now and deal with the rest later.

In the midst of this plenty, there is one thing we do need, however—a new bed. After all the strange beds we've slept on in the past nine months, you wouldn't think it would matter what the bed feels like. But it does. We now appreciate as never before the value of a firm, comfortable mattress.

JUNE 10
How could she have done it? What could possibly have possessed her? I told my sister she could use my computer while I was gone—just be careful not to touch any of my documents. I went over to

alert her I'd need to use the computer because my corporate income tax return is due by the end of the month, and she pointed to a metal box and told me all my files are in there! She upgraded the computer, removed my files, and now the computer store tells me they are irretrievable. Seven years of corporate files. And, according to Liz, I'm overreacting because she "didn't touch them; they're all there." She thought it would be an easy matter to hook them in again, and it's taking her a while to grasp the fact that I can't get to them. It's like the sound of a tree falling in an empty forest. If computer files are inaccessible, do they continue to exist?

Okay, Lynda, get a grip. Calm down. Find a quiet spot inside. Take a breath. Put yourself back on the trip. Find a place. The desert, the heat, the silence. Pull it back. Imagine the red glow of Uluru at sunset. Remember the peace. The trip will only have meaning if you can use it to stay centred. It's not that important. Breathe. Slowly. Hold it. All right, I'm calmer now.

But how could she?

JUNE 14

Barbara took wonderful care of the house and cats, but gardening is clearly not her strength. She informs us that she has no desire to own her own home—a condo, maybe, but nothing with a lawn. Actually, I'm thrilled that she's done so little. There is nothing more satisfying than planting my hanging baskets and putting my veggies in. Playing in the dirt, the feel and smell of earth between my fingers, grounds me. And I desperately need grounding.

Something weird has happened. I can't settle. I expected to come home to quiet days of lazing in the hammock, reading and soaking up the sun. I set up the hammock the first week we were home, but I can't lie still in it for more than ten minutes at a time. I constantly leap to my feet, needing to do something, anything. I plant my flowers. Back to the hammock. I water the roses. Back to the hammock. I run to the hardware store to buy those picture hooks. Back to the hammock. I put the pictures in albums. An hour later, I'm back in the hammock. Until Peter returns from golf. We'd better rush out and get that painting framed. On and on and on. By the time ten o'clock at night rolls around, I'm exhausted.

I think I have become addicted to constant stimulation. When you're on the road, there is always something new happening, something different assaulting your senses. Here, at one level, everything feels different while nothing really has changed. Everything continues as it was. We run into friends on the street, and it's as if we had spoken with them yesterday, not a year ago. They're doing the same jobs, dealing with the same crises, talking about the same issues. I feel as though I'm racing at fast forward through a video that's on pause. My engine is still revving, but there's nothing happening, so I have to manufacture activity to keep from blowing up. Peter keeps saying, "I thought you were going to use this time to just unwind and do nothing." I was. I want to. But I can't.

Peter feels some of this need for activity, but he has arranged better to deal with it. He had always planned to use this part of the year to improve his golf game. So, three or four mornings a week, he's out there doing something physical, hitting balls or playing a round. My plans for this time were determinedly non-physical, but I can't pull it off.

I'm trying to divert my attention from mindless running around by concentrating on my garden. But with only limited success. It's starting to look and feel like home again on the outside, but the inside of the house is pathetic. We brought up the old couch from the basement because we need something to sit on, but it's horrible. I don't think I've ever really seen it before. It's dirty and worn and sagging and scratched by the cats and totally embarrassing to have around. I know we shouldn't be going any deeper into debt, but I can't live with this. We need new living-room furniture. Here I go again.

JUNE 22

Last night was our annual summer solstice dinner with Bob and Mary at the Aerie. A beautiful evening, warm enough to have our drinks on the balcony high above Finlayson Arm, catching up on each other's lives. It is wonderful to be with old friends again. So, it amazes me all the more how slowly we have reached out to other people since returning home. We've spent time with Barbara and our mothers and been over to Jack and Jill's. I've had a couple of short visits with Linda. But that and last night's dinner have been about it. We're pleased to be home and love seeing our close friends, but we are in no hurry to be sociable. It's as if we've undergone some enormous shock and need time to adjust. With Peter trying to improve his golf game, we are seeing less of each other than we did on the trip. So we need the rest of the time just to find our centre again before we open ourselves to the world. We go for long walks together but in different frames of mind. For me, it's a necessary way to burn off energy. For Peter, it's just relaxing. The first time Linda saw me, she took one look and said, "You're not really home yet." She may be right.

The part of me that is home is still busy. I don't know where I'm finding all these chores, but there always seems to be something to be done. The trip photos have been culled and arranged in three albums, even if no one seems to want to look at them but us. Oh well, we get a lot of pleasure out of them. We've been shopping— new furniture on order—and soon we'll be redecorating. The colour of the living room doesn't go with the new sofa and chair, so we'd better get busy and repaint before they arrive.

JULY 15

Painting provides a wonderful opportunity for reflection. I'm beginning to realize that I have been a crazy person for the past six weeks. I've been using activity as a substitute for thought, spending as a way of denying reality. Fortunately, painting has forced me to stay in one place for a few days and given me time to find some calm. I'm mellowing out. Finally. As a bonus, four days of hard work have resulted in living room beautiful. The new furniture is in. The pictures are hung. In the rest of the house, everything that's going to come up from the basement is in place. The flower pots are in full bloom. The veggie patch is looking good. Everything there was to be done—and many things that didn't need doing—are done. I'm ready for the hammock. It's about time.

AUGUST 3

Our year is almost over. I can hardly take it in. Peter and I had a long talk this weekend about what we were going to do come September. We talk a lot about the importance and the impact of the trip. We know that it has made a difference to us, to the way we feel about ourselves, each other and the world. Now we feel an obligation to do something with it—to make it more than simply an extended holiday. Peter wants a job that stretches him, something with social value, something worth doing. I've decided to put off looking for work and devote the time from now until Christmas to see if I really can write a book about our experiences.

This morning, Peter started the process of firming up a job. He's set up appointments for later in the week to see what's available. It feels so weird. This year has been such a gift. I know that we've had the opportunity of a lifetime, and I am truly grateful for it. Is it too selfish of me to feel sad that it is about to come to an end?

AUGUST 15

My fiftieth birthday isn't until September, but my present has arrived early. A 1990 fire-engine-red Miata convertible sports car is sitting in the driveway. Peter thought I should have the pleasure of using her before summer ends. What a wonderful man! She is perfect. Her name is Carmen. We've bonded.

This is, of course, totally insane. We can't afford to be spending money like this. All our normal, careful financial instincts have deserted us since we've been home. We seem to have lost touch with the meaning of money. First the furniture, now Carmen. The line of credit we took out but didn't need to use for trip emergencies has been used at a truly alarming rate since our return. But, as Peter says, he'll soon be back at full salary and we can start paying it down. And how many times am I planning on turning fifty?

When I was in my mid-forties, thinking of turning fifty, all my images were grey and brown, drab and shrivelled. Now, I see myself in vibrant Technicolor, striding purposefully into the future. I remember having my fortune told in Greece almost thirty years ago and being informed that the years after fifty were going to be the most creative, most exciting, most rewarding period of my life. I have embraced that prediction through some difficult times along the way, but I'm not sure I ever really believed it. I do now.

Peter's job situation is somewhat confused, but he's refusing to allow it to get him down. He headed off on the trip with the guarantee of a job on his return. It sounded great. It is great. But we foolishly thought that meant there would be a specific job for him to return to. Instead, despite eleven months to plan for his return, nobody seems to have a clue what to do with him. Peter's a bit bemused by it all but remarkably unruffled. He's now off on a concerted job hunt, talking to contacts about what's happening in town, what's available, and what he can invent for himself.

I find fascinating the extent to which none of this really matters. Peter is impressively nonchalant about it. And even I, Ms. Security Freak, am quite content to let things unfold as they will. At its most basic, the trip has somehow taught us that there's no point worrying. Things will work out. One way or another. We're together. We're healthy. We're happy. The future will be fine. And we're certainly not going to allow a few glitches now to take away the pleasure of our remaining few weeks of freedom.

AUGUST 27

We have been gathering up the joys of our time together and clasping them tightly. Our days are spent in the neighbourhood and around the house and garden. We have no desire to stray too far afield. We want to savour every moment. We sleep in and have long lazy breakfasts on the back porch, reading the papers. Peter may golf and I do a bit of gardening, or we'll head out for a stroll along the Dallas Road cliffs and rejoice in the seals playing in the ocean, the heron fishing at the water's edge, and eagles soaring overhead. Late afternoon finds us in the backyard, reading peacefully or visiting with friends who've dropped by. We'll cook something simple for dinner and maybe go out for a movie or watch TV for a while before climbing into our luxurious new bed. This is what I had hoped our time at home would be like. It may have taken me a while to find it, but it was worth the wait. If this is what retirement will be like, we have a lot to look forward to. But, first, there is some interesting work to be done.

SEPTEMBER 1

What a strange, sad, and exciting morning. The next stage of our lives officially begins today. It's the first day of work in a year. We kissed each other goodbye at the front door and hugged for longer than usual. I watched Peter striding down the street to his new job, tall and handsome and happy, and thought, a little wistfully, how much I will miss spending my days with him. We've had such a wonderful time being together, playing together, laughing and crying together, finding out new things about each other. To some extent, we've shared one life for the past year. It's going to be a wrench to build independent lives again. At the same time, we're both feeling wonderfully upbeat. We're filled with energy and a desire to put it to work. We have absolutely no doubt that exciting times lie ahead and that, when bad things happen, as they inevitably will, we will be able to face them with courage. I suspect it will take some time, perhaps years, to understand fully what impact this year has had on us. But a clear and immediate legacy is our sense of confidence in ourselves and optimism about the future.

When Peter turned the corner, I closed the door, headed to my desk, turned on my new computer, took a deep breath, and started to type. "Have you ever wanted to run away from home?…"

TWELVE
WHAT A DIFFERENCE
A YEAR MAKES

A year can change your life. It did ours. We left Victoria in September feeling middle-aged, worn-out, tired, and frustrated. We were bored with our jobs—possibly with our lives—and wondered if the next twenty or thirty years were simply going to be more of the same. We returned home in June revitalized, invigorated, and filled with optimism about our futures.

And this was without either of us experiencing the eureka moment. There was no sudden revelation of what we want to be when we grow up. No light bulb of brilliance illuminated the future. There is simply a quiet absolute certainty that life offers innumerable opportunities, that you are never too old to dream, and that we still have plenty of time to fulfill those dreams.

I set off hoping to discover some buried portion of my lost youth. I found something better. I discovered the reality of who I am and a comfort with that reality.

We are all the stars of our own movies. More convincingly than any high-tech wizardry, we fashion our self-images to become the person we wish we were—younger, more attractive, more adventurous, more intriguing. What I and others found instead was the real thing.

> My big realization was that I am not invincible. I do have weaknesses like everybody else. So I deal with them.
>
> Suzanne

In some indefinable way, the trip—or perhaps more precisely, taking the trip—clarifies your image of yourself. Choosing to do something different, leaving what's familiar, causes you to examine your life in whole new ways. What you find is sometimes unexpected. Not everything is positive. But you also discover some very real and important strengths.

When we came back, I was diagnosed with cancer. But, having had the trip, I knew we could handle it. After all we'd gone through, I didn't think there was anything we wouldn't be able to survive together. And then this happened. I'm not sure how I would have handled the cancer if I hadn't known that we're okay. The family unit is strong enough to handle this.

Jocelyn

Few travellers' discoveries are as direct and dramatic as Jocelyn's, but they are just as powerful. As I interviewed people, I was astonished by the similarity of their emotional experiences and development. Over and over again, they described themselves as "more confident," "freer," "more courageous," "younger."

With the single exception of Janet, whose marriage breakup coincided with her year off, every person I spoke to remarked about feeling more personally confident. In some cases, like Marie building her house, it was partly a matter of achieving a set objective. But often, it's more than that. For some, the confidence came from discovering the ability to do practical and useful work. For others, it was a result of discovering themselves, away from other people's definition of who they are or should be.

I found out that you have more control over your life than you think. I found out that I could make decisions, I could take time off and do some things I wanted to do and still come back and the sky wasn't going to fall. I found out that, when I was able to let go of the security blanket, I didn't need it anymore.

Marie

I'm more confident. I've learned that I'm allowed to do things other people don't agree with or approve of. I'm sometimes way too driven by what other people think. The trip has led me to think it doesn't really matter ultimately. Being removed from influences in my life that channel me in a certain direction helped me to develop and learn more about who I want to be, rather than who I thought I should be.

Heather

For most of us, it's simply a case of accomplishing a goal, however nebulous, and discovering that we can take care of ourselves in a variety of environments. By the time you've negotiated your way around the world or through a developing country, encountered all manner of people and situations, experienced illness, loneliness and discomfort, and continued, you begin to understand that you can do anything.

The year after we got back, we sold our place in town, bought nine acres, and moved out to East Sooke. This was something we'd thought we might like to do, but the idea that we could learn a new place and scratch a living out of it was reinforced by the experience we had when we were away. It made us realize we could do it.

Margaret

Memories become symbolic. You remember a moment. It triggers a feeling. And suddenly you're back in the mood you want to be. Your head slows down a bit and things become a little clearer.

I liken the trip to those three years I spent in a cancer clinic. The stuff I learned about the value of life dissipates over time. But, every once in a while, there's something that reminds me of it and then I go back to that place. And at least I've got that place to go back to.

Patrick

After two and a half years, I still find myself reflecting on the trip and the meaning of the trip and the emotions it conjures up in me—deeper, more personally significant kinds of things. I guess we are peeling off some layers.... It's a sort of reality check. You remember that you were there and what it meant and what it should mean now.

Rita

Sometimes, memories can be directly applied to help you deal with difficult situations.

> The trip gave me some of the strength that I needed to do what I needed to do. Going through cancer treatments, I could transport myself to one of my favourite places of the trip. There were many I could choose from. And I could just daydream about them and pretend this wasn't really happening. So I had a lot to draw from.
>
> Jocelyn

I find it ironic that, for me, what started as a quest for lost youth should result in acceptance of—even revelling in—middle-aged reality. I discovered that travelling in middle age could be even more fun than doing it when you're young. What I craved were not the trappings of youth—I don't want to stay in youth hostels, travel on third-class trains, and party all night. I wanted the freedom. And that is available to anyone who goes after it—at any age.

My greatest surprise was how much I like being middle-aged. I like the knowledge and perspective it gives me. I like the connection it provided to people we met along the way. And to be truthful, I like the cachet it bestowed because we were middle-aged people doing something different.

Youth may be unrecoverable, but I, and others, did rediscover a sense of youthfulness.

> I feel like, even though I'm 50, life is more of an adventure. I think that lots of interesting things are going to happen to me in the last part of my life. I don't feel like I'm waiting around for old age and the nursing home.
>
> Marie

As an added benefit, that feeling of youthfulness has external ramifications. On their return, almost everybody had the flattering experience of being told they looked ten years younger. And it's true. The lines on the face seem to have receded; the bags under the eyes are gone; the visible tensions of working have disappeared. To be replaced by a spring in the step and an alertness in the eyes that comes with feeling truly alive.

PERSPECTIVE ON RETIREMENT
In addition to the personal benefits, there is at least one very practical reward for the midlife runaway. The time away gives you direct experience of what retirement may be like. It allows you to test out not working and to see how you adjust to not having a job to define you.

> It was great retirement preparation. I thought I'd love to be retired—I'd go to the library and do this and do that. Now I understand how people are lost when they retire.
>
> Janet

> It made me realize that one day I won't be working anymore. I remember when my dad retired. He drove my mum nuts because he wandered around the house like a big lost kid. He didn't know what to do with himself. . . . I can start thinking now about what I want to do and how I can set myself up. So, not only did I move one of my retirement years from my 60s into my 40s, but my retirement years are probably going to be an awful lot better.
>
> Patrick

> I think I found a different way to live, a simpler way to live. I'm not able to afford it yet, but now I'm motivated to come back and do the old stuff to be able to retire earlier and live that way again.
>
> Marie

If you're in a relationship, the time away together provides a chance to see how that relationship functions when the two of you are on your own. If you're lucky, it will reinforce a bond between you. If not, maybe it's better to know now.

> We won't have any problem finding things to do when we retire. We can't wait.
>
> Helen

I was sitting there with my husband and thinking—this is what it's going to be like when we retire. I can't do this.

Janet

To those of us for whom retirement is no longer a distant vague unimaginable land, an advance year to get a taste and feel of our futures is valuable indeed.

EVERYTHING TO GAIN

Confident, free, courageous, proud, young, adventurous. Are these not wonderful things to feel about yourself at any age? Perhaps more wonderful than ever in midlife.

I'm tempted to encourage all middle-aged people around the world to rise from their couches, leave their jobs, and go in search of their dreams simply to be able to feel this way about themselves.

It re-energized me. It allowed me to get beyond some irrational fears I had about risk-taking. It allowed me to heal and recover from burnout.

Marie

The irony is glaring. Our society's assessment of accomplishment and our sense of self-worth are so tied to what we do for a living. We define ourselves through our jobs. We assume that the good, normal, middle-class working life will reward us and make us feel good about ourselves. Then we do the complete opposite—run away from our jobs, our families, our responsibilities—and we feel great about it.

In thirty years of working for a living, I have never felt as proud, as good, as confident in my own abilities as I do after a year of slouching off around the world.

I uncovered character traits I hadn't recognized previously or had forgotten about. I'm a person of strong emotions; I love and loathe to equal depths. I'm capable of great joy. I'm funny and fun to be around. And, after I finish pouting when things don't go my way, I usually make the best of a situation. I may have discovered that I am not quite as adventurous as I thought I was or wanted to be, but I'm a lot more adventurous now than I was when we set out. I learned a lot about compromise and patience and flexibility and letting go, and most of those lessons are staying with me.

Despite all my flaws—which stood out glaringly in alien environments—I like myself. In fact, I'm proud of myself—of both of us. Peter and I had the imagination to have a dream and the courage to follow it through.

> If you've got a dream, just do it. You'll never regret it. Don't let anything get in the way. Whatever it is you have to risk, risk it.
> Suzanne

It may feel risky. It may be risky. But think how much riskier it is to do nothing and always to wonder what might have been.

> I'm a nurse, and I've stood by a lot of deathbeds. The most common regret is that most people wish they had taken more risks.
> Ruth

After almost a year back home, Peter and I are happier—with ourselves and with each other—than we have ever been. Individually and as a couple, we have confronted our weaknesses and feelings of insecurity and vulnerability. We emerged more balanced, stronger, fuller human beings. Peter found the strength to focus on a sense of accomplishment rather than career status. I found the courage to try writing this book. Our newfound confidence and sense of security have nothing to do with expectations that things will remain the same and everything to do with embracing change and growth.

And on top of all that, we had fun. We laughed, we joked, we smiled, we played. We just plain had a great time. And we still are.

To all of you who have ever considered running away from home, I say, if you're thinking about it, you should do it. There were moments I hated. There were times I wondered what the hell I was doing. But I never fundamentally regretted it for a minute. The bad times were far outweighed by the wonderful. And only good has resulted.

So, don't be afraid. Gather up your dreams. Run away with them.

Index

The Runaway Route